I0005048

Windows 8

Superguide

Third Edition

By Matthew A. Buxton

The materials contained in this book are provided for general information purposes only and do not constitute legal or other professional advice on any subject matter. Top-Windows-Tutorials / ACEL Systems does not accept any responsibility for any loss which may arise from reliance on the information provided in this product.

While the information provided has been carefully reviewed, no guarantee is given that the information in this product is correct, complete, and/or up-to-date.

Windows, Windows 8 and Windows 8.1 are registered trademarks of Microsoft corporation. This publication is not affiliated with or endorsed by Microsoft corporation.

About the Author

Matthew A. Buxton holds a degree in computer studies and has several years experience working in programming and technical support. He is the author and webmaster of the popular Windows website Top-Windows-Tutorials.com as well as two new sites for videogamers, Videogameperfection.com and Play-Old-PC-Games.com. His previous book and training course, the Windows 7 Superguide, is used by individuals, businesses, schools and colleges around the world to help teach Windows 7 to computer users of all experience levels. Matthew also writes about video games on blogs and forums and is a passionate game player across several different formats.

He currently works as a self employed webmaster and computer consultant. You can contact him by visiting his website, http://www.Top-Windows-Tutorials.com/

on Facebook at https://en-gb.facebook.com/top.windows.tutorials

or on Twitter at https://twitter.com/TopWindowsTuts

Authors Acknowledgements

First and foremost, I'd like to thank my family, especially my mother whose tireless dedication to proof reading and checking has made this book into the professional document that it is.

Secondly, I'd like to thank the folks at Foliovision, for helping transition Top-Windows-Tutorials.com to Wordpress and for giving the old website a new lease of life with a much more modern look and feel.

Once again I would also like to thank Seniornet New Zealand for helping to fund the writing of this book and for their input and suggestions. We hope you find this course as useful as the Windows 7 Superguide was.

Thank you also to Rachel Mcneill for our new improved cover design for the second edition.

Finally, I want to thank you, for purchasing my book and (hopefully!) visiting my website. I sincerely hope you will find the material easy to understand and that it helps you get the best out of your Windows 8 computer, whatever size and shape it might come in!

Table of Contents

Foreword...**13**

Foreword to the first edition...**14**

Introduction...**16**

Chapter 1 – The Beginning...**19**

Before You Begin..**20**

What is Windows 8? 20
    Do I need Windows 8?..20
Choosing the right version..20
Windows 8.1 retail DVDs..22
    32-bit or 64-bit?...22
Taking the plunge...23
    The easy way – Choosing a new computer with Windows 8 installed.................23
    The hard way – Upgrading an existing computer..................25
    Custom install versus in-place upgrade................................25
    Is my old PC capable of running Windows 8?.......................26
    Upgrading to Windows 8.1...26
    Is that all?..27

Lesson 1 – Starting your new Windows 8 PC...............**29**
1.1 – Initial personalisations...29
1.2 – Choosing a Microsoft or a local account...........................31

Lesson 2 – The new Start screen..................................**35**
2.1 – Logging in..35
2.2 – Getting to grips with tiles..38
2.3 – Navigating between tile apps...39
2.4 – Apps view..41

Lesson 3 – Multitasking with tiles.................................**43**
3.1 – Switching between apps...43
3.2 – The taskbar and tile applications.......................................46
3.3 – Meet the Charms Bar...46
3.4 – Closing tiles...47
    3.4.1 – Closing tiles the touch-friendly way..........................48
    3.4.2 – Closing tiles the mouse-friendly way.........................49

Lesson 4 – Searching your Windows 8 PC....................**50**
4.1 – Starting a search...50
4.2 - 'Everywhere' search limitations..52
4.3 – Apps view..54
4.4 – Search Charm in Windows 8.1...56

Lesson 5 – The Settings Charm....................................**57**
5.1 – Start screen settings Charm..57
5.2 – The basic PC settings icons...58

5.3 – Account options..60
5.4 – Settings in other programs..61
Lesson 6 – The Share Charm..**62**
6.1 – Sharing in the Photos app...62
6.2 – Sharing in Internet Explorer...63
Lesson 7 – Multiple tiles...**66**
7.1 – Inserting with a right-click..66
7.2 – Resize control 67
7.3 – Opening further apps..67
7.4 – Arranging apps by dragging..68
7.5 – Arranging apps with the title bar...69
7.6 – Arranging apps with the keyboard...70
7.7 – Using insert with the desktop...70
Chapter 2 – Getting Social...**72**
Lesson 8 – Mail...**73**
8.1 – Introducing Windows 8 Mail..73
8.2 – Replying and composing...75
8.3 – Adding new accounts..77
8.4 – Moving messages..79
Lesson 9 – The People app...**81**
9.1 – Linking social network accounts...83
9.2 – Other People app options...86
9.3 – Working with contacts...87
9.4 – Editing contacts...89
9.5 – Linking contacts...90
9.6 – Other contact options...91
9.7 – What's new...92
Lesson 10 – Photos...**94**
10.1 – Browsing pictures...96
10.2 – Picture browsing tools..97
10.3 – Fun with pictures..98
Chapter 3 – More Tile Apps..**100**
Lesson 11 – The App Store..**101**
11.1 – Free and paid apps..102
11.2 – Finding more in the store...105
11.3 – Installing a new app..105
11.4 – Rating an app...106
Lesson 12 – Music and Video...**108**
12.1 – Playing music 109
12.2 – Creating playlists...111
12.3 – Playing music outside the music folder......................................113
12.4 – Radio..113
12.5 – Browsing music to buy..113
12.6 – The Video app...117
12.7 – Browsing video to buy...118

   12.8 – Viewing options..120

Lesson 13 – The News and Sport apps................................122
   13.1 – News...122
   13.2 – News sources..124
   13.3 – Customise your news...125
   13.4 – News videos..128
   13.5 – Sport...128
   13.6 – Favourite Sports...129
   13.7 – Favourite Teams 130

Lesson 14 – Travel, Finance, Weather................................132
   14.1 – Travel...132
   14.2 – Finance..135
   14.3 – Weather..137
   14.4 – World weather..140

Lesson 15 – Maps...142
   15.1 – Map options..143
   15.2 – Pins and favourites..144

Lesson 16 – OneDrive...146
   16.1 – Working with OneDrive...147
   16.2 – OneDrive on the desktop..151

Chapter 4 – Back to the Desktop..153

Lesson 17 – Introduction to the desktop............................154
   17.1 – Desktop elements..154
   17.2 – Notification area..156

Lesson 18 – Windows on the Windows 8 Desktop...............158
   18.1 – A Windows 8 desktop window...158
   18.2 – Moving and resizing..159
   18.3 – Ways to work with windows..159

Lesson 19 – Tweaking Windows 8 for desktop systems 162
   19.1 – Secret Start button shortcuts..162
   19.2 – Basic desktop PC tweaks...163
   19.3 – Alternative ways to access apps.....................................165
   19.4 – Changing default programs...168
   19.5 – Restoring the Start menu and other third-party tweaks.......169
      19.5.1 - ModernMix...172

Lesson 20 – Exploring File Explorer....................................174
   20.1 – Your personal folders..174
   20.2 – The individual elements of a File Explorer window.............177
   20.3 – Introducing the ribbon...179
   20.4 – Breadcrumbs..180
   20.5 – Folder views...181

Lesson 21 – Advanced File Explorer techniques..................188
   21.1 – Delving into details view..188
   21.2 – Preview pane..189
   21.3 – Details pane...190

21.4 – Navigation pane...191
Lesson 22 – Working with Files and Folders.............................193
22.1 – Working with folders...193
22.2 – Making your own folders...194
22.3 – The context menu in File Explorer.....................................195
22.4 – Send to...196
22.5 – Cut, copy and paste..197
22.6 – When file names collide...199
22.7 – Renaming or deleting files and folders..............................200
Lesson 23 – Working with multiple Files and Folders.............202
23.1 – Dragging and dropping...202
23.2 – File name collisions revisited...202
23.3 – Desktop Snap and multiple File Explorer windows...............206
23.4 – Working with multiple files at once...................................210
23.5 – Keyboard short cuts for working with multiple files............211
Lesson 24 – Libraries...213
24.1 – Activating libraries..213
24.2 – Working with libraries 214
24.3 – Sorting data in libraries...220
24.4 – Pictures library...222
24.5 – Open file/folder location..223
Chapter 5 – Deeper Into Folders..225
Lesson 25 – Folder properties..226
25.1 – Accessing folder properties..226
25.2 – Customise tab...229
25.3 – Folder pictures and folder icons.......................................231
Lesson 26 – Folder options..233
26.1 – Folder options window...233
26.2 – General folder options...234
26.3 – View tab...238
26.4 – Hidden files and folders...239
26.5 – Hide extensions for known file types 242
Lesson 27 – The Recycle Bin..246
27.1 – Into the Recycle Bin..246
27.2 – Sending files to the Recycle Bin.......................................248
27.3 – Files that are not sent to the Recycle Bin..........................249
27.4 – Recycle Bin folders 250
27.5 – Recycle Bin Properties 251
Chapter 6 – Polishing Your Skills...253
Lesson 28 – This PC...254
28.1 – Inside This PC...254
28.2 – Personal folders..255
28.3 – Devices and drives..255
28.3.1 – Hidden drives..258
28.4 – Network Locations..259

28.5 – Other devices...259
Lesson 29 – More about the taskbar.................................261
29.1 – Jump lists and the taskbar...261
29.2 – Moving the taskbar..263
29.3 – Adding toolbars to the taskbar.....................................264
29.4 – Other taskbar customisations.......................................265
29.5 – Multi-monitor support...268
Lesson 30 – The notification area.......................................270
30.1 – The new notification area versus the old........................270
30.2 – Customising the notification area..................................271
Lesson 31 – Search is everywhere.......................................274
31.1 – Tags and other meta data..274
31.2 – Indexing options...276
31.3 – Tips for searching in Windows 8...................................281
Chapter 7 – Securing Your PC and Your Data.......................283
Lesson 32 – Planning a backup strategy..............................284
32.1 – Backup methodologies...284
32.2 – Do you have operating system recovery media?..............285
32.3 – Where to backup...285
32.4 – A note about storing your backups................................289
Lesson 33 – Configuring File History backup........................290
33.1 – Choosing a File History drive.......................................290
33.2 – Starting the backup...292
33.3 – Advanced settings...295
Lesson 34 – Restoring files from File History.......................297
34.1 – Restoring a file...297
34.2 – Other ways of working with File History.........................301
34.3 – Limitations of File History..303
Lesson 35 – Creating system repair media..........................304
35.1 – System repair USB device..304
Lesson 36 – Creating and modifying user accounts..............310
36.1 – Adding a user...310
36.2 – Microsoft accounts vs local accounts.............................311
36.3 – Standard users and Administrators.................................314
36.3.1 – Changing account security levels................................315
36.4 – Creating local accounts...317
36.5 – Running as a standard user..320
Lesson 37 – The low down on User Account Controls............321
37.1 – Halt! Who goes there?...321
37.2 – User Account Controls to the rescue..............................322
37.3 – Changing User Account Control settings.........................323
37.4 – User Account Controls and standard accounts.................325
Lesson 38 – Updating your PC...327
38.1 – Manually checking for updates......................................327

38.2 – Advanced update options..329
38.3 – The maintenance window 332
Lesson 39 – Privacy options...335
39.1 – Configuring privacy options..335
39.2 – General privacy settings..336
39.3 – Location privacy settings...337
39.4 – Webcam, Microphone and Other devices......................339
39.5 – Desktop software and privacy.......................................339
Lesson 40 – Windows Firewall..340
40.1 – About the Windows 8 firewall..340
40.2 – Changing firewall settings...342
40.3 – Windows Firewall with Advanced Security...................343
40.4 – Third party firewalls...344
Lesson 41 – Windows Defender...346
41.1 – What is antivirus software?..346
41.2 – Starting Windows Defender..346
41.3 – Windows Defender Options...348
41.4 – Manually scanning your computer..................................349
41.5 – Automatic scanning..351
41.6 – Third party antivirus packages......................................352
Chapter 8 – Your PC your Way..354
Lesson 42 – Customising the mouse..355
42.1 – Left handed use and other button options.....................356
42.2 – Pointers and pointer options..357
42.3 – Mouse wheel options...359
Lesson 43 – Customising Start screen tiles...........................361
43.1 – Rearranging tiles and groups...361
43.2 – Options for individual tiles..363
43.3 – Other Start screen options...364
43.4 – Adding tiles from the desktop..365
Lesson 44 – Customising Start and Lock screens..................366
44.1 – Start screen personalisations...367
44.2 – Customising the Lock screen...368
44.3 – Lock screen apps..371
44.4 – Lock screen camera..372
44.5 – Setting an alarm...372
Lesson 45 – Notification options...374
45.1 – Accessing notification options.......................................374
45.2 – Quiet Hours..375
45.3 – Notification settings for individual applications............375
Lesson 46 – Installing new desktop software.........................377
46.1 – Choosing software..377
46.2 – Free software versus paid...378
46.3 – Starting installation from optical media........................379
46.4 – Installation examples...380

Lesson 47 – Legacy software and compatibility.................................**384**
    47.1 – Windows 8 64-bit edition..384
    47.2 – Using compatibility options..385
    47.3 – My software still won't run...389
Lesson 48 – Changing the desktop background **391**
    48.1 – Getting started with desktop backgrounds.........................391
    48.2 – Picture positioning options...394
    48.3 – Slideshow backgrounds..394
    48.4 – Desktop backgrounds from the internet.............................395
    48.5 – Desktop backgrounds on the Start screen.........................396
Lesson 49 – Changing screen savers...**398**
    49.1 – Windows 8 and screen savers..398
    49.2 – Configuring screen savers...399
    49.3 – Downloading new screen savers..401
Lesson 50 – Windows 8 desktop themes......................................**404**
    50.1 – The desktop theme manager..404
    50.2 – Automatic colours...405
    50.3 – Saving themes...406
    50.4 – Downloading themes..407
Lesson 51 – Devices and Printers..**409**
    51.1 – Delving into Devices and Printers.....................................409
    51.2 – Using Devices and Printers...412
Chapter 9 – Networking and the Internet....................................**413**
Lesson 52 – Choosing an ISP and networking hardware...............**414**
    52.1 – Types of internet connection..414
    52.2 – Choosing an ISP...416
    52.3 – Types of internet hardware..416
    52.4 – Connecting it all up..417
Lesson 53 – Internet Explorer 11 on the desktop.........................**419**
    53.1 – Starting Internet Explorer 11..419
    53.2 – Your first Internet Explorer 11 session..............................419
    53.3 – Home page...421
Lesson 54 – More on Internet Explorer 11...................................**422**
    54.1 – Tabs...422
    54.2 – Favourites..423
    54.3 – Advanced IE11 options..425
    54.4 – Download manager...428
Lesson 55 – Internet Explorer 11 – Tile version..........................**431**
    55.1 – Navigating with IE11 on the tiles......................................431
    55.2 – Searching with Tile IE...431
    55.3 – Tabs in the IE11 tile..433
Lesson 56 – Homegroups..**434**
    56.1 – Creating a homegroup...434
    56.2 – Restricting access to files or folders.................................436

56.3 – Joining an existing homegroup..438
56.4 – Browsing a homegroup...439
Chapter 10 – Windows Media Player...**441**
Lesson 57 – Introducing Windows Media Player 12.........................**442**
57.1 – Running Media Player for the first time....................................442
57.2 – Playing video...444
57.3 – The media library...446
Lesson 58 – Ripping CDs...**447**
58.1 – Setting ripping options..447
58.2 – Ripping a CD...449
58.3 – Copy protection options..452
Lesson 59 – Wrapping up Media Player...**455**
59.1 – Browsing libraries...455
59.2 – Viewing pictures...458
59.3 – Making Windows Media Player the default player......................459
Chapter 11 – Troubleshooting and Maintenance............................**460**
Lesson 60 – Uninstalling software..**461**
60.1 – Uninstalling tile software...461
60.2 – Uninstalling desktop software..462
Lesson 61 – The Disk Cleanup utility...**465**
61.1 – Starting a disk cleanup..465
61.2 – Choosing cleaning options...465
Lesson 62 – Disk defragmentation...**468**
62.1 – The Optimize Drives window...468
62.2 – Setting a schedule..470
62.3 – Manual defragmentation..471
Lesson 63 – System Restore utility..**473**
63.1 – Starting a System Restore..473
63.2 – Choosing a restore point..475
63.3 – Restoring from a restore point..476
63.4 – Undoing a System Restore..478
63.5 – Creating your own system restore point...................................479
Lesson 64 – Refresh your PC...**481**
64.1 – Refresh your PC...482
64.2 – Remove everything and reinstall Windows................................484
Lesson 65 – The Task Manager..**486**
65.1 – Starting the Task Manager..486
65.2 – Managing tasks...488
65.3 – Processes...489
65.4 – Other Task Manager tabs...490
65.5 – Running a program from the Task Manager...............................496
Chapter 12 – And Finally..**497**
Popular Windows Software...**498**
66.1 – Software recommendations..498

E-mail..498
Games...498
Image and photograph editing...498
Instant messaging, video and voice chat...............................499
Music and Multimedia..499
Music creation..500
Online safety...500
Password Management...500
Social networking...501
Web browsing...501
Word processing and office..502
Appendix – Using Touch Gestures......................................503

Foreword

A year on from the launch of Windows 8 and Microsoft's vision seems as muddled as ever. The hybrid OS continues to bewilder and frustrate newcomers to Windows and experienced users alike and a lack of compelling and affordable hardware to showcase the OS is still a problem. With Windows 8, have Microsoft really produced a dud?

While sales of Windows 8 tablets may be slow, there's little doubt that the PC market is diversifying. Casual users are finding that tablets and smartphones carry out all the computing tasks they need. Indeed, shipments of tablets and similar devices are up, while shipments of PCs are down. This fact alone has led some of the more over-dramatic IT news sites to declare the PC dead, but that seems unlikely. For many users, the tablet is a bad fit for some or all of the computing work they do. For instance, your author does not relish the idea of trying to write this book using only a tablet PC, even one with a keyboard attached!

Windows 8 may have identity issues, but with just a few tweaks it is actually the most versatile version of Windows yet. On a desktop PC it offers the best support for multi-monitor systems ever, as well as a highly streamlined fully Windows 7 compatible desktop. For tablet users, Windows 8.1 brings improvements that make it the most powerful and versatile tablet OS in the market today. For anyone running a portable machine, Windows 8.1 offers fantastic battery life and performance.

So what does Windows 8.1 still get wrong? Several things, most notably, the lack of really good quality apps for tablet PC users in the Windows store. While better, the shunting between the tile/touch interfaces and the desktop is still too frequent and there's still the concern from many users that the desktop will be dropped entirely (though this seems extremely unlikely).

Windows 8.1 is the best version of Windows ever, but it's also the version most likely to need tweaking or configuring for the way you want to work. Luckily this Superguide covers everything you need to know to get on with Windows 8.1.

A quick note about the third edition – The third edition of this book has some minor alterations to a number of the lessons to account for the changes Microsoft introduced with Windows 8.1 update 1.

Foreword to the first edition

Windows 8 is far from just another entry into the ever growing list of Windows operating systems, in fact, this version could be the most controversial yet! Then again, perhaps not, now that the anticipating and second guessing is done and we have a final version of the operating system in our hands, clearly a lot has changed, but a lot has stayed the same too.

Windows 8 lays out Microsoft's vision for the future of computing devices. Microsoft believe that touch devices like tablets will make up a significant chunk of the devices people buy and use in the near future. To that end, Windows 8 is Microsoft's second attempt to marry the desktop operating system to the tablet PC experience, creating an operating system that's just as much at home on a touch screen only slate as it is on a desktop power-house.

Notice I said second attempt. Many users don't even realise that tablet PCs were around long before the Apple iPad. In fact, back in 2002, Microsoft launched Windows XP Tablet PC Edition. The tablet PCs of the time were larger and bulkier than the sleek slates we have now and typically they used a pen or stylus for input. Windows XP Tablet PC Edition didn't include any tiles on its interface, instead it simply added basic touch and handwriting support to the operating system. While these machines carved out a niche in certain enterprise, education and research markets, for consumers they were a total flop. There were several reasons for this. Early tablets were often too heavy and bulky, they were also expensive compared to similar specification machines in other form factors. Most crucially of all, there was little compelling software to encourage the masses to take up tablet PCs.

Fast forward ten years and advances in technology have taken care of the bulk and weight issues that plagued early tablet PCs. Microsoft is doing its utmost to learn from competitors like Apple and provide a good selection of tablet-centric software in its new Windows Store. The high costs of Windows tablets remains a concern though, for the privilege of owning a tablet that's also a full Windows 8 PC, expect to pay high-end laptop prices.

Despite the obvious changes though, underneath it all Windows 8 is still the same power house desktop operating system that made Windows 7 such a success. The Start menu may have gone (although thanks to third party developers it's easy to add back in if you want to), but that doesn't mean the desktop is any less powerful. In fact, there are a number of significant improvements for desktop users. While it might feel initially like Microsoft wants us all to abandon our keyboards and mice, really nothing could be further from the truth.

Windows 8 really opens up possibilities for new ways to use your computer.

Want a powerful desktop system for productivity? No problem, Windows 8 is even better than Windows 7. Want a tablet that you can convert into a laptop by clipping on a keyboard? again, Windows 8 gives you the best of both worlds. One of the phrases that the Windows 8 marketing team liked to throw around was "no compromises". Now your touch enabled devices can be as flexible as your laptop or desktop. While this might be an exaggeration, Windows 8 certainly opens up exciting possibilities and could make the operating system even more ubiquitous!

Introduction

Welcome to our newest Top-Windows-Tutorials.com Superguide. The Windows 8 Superguide has been especially challenging. Windows 8 is almost like two operating systems in one and as a result this guide is significantly bigger than our best selling Windows 7 Superguide. Thousands of users across the world have benefited from our other Superguides and we sincerely hope that this latest guide will help you get to grips with Windows 8. Even after the tweaks Microsoft made in Windows 8.1, Windows 8 can still be initially quite frustrating for users who are accustomed to older versions of Windows, so don't dismay, we feel your pain and we're here to help.

About this book (physical and e-book edition)

The Windows 8 Superguide is designed as a complete training course, this includes video content as well as an e-book. Physical copies of this e-book are also available, as well as e-book copies for devices such as the Amazon Kindle. We originally started offering these additional services at the request of our customers, with the Windows 7 Superguide. With the Windows 8 Superguide, the physical and e-book editions will launch at (or around) the same time as the full training course. We understand some people prefer to have a traditional reference book, while others prefer a full video course. To find out more about all the ways you can get Windows 8 Superguide, visit this page on our website:- http://www.top-windows-tutorials.com/windows-8-superguide.html

Prerequisites

Apart from a desire to learn about Windows 8, there are a few things you should have before you start this course.

You should know some basic computer skills, such as how to turn your machine on. Knowing how to operate a keyboard and mouse is also very useful. Windows 8 is designed to work both with touch and with keyboard and mouse input. This guide was written using a keyboard and mouse but if you have a touch screen PC, the controls are very similar and you should still be able to follow the content without too much difficulty. If you plan to use a touch enabled PC, please read the appendix "Using touch gestures", at the back of the book before you begin the course. Customers who purchased the full Windows 8 Superguide course can also print this from the main menu as a quick reference sheet.

Remember that Microsoft themselves provide plenty of additional help for Windows 8. To access it, open the Charms Bar (see lesson 3.3) then select the Settings Charm. Now, click on "Help".

If you are not familiar with using Windows or desktop operating systems of any kind, you may want to see Microsoft's guide to using menus, buttons, bars and boxes. This information is most relevant to using Windows 8 in desktop mode. You can access this guide on the internet here:- http://windows.microsoft.com/en-US/windows-vista/Using-menus-buttons-bars-and-boxes.

Access to a Windows 8 machine, while not absolutely essential, is also extremely helpful for practising your skills. You should make sure that the Windows 8 machine you are using is updated to Windows 8.1. For a quick tutorial on how to do this, see "Upgrading to Windows 8.1" at the end of the "Before you Begin" section.

Conventions used in this book

We have aimed to keep this book free of jargon and technical terms wherever possible. One convention we did decide on is regarding the use of the mouse. This book is written assuming a right handed mouse configuration. When we instruct you to click on an item, we are talking about clicking with the primary mouse button. When we talk about right-clicking, we mean the secondary mouse button. We did consider using different terminology, such as "alt click" or something similar, but nothing was as clear as simply using "click" and "right click". We hope left handed users will forgive us this bias. If you're a touch screen user, see the appendix at the end of the book which explains how to "right click" with a finger!

How to use this book

Windows 8 is a versatile operating system and we realise that people want to use it in different ways. We've considered three main groups of user when making the guide. Choose whichever option describes you best and work through the lessons accordingly.

I want to learn all about Windows 8, both on the new interface and on the desktop, or I'm new to Windows entirely – That's great! In this case simply work through the entire guide at your own pace. If you've never used Windows before, you should learn about both the desktop and the tiles so you can use whichever mode suits you best.

I am a confused and frustrated user of an earlier version of Windows, or I just want to get to work on my desktop or laptop PC – We feel your pain, honestly. We love Windows 8 tiles on a touch screen, but rarely use anything other than the occasional game tile on our desktop PCs. You should complete lessons 1 through to 5, since you will need to learn some of the new techniques Windows 8 introduces. After you have completed these lessons, jump forward to lesson 17 and pay particular attention to lesson 19. You can also skip lesson 55.

I have a touch PC and/or I prefer to use the tiles – You should complete lessons 1 through to 16. You may find that you need to use File Explorer to manage files on your PC, so in that case complete at least lessons 17, 18 and lessons 20 through to 23 at a minimum. We also recommend you complete lessons 32 to 35 as everyone should have a backup strategy. You can tackle the other lessons as and when you need to access that extra functionality on your device.

Chapter 1 – The Beginning

It is time to start your journey. A whole new, exciting modern operating system holds so many possibilities for you and your PC. Windows has always been about versatility and with Windows 8 that goes even further. Now Windows 8 can be at home on your desktop PC, your laptop, on a tablet or on a touch screen anywhere. Never before have there been so many exciting ways to interact with your Windows PC!

Before You Begin

Arriving with much controversy, Windows 8 is finally here and on sale to the public. While Windows 7 stayed true to the traditional Windows formula, Windows 8 adds a whole new interface and several other new exciting and often opinion dividing features.

What is Windows 8?

Windows 8 is still the same Windows operating system that users around the world know and love. The traditional desktop is still available and virtually all the software designed for Windows 7 is fully compatible. Windows 8 brings several improvements for desktop users, including faster boot times, an improved Task Manager and a new improved Windows Explorer called File Explorer.

Windows 8 is also something entirely new. Gone is the old Start menu that we've been used to since Windows 95. Instead, there's a fresh new Start screen populated with tiles. This interface (previously known as Metro) represents a whole new way to work with your PC, using touch screens and devices like tablets. As we said in the introduction, Windows 8 is almost two operating systems in one. This whole new way of working allows for some fantastic new PC designs and opens the door to all kinds of possibilities in the future.

Do I need Windows 8?

If you are reading this guide then we will assume that you have already purchased Windows 8 or you are strongly considering an upgrade. If you are planning to purchase a new Windows PC, you should absolutely make sure that it ships with Windows 8 already installed. If you are planning to upgrade your existing computer, things are a little more complicated but we will discuss the options later.

Choosing the right version

Buying Windows 8, either pre-installed or as an upgrade to an existing PC, might not be as straightforward as you think. There are a total of four different versions of Windows 8 available and each (apart from one) is available in 32-bit and 64-bit versions, but more on those later. For home users, the correct choice is usually the standard Windows 8, but we'll take a look now at each version of the operating system and describe what it offers.

Windows 8:- This standard version of Windows 8 is designed for the home user and therefore sacrifices some of the advanced features available in the pro version, such as Bitlocker encryption. As with Windows 7 home versions, computers running this version of Windows 8 cannot join a corporate "domain" network. Microsoft have also dropped Windows Media Center from this edition of Windows, though it is still available in Windows 8 Professional as a free download.

Windows 8 Professional:- This version replaces both Windows 7 Professional and Ultimate and includes all the features of the standard edition as well as several features targeted at enthusiasts and business users. Windows 8 Professional users can join a domain based network (common in businesses around the world), as well as use advanced features like Bitlocker and virtual hard disks. We do not cover these features in this guide.

Windows 8 Enterprise:- Available to Microsoft's corporate customers and registered software developers only, the Enterprise edition has the same features as the Professional edition (except for Windows Media Center) and can also run prototype/development builds of tile applications. Normally tile software can only be downloaded and run from the Windows Store.

Windows RT:- This is a special, new edition of Windows that is different from any version that has appeared before. The RT version of Windows 8 is only available pre-installed on tablet PCs and other portable devices which run a certain type of processing chip called ARM. ARM chips are very popular for portable devices such as phones, handheld games consoles and tablets because they offer superb computing performance while consuming relatively little power. For bigger devices, such as Laptops or Desktop PCs, ARM CPUs are rarely used because they lack the raw computing power of their hotter, more power hungry x86/x64 cousins. ARM processors are also incompatible with software designed for x86/x64 based CPU's, meaning the Windows RT machines will only run software specially designed or converted for them. Software for Windows RT machines can only be purchased in the Windows Store tile. Tile-based software that you purchase from the Windows Store will work on both Windows RT and the other versions of Windows, while desktop software will not work on RT machines unless it has been specially converted/reprogrammed first.

If you're still confused as to which version you need, then chances are that the standard Windows 8 is the right version for you. The Enterprise edition is not widely available to the public and if the extra features that come with the Professional edition sounded like another language to you then it is unlikely you will ever need them. If you do, it is possible to upgrade through Windows Anytime Upgrade, as long as you have an internet connection and a means of electronic payment such as a credit card. Be warned though, the prices for Anytime Upgrade are not always as economical as simply buying the correct version of Windows in the first place.

Windows 8.1 retail DVDs

Windows 8.1 is the latest upgrade to Windows 8. Windows 8.1 includes new features as well as bug fixes, so if you are planning to buy a copy of Windows 8, you should make sure it is Windows 8.1. Having said that, if you find a bargain priced copy of Windows 8, you can upgrade it to Windows 8.1 for free. We discuss upgrading to Windows 8.1 at the end of this section.

32-bit or 64-bit?

When discussing this subject, it is easy for technical authors such as myself to begin reminiscing about our childhoods and the amount of memory and storage space the early computers of the time had. I decided I would spare you that this time and get to the point. 64-bit versions of Windows can access more memory than their 32-bit counterparts, but the 32-bit versions tend to have better overall compatibility especially with older hardware and software. The 32-bit versions of Windows 8 can access a maximum of 4 gigabytes of RAM. RAM is the primary storage area on your computer that Windows uses for programs and data that it is currently working on. It is not the same as the hard drive which is used to store programs and data that are not currently being used. If you're confused, we will discuss these terms in more detail later, when we talk about choosing a computer for Windows 8 or upgrading an existing machine.

The 64-bit versions of Windows 8 can access either 16gb on the standard edition or up to a whopping 192 gigabytes on the Professional edition. Again, I want to tell you how many hundreds of times more capacity that is than the first hard drive I owned, but I wont.

Now, 4 Gigabytes of memory might seem like a lot and for many users it will be adequate. 4 gigabytes must have sounded like a lot when the first 32-bit versions of Windows were developed, but by today's standards it's quite modest. For instance Windows PCs have the most cutting edge games in the world and many of these games will benefit from machines with large amounts of RAM. It is important to note that this maximum memory allocation includes memory on your graphics card too. Were you to purchase a high end graphics card for gaming, with 1 gigabyte of memory, the most RAM you could then use with a 32-bit version of Windows would be 3 gigabytes. With graphics cards now shipping with even more memory than that and with top-spec gaming motherboards giving the option of attaching two or more graphics cards at once, enthusiasts should seriously consider going 64-bit to get the most out of their machines. Even regular users should probably choose the 64-bit version of Windows 8 unless they have a particular piece of old software that isn't compatible.

Just like Windows 7, the retail editions of Windows 8 will ship with both 32-bit and 64-bit versions in the same box. However, you can't switch between versions without either reinstalling your operating system or configuring some kind of dual booting system.

Taking the plunge

So, you have decided on which edition of Windows 8 to purchase, how do you go about getting it? Before you tear off to the store with your shopping list, let's look at a couple of options.

The easy way – Choosing a new computer with Windows 8 installed

Buying a computer with Windows 8 pre-installed is the easiest way to get the operating system. The hard part is done and you can get right on with discovering your new PC. Which PC you choose is largely down to your personal tastes and requirements. Do your homework, look for reviews on the internet if possible and think carefully before parting with your cash. Here are a few pointers to look out for when buying a Windows 8 PC.

Memory:– Windows 8 requires 1 gigabyte of computer memory (2 gigabytes for the 64-bit version). Memory is usually shortened to RAM, it can also be referred to as "primary storage". RAM is where the computer stores programs and data it is currently working on, this is different to the hard disk or drive which is generally only fast enough to store programs and data you are not currently using. One gigabyte of memory is just about adequate for regular computing tasks such as surfing the internet, word-processing or writing e-mails. If you work with lots of programs at once, or you do more demanding tasks on your computer such as gaming, you may want to go for a machine with 2 or more gigabytes of memory. Memory can easily be upgraded in almost all computers, including laptops.

Hard Drive Capacity:– Your hard disk drive is used to store all the programs and data you keep on your PC. Hard drive sizes are measured in gigabytes too, but they are considerably larger than memory or RAM capacities. Windows 8 requires 20 gigabytes of hard drive space all to itself. The remaining space is filled up with any other programs you install and any files you create yourself or download from the internet. If you have a large collection of multimedia files, you will want to make sure to purchase a machine with an equally large hard drive. Don't forget that hard drives are prone to sudden, random failures. Always keep a backup of your data if it is important, we discuss backup and the Windows 8 backup utility in chapter 7.

Hard Drive Type:- There are two types of hard drive available to consumers, solid state and magnetic. Solid state drives or SSD's are extremely fast and can give your computer a noticeable speed boost. However, they have a much less attractive cost to capacity ratio when compared to traditional, magnetic media hard drives. In a desktop PC or larger laptop, you may be able to choose an SSD for Windows and a second, traditional magnetic media drive for secondary storage. In a smaller form factor PC where weight is an issue, you will usually be limited to choosing one or the other.

Graphics Card:– The graphics card or graphics chip in the computer you buy is often overlooked by consumers when shopping for a new computer. You should make sure to check that the graphics card in the machine is capable of running DirectX 9 and WDDM 1.0 or higher. If you plan to play the latest games on your machine, you will need a PC with a more powerful graphics chip. Be sure to budget for this and check the requirements for the games you want to play to make sure your new PC matches up.

Internet connection:- Remember that to use the Windows store and many of the features of the tiles we demonstrate, you will need some kind of internet connection. Typically new PCs come with wired and wireless connections. We discuss types of internet connection in lesson 52. If you aren't planning to connect to the internet, you can still buy and use desktop software from various retailers, but you won't be able to buy any of the new tile software as it is only available online through the Windows store.

All shapes and sizes:– Modern PCs come in all kinds of different shapes and sizes, from tiny ultra-portables to huge, powerful desktops and this has never been more true than with Windows 8 machines. Again, the machine you choose comes down to personal taste and requirements. As a general rule, desktop computers have better upgrade options, larger displays and give more "bang for the buck" in terms of performance. Laptop, netbook (very small laptops, sometimes called ultra portables) and tablet PCs can, obviously, be transported and used almost anywhere. That could be up and down the country as you travel on business or up and down the house and garden as you work and play at home. Laptops and ultra-portables also take up less space but aren't quite so suited to heavy computing work as desktop PCs are and the smaller the PC gets the less powerful it is likely to be. Tablets can be great for reading or watching a movie, but not so great for when you want to get some work done. Many Windows 8 tablets have docking stations that turn them into mini-laptops, making them very flexible devices indeed.

Should I consider a Windows 8 RT machine?

Remember that if you are considering a Windows RT machine, it will not be compatible with any desktop software or existing Windows software. Windows RT machines will only run software available from the Windows Store tile, this includes specially modified versions of desktop apps such as Office. Don't write off Windows RT altogether, although it has this significant drawback, Windows RT tablets are lighter and cheaper than the machines that run the regular version of Windows. Remember too, that software you buy on your Microsoft account will work on any other Windows 8 machines you have access to, as long as you can sign into them using your Microsoft account. For instance, you could have a heavyweight, super powerful notebook PC for business and a lighter Windows RT machine for those weekends away. Both these machines would have access to your Windows store purchases.

The hard way – Upgrading an existing computer

Windows 8 is a compelling upgrade for many existing computers too, particularly for those die-hard Windows XP users who want to take advantage of the newer features that Windows 8 brings. For Windows 7 users, there's less incentive to upgrade this time, but even for desktop users, Windows 8 still brings some good new features. Upgrading an existing computer to Windows 8 is a little more tricky than just going out and buying one with Windows 8 preloaded. Care must be taken to backup all your data and you may have to reinstall all of your programs once you have finished upgrading your operating system.

Custom install versus in-place upgrade

There are two ways in which you can change operating systems on your PC, custom install and in-place upgrade. An in-place upgrade changes your current operating system from one version to another. So, in theory at least, all you need to do is insert the Windows 8 DVD or other installation media and wait for the process to complete. In practise it is not always that simple. Problems can and do occur since no two Windows installations are exactly alike. Many IT professionals prefer to do a custom installation instead. You should definitely make sure that you have a full backup of your system before you begin.

When you perform a custom installation, your entire existing operating system is removed and replaced with the new one. Usually during this process, you will lose any programs and data that you have not backed up. This is the big disadvantage of a custom installation.

When choosing which type of installation to perform, in lots of cases, Microsoft have already made the decision for you. If you are upgrading from Windows XP or Windows Vista, you only have the choice of a custom installation. Similarly if you are upgrading from a 32-bit version of Windows to a 64-bit version then a custom installation is also the only way to go. Finally, Windows 8 Professional can in-place upgrade any version of Windows 7, but the standard edition of Windows 8 can only in-place upgrade from Windows 7 Home Premium.

Is my old PC capable of running Windows 8?

Windows 8 requires a 1 gigahertz processor and 1 gigabyte of RAM (2 gigabytes for the 64-bit version). You will also need a DirectX 9 graphics device. The easiest way to see if your computer meets these requirements is to use the Windows 8 Upgrade Assistant. To obtain this tool, visit the Update to Windows 8.1 FAQ online here:- http://windows.microsoft.com/en-US/windows-8/upgrade-to-windows-8

Now, click on "Will my devices and apps be compatible with Windows 8.1?". You should now see a download link for the Upgrade Assistant. Run the Upgrade Assistant to evaluate your current PC and see if it meets the requirements for installing Windows 8.1.

Upgrading to Windows 8.1

If you're running a Windows 8 machine, you will need to upgrade to Windows 8.1 in order to use this guide. Fortunately, upgrading is super easy. Upgrading is done by using the Store tile, rather than Windows update as you might have expected. On most Windows 8 machines, all you need to do is connect to the internet then open the Store tile by clicking it on the Start screen. The option to upgrade to Windows 8.1 will appear instantly.

If you are running Windows 8, this tile should appear in the store

Click this tile then follow all on-screen prompts. The Windows 8.1 upgrade will now download and install automatically. The download is quite large so be prepared to wait for a while.

If you don't see the tile, you may need to update your PC. Try restarting your machine first, so that Windows can apply any pending updates and then try again. If you have the full version of the Superguide, you can also watch a brief video that discusses how to upgrade from the guides main menu. Alternatively, watch our guide to upgrading Windows 8.1 on Top-Windows-Tutorials.com here:- http://www.top-windows-tutorials.com/installing-windows-upgrade/

Is that all?

We did consider covering installation and upgrading to Windows 8 in this guide. However, we decided that it was beyond the scope of a book aimed at beginners. We would want to cover dual booting (installing two or more operating systems at once) and various other options to really cover the subject in the kind of detail that Superguide readers would expect. If you want to upgrade your existing computer to Windows 8, discuss the options with a local IT professional or computer workshop. They will be able to asses all your upgrade options.

Lesson 1 – Starting your new Windows 8 PC

Even starting a Windows 8 PC can cause some surprises. In this lesson we will take a look at what happens when you first power on a factory fresh Windows 8 machine. Don't worry if you've already gone over these steps, there is nothing here that you can do wrong or can't change later.

1.1 – Initial personalisations

The very first thing to do on your Windows 8 PC is choose a colour scheme, figure 1.1 shows the colour scheme picker.

Figure 1.1 – Choose your favourite colours with the colour picker

Click (or tap) on any colour to select it. Simply choose the colour scheme you like best. If other users are sharing the PC with you, they can choose their own colour scheme later, after you have set them up their own user account (we cover user accounts in lesson 36).

Next, choose a name for your PC and enter it into the text box below the colour picker. The PC name can be anything, it can be used to identify your PC on the home network and also can be seen by Microsoft if you link your PC to your Microsoft account, which we cover later in this lesson. When you have made these changes, click on the "Next" button in the bottom right corner of the screen. The screen shown in figure 1.2 will then appear.

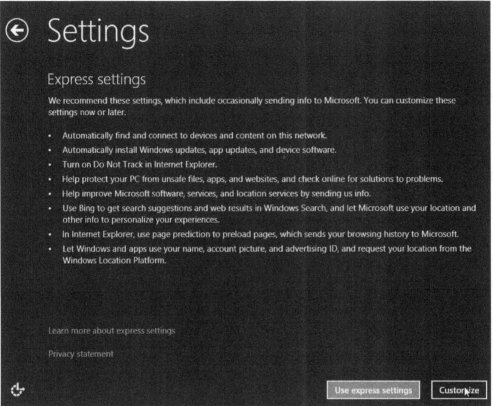

Figure 1.2 – Choosing options and reviewing privacy policies

The screen shown in figure 1.2 will offer the choice of "Express settings" or "Customize". For simplicity, new users should choose "Use express settings". All settings can be changed later once you're more comfortable working with your PC. If you want to know exactly what express settings will configure, there are two links at the bottom of the screen. The first link reads "Learn more about express settings". You can also review Microsoft's privacy policy by clicking on the second link, which reads "Privacy statement". We only cover the express settings in this guide, but we do show you how to change some of those settings later. Click on "Use express settings" to proceed to the next screen, which contains the information shown in figure 1.3.

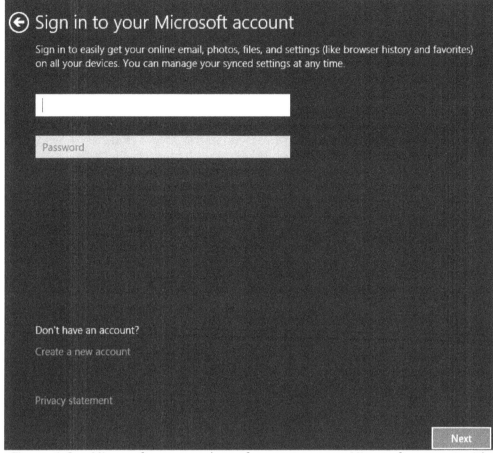

Figure 1.3 – Microsoft are very keen for you to use a Microsoft account with Windows 8, but you don't have to

1.2 – Choosing a Microsoft or a local account

The setup process now presents you with an important choice. You can sign in to your PC using a Microsoft account or you can use a regular Windows login.

What is the difference between each type of account, and why was this change introduced? Microsoft are keen for users to sign in with a Microsoft account. When you do this, settings will be synchronised between all the PCs you own and you will be automatically signed into the Windows, Music and Video stores. This can be very convenient of course. You might already have a Microsoft account and not even be aware of it. If you use Hotmail or Outlook.com, your login for these services is your Microsoft account. The same login is used for OneDrive and Xbox Live too. If you don't have a Microsoft account, you can sign up for one at this point too, by clicking "Create a new account".

Why might you want to use a regular Windows account instead? You may consider that linking all of your Microsoft services like this to be a security risk. Malware designed to steal Windows login credentials has appeared in the past and now that Windows credentials can be linked to online accounts too, they become even more valuable. Although Microsoft take steps to mitigate logins being stolen, as we've seen in the media there's always that danger. Personally, I prefer to keep my Microsoft password in a password manager and use a standard login for my PC, this means I can use a much longer password than I could normally remember for my Microsoft account. We cover password managers briefly in the last chapter.

The other reason you might not want to login with a Microsoft account is if you have a home network setup. Perhaps you or a technician or family member has configured devices like media streamers or network attached storage (NAS) boxes in your home. In this setup, these devices may be protected with usernames and passwords that prevent certain family members from accessing each others files. In this case, you might want to continue using a regular, old fashioned Windows account rather than reconfiguring all of your network to accept new user names and passwords.

The choice of which type of account you use is entirely up to you. You can add new accounts of both types later, or even switch an old style account to use a Microsoft account instead. Even logging in without a Microsoft account, you can still access features like the Windows store, you will simply be prompted to enter Microsoft account credentials when you access the store.

If you sign in with a Microsoft account now, you will be asked for your password and, if security information does not exist on file, you will be asked to add some. Usually you will be asked to add a phone number, alternate e-mail and secret question. Make sure not to make the answer to your secret question too easy to guess! Remember that your Microsoft account could be linked to many services so always take extra care with it.

What if you don't want to use a Microsoft account? With Windows 8.1, Microsoft have made it harder to create a standard Windows account and you will have to jump through some hoops if you want to do so. In the top text entry box shown in figure 1.3, enter a fictitious e-mail address. Try to pick one that is unlikely to be in use by anyone else in the world. A random mashing of your keyboard, followed by @hotmail.com usually works best. Then, in the password box, enter sixteen characters or less of random letters and numbers. See figure 1.4 for an example.

Figure 1.4 – Entering a random address and password to skip the Microsoft account login requirement

By entering a false e-mail address like this, Windows will fail to connect to your Microsoft account. It will then relent and give you the option of creating a local account. Figure 1.5 shows this.

Figure 1.5 – Finally we have the option of creating a local account

Click on the "continue without a Microsoft account" link, then click on the button labelled "Create a local account". The screen shown in figure 1.6 will then appear.

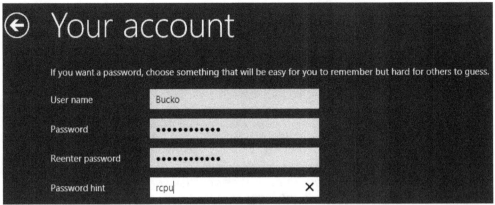

Figure 1.6 – Creating a local account

Fill out a username, password and password hint for your local account. These details will then be stored locally on your PC. Remember that the password hint can be seen by anyone who has access to this PC, so don't make the hint too obvious.

Once you are done configuring accounts and adding security information for either a local or a Microsoft account, Windows will prepare your account. While it does this, you can watch a little tutorial on how to use the new interface. Don't worry if you miss this though, we will be covering it extensively in the next few lessons. When the configuration is complete, the new Start screen will appear. You've now set up your new Windows 8 PC and you can proceed to the next lesson.

Lesson 2 – The new Start screen

Time to say farewell to the Start menu and meet Microsoft's new Start screen. Working with the Start screen is easy and in this lesson you will learn how to get around.

2.1 – Logging in

When you power on your Windows 8 PC, you will need to log into the machine. This works slightly differently to previous versions of Windows. Initially, you will see the Lock screen. Figure 2.1 shows a typical Lock screen, though as you will see in lesson 44.2 you can actually customise it to display any picture you want to.

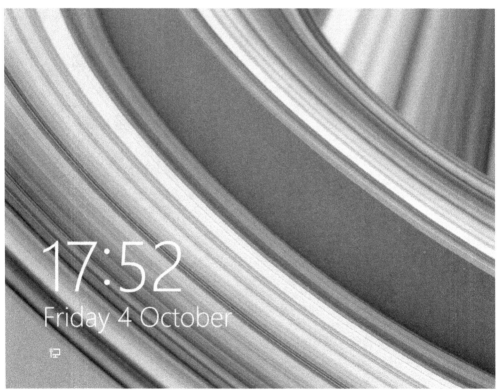

Figure 2.1 – The Windows 8 Lock screen

To unlock your PC, either click once with the mouse or swipe your finger upwards. The Lock screen will then disappear, revealing the login screen shown in figure 2.2.

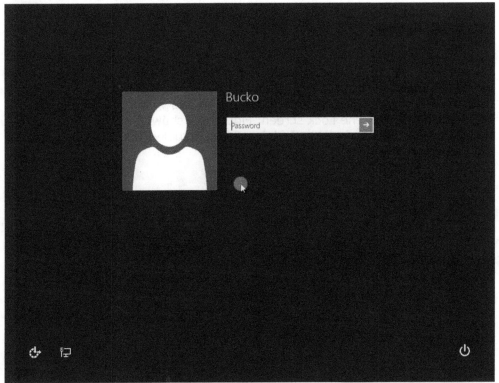

Figure 2.2 – Once the Lock screen has been dismissed, you can log in

Enter your password into the text entry box shown in figure 2.2 then press enter or click the right-pointing arrow. You will then be logged into the PC. What happens next depends on what kind of PC you are running. If Windows does not detect a touch screen, you will be taken directly to the desktop. The desktop is where most users who have keyboard and mouse equipped systems will spend most of their time.

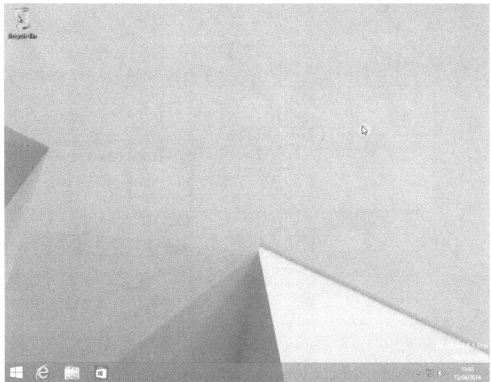

Figure 2.3 – The desktop is one of the computing environments Windows 8 offers

If you do have a touch screen however, the Start screen will appear, as shown in figure 2.5.

Whenever you are on the desktop, you can always access the Start screen by moving your mouse pointer to the Start button (shown here) and clicking. The Start button is the button located in the bottom left hand corner of the desktop.

Figure 2.5 – The new Windows 8 Start screen

2.2 – Getting to grips with tiles

Figure 2.5 shows the new Windows 8 interface which you will see on a clean installation of the operating system. Windows 8 gives you two distinct ways to work with your PC. There's the new tiled interface that you see on the Start screen, as well as the traditional desktop interface that users of previous versions of Windows will be familiar with. The tiles also replace the old Start menu, so even if you primarily run desktop applications, you will want to familiarise yourself with the Start screen so that you can search your PC and launch your programs.

The tile applications were originally called "Metro" apps. Due largely to a trademark dispute, Microsoft changed their mind and since then they have been referred to as Modern apps or Windows Store apps. To save confusion, we will refer to them as "Tile" apps in this guide.

Notice the large message in the top right hand corner? In Windows 8.1, Microsoft have added these messages as a quick-start tutorial, to help the many bewildered users that have migrated to Windows 8 from an earlier version of the operating system. To make the message go away, simply do as it says. These messages only appear once and we will cover the techniques they demonstrate in much more detail as we go through the guide.

Each tile on the interface represents a program. In figure 2.5 the tile near the bottom right of the screen has a picture on it. This is the News tile, and the picture is of the infamous mother of the "mummified boy" that was sadly in the news at the time the picture was taken. The pictures and information on the tiles are constantly changing, unlike icons that usually remain static.

Many tiles on the interface can show information. As you work with Windows 8 the Start screen will "come alive". Pictures from your Pictures library will appear on the Pictures tile, photos of your friends will appear on the People tile and so on.

To start a program from the tile interface, just click (or tap) the tile once.

Usually, to browse through content in a tile application or on the Start screen, you use the scroll bar at the bottom of the screen, or swipe with your finger. Figure 2.6 shows a close up of the scroll bar.

Figure 2.6 – Browsing the store using a mouse, with the scroll bar

2.3 – Navigating between tile apps

While you can close tile programs, you don't generally need to. Windows will make sure that they don't consume computing resources when they are not actively running. There are several ways to navigate back from an open tile to the Start screen. You can press either the left or right Windows key on your keyboard, figure 2.7 shows the Windows key on a typical keyboard layout.

Figure 2.7 – The Windows key is used as a shortcut back to the Start screen and also for several other keyboard shortcuts.

You can also use the hot corner in the bottom left hand corner of the screen. Move your mouse to the very bottom left corner of the screen. Figure 2.8 shows the icon that will then appear.

Figure 2.8 – Accessing the Start 'hot corner'

Simply click on the Start button that appears and the Start screen will reappear. Note that if you see a small image of the Start screen in the hot corner, instead of the Start button, you are still running Windows 8. Follow our quick tutorial at the start of the guide to upgrade to Windows 8.1. It's free, so there's no reason not to.

If you are using a PC with a touch screen, then to get back to the Start screen, swipe your finger from the right of the screen to open up the Charms Bar and then tap the Start Charm. We cover the Charms Bar in more detail in lesson 3.3.

2.4 – Apps view

If you move your mouse pointer to the bottom of the screen, or press your finger near the bottom of the screen, you should see a small downward pointing arrow icon. By clicking or tapping this icon, the Start screen will change to "Apps" view. Figure 2.9 illustrates this.

Figure 2.9 – Apps view

Apps view was introduced to make the Start screen behave a little more like the traditional Start menu from earlier versions of Windows. From here, you can browse all the apps, both tile and desktop, installed on your PC. To change the sorting order, click on the text next to the word "Apps" at the top left of the screen. The menu shown in figure 2.10 will then appear.

Figure 2.10 – Changing the sorting criteria for Apps view

You can also search your apps using the search box in the top right of the screen. We cover searching your PC in lesson 4.

To go back from Apps view to the regular Start screen, look for the up pointing arrow at the bottom of the screen.

Most tile applications have a command bar. To access this on a touch machine, swipe upwards with your finger from the bottom of the screen (or the top of the screen on some apps). On a machine with a keyboard and mouse, simply right click on an empty area on the app.

Congratulations, you now know the basics of getting around the new interface. In the next lesson we will look more closely at the other elements of the new interface.

Lesson 3 – Multitasking with tiles

Windows 8's new tile-based interface has several shortcuts that make it easier to navigate using either a touch screen or a more traditional keyboard and mouse. In this lesson we will take a look at how to get around the tiles primarily using your keyboard and mouse. Where touch screen navigation differs significantly, we'll cover that too.

3.1 – Switching between apps

In the last lesson we used the hot corners to switch back to the Start screen. Windows 8 also has a simple program switcher that can be accessed from the same corner. When you have several tile programs running, move your mouse to the bottom left corner of the screen and then slide the mouse upwards. If you complete the gesture correctly, the task switcher shown in figure 3.1 will appear.

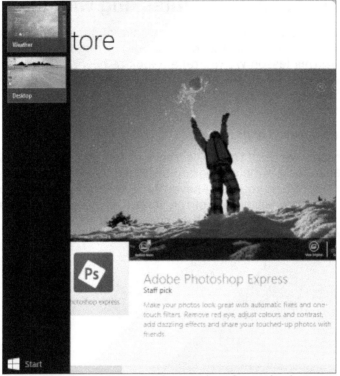

Figure 3.1 – Accessing a task switcher from the hot corner

You can now click or tap the application you want to switch to. Alternatively, if you want to quickly flip between open tiles, move your mouse pointer to the top left hand corner of the screen. A small thumbnail sized picture of another tile application will then appear. Click on the thumbnail to flip to that application. You can keep clicking and the applications will shuffle, as if shuffling through a stack of papers.

Touch Users – Accessing this task switcher is a little more tricky on touch screens, at least initially. To do so, swipe your finger in from the left of the screen, then when the first app thumbnail appears, swipe back towards the left.

Many users find the hot corners difficult to use. Remember that to get back to the Start screen, you can press the Windows key on your keyboard instead of using the hot corner. You can also use the Alt-Tab keyboard shortcut to access a different task switcher. Simply hold down either of the Alt keys and then press and release the Tab key. Figure 3.2 shows the correct keys to press.

Figure 3.2 – Press the Alt and Tab keys to access a task switcher

When you press the key combination shown in figure 3.2, the window shown in figure 3.3 will appear.

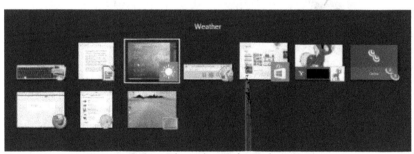

Figure 3.3 – The Alt+Tab task switcher

The task switcher window shows your currently running tile and desktop applications. While using the task switcher, keep the Alt key pressed. You can then either click on a program with the mouse or press and release the Tab key again to shuffle through the programs.

There's one important difference between the Alt-Tab task switcher and the task switcher we discussed at the start of the lesson. With the task switcher you access from the hot corner, all desktop apps are treated as a single app, called simply "Desktop". With the Alt-Tab activated task switcher, each desktop app is selectable individually.

3.2 – The taskbar and tile applications

In the latest Windows 8.1 update, Microsoft have also added the option to use the Windows taskbar while working with tile applications. Tile applications will now appear on the taskbar when using the desktop. Furthermore, when working with a tile, move your mouse to the bottom of the screen and the taskbar will appear.

Figure 3.4 – Accessing the taskbar from within a tile application

With the taskbar open, you can switch instantly to any other program, desktop or tile, just by clicking on its icon.

3.3 – Meet the Charms Bar

As you might have guessed, there's a hot corner in the right hand side of the screen too. Move your mouse to the top right or bottom right and then the Charms Bar will appear. Move the mouse pointer towards the Charm icons to open the Charms Bar fully. Touch screen users can swipe in from the right of their screen to open the Charms Bar. Figure 3.5 shows the Charms Bar.

Figure 3.5 – The Windows 8 Charms Bar

You can click or tap the Start Charm to return to the Start screen at any time. We will be exploring the Charms in more detail in later tutorials.

3.4 – Closing tiles

You generally don't need to close tile applications when you are done working with them. Windows will intelligently manage tiles you are not using, ensuring that they consume only minimal resources while running in the background. If you find you have dozens of tiles open and it is starting to become difficult to navigate through them, you can close them manually. In the latest Windows 8.1 update, there are two ways.

3.4.1 – Closing tiles the touch-friendly way

Move your finger or mouse pointer to the top middle of the screen. The mouse pointer will change into a hand icon. Press and hold the mouse button or hold your finger to the screen and drag downwards. You will notice that the currently active tile then becomes smaller, see figure 3.6 for an example.

Figure 3.6 – Manually closing a tile application

Drag the tile to the very bottom of the screen and let go of your mouse button or release your finger. The program is then fully closed and you will be returned to the Start screen.

3.4.2 – Closing tiles the mouse-friendly way

This method of closing a tile app should be familiar to anyone who has used Windows before. When working with a tile, move your mouse pointer to the top of the screen and a title bar will appear.

Figure 3.7 – Accessing a tile applications title bar

To close the application, click the cross in the top right hand corner. Alternatively, click on the icon to the left of the cross to leave the application without closing it. If you use these controls to close or dismiss a tile application, you will be returned to the desktop rather than the Start screen.

You now know how to multitask and switch between tile applications on your Windows 8 PC. In the next lesson we will look at the important topic of searching your computer.

Lesson 4 – Searching your Windows 8 PC

Searching in previous version of Windows was done from the Start menu and since the tile-based Start screen is the new Start menu, you can search from the Start screen too.

4.1 – Starting a search

There are two ways to start a standard search on a Windows 8 PC. You can open the Charms Bar (see lesson 3.3) and click on the Search Charm, the Search box will then open. Alternatively, go to the Start screen and simply start typing on the keyboard. Search will then open automatically. Figure 4.1 shows a typical search in action.

Figure 4.1 – Searching on a Windows 8 PC

Search in Windows 8.1 has changed significantly since Windows 8. Searches take place across several categories. Notice in figure 4.1, below the word "Search" on the top right, we are searching "Everywhere". Searching everywhere will search all the programs and files on your PC, it will also bring back search suggestions for the web, which are displayed in the bottom part of the search bar below the dividing line.

Figure 4.2 shows the other search categories that can be selected.

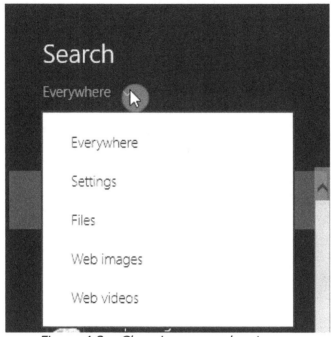

Figure 4.2 – Choosing a search category

Each search category narrows your search results accordingly, the categories are as follows.

Everywhere:– Searches all programs and files on your computer and for websites related to the keyword you enter.

Settings:– Specifically searches for PC settings related to your keyword.

Files:– Searches only for data files on your PC, such as pictures, videos or text files.

Web images:– Searches online for pictures.

Web videos:– Searches online for videos.

4.2 - 'Everywhere' search limitations

When searching your Windows 8 PC, remember that searching "everywhere" may limit the number of results you get. Consider figure 4.3, it shows the search results for the term "display" with the search category set to "Everywhere".

Figure 4.3 – Search results may be limited when searching "Everywhere"

Now, compare figure 4.3 with figure 4.4, which shows the same search term but this time with the "Settings" category.

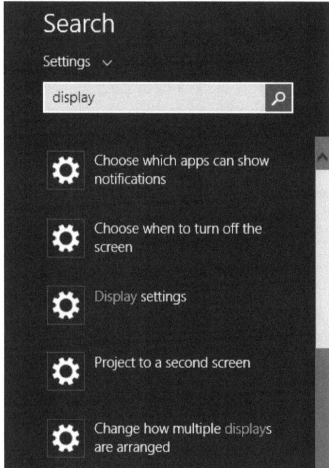

Figure 4.4 – Choosing a specific search category helps get more results

As you can see, there are many more results when searching in a specific category rather than just "Everywhere". When there are too many search results to fit on the screen, a scroll control will appear on the right. Use your finger or the mouse to move this control and scroll down the results.

Another technique you can use to get more search results, for any category of search, is to press enter after your search or to click or tap on the magnifying glass icon at the right of the search box. Doing this will open a full-page of search results. Figure 4.5 shows an example of this.

Figure 4.5 – Full screen search results for "Display"

4.3 – Apps view

As we saw in lesson 1, if you are searching for an app on your PC, you may prefer to use the apps view. To access apps view, click on the downward pointing arrow at the bottom of the Start screen, or swipe the screen upwards with your finger. This arrow is circled in figure 4.6. If you don't see it, click or tap near the bottom of the Start screen and it should appear.

Figure 4.6 – Click or tap on the arrow circled to access Apps view

Figure 4.7 shows the Apps view screen.

Figure 4.7 – Apps view is new to Windows 8.1. Use the search box in the top right to search through your apps

Using Apps view, you can search apps directly by typing into the search box at the top right of the screen. You can also scroll through all your apps using either the mouse or your finger. This view is closer to the old Start menu that users of previous versions of Windows are used to.

4.4 – Search Charm in Windows 8.1

The behaviour of the Search Charm has changed a little in Windows 8.1. In Windows 8, if you opened the Charms Bar and selected the Search Charm while you were working in an app, such as the store, Windows would open up a search for the current app. In Windows 8.1 this doesn't happen. To search the store in Windows 8, you simply use the search box that appears in the Store app, as we'll see in lesson 11.

That's all it takes to search in Windows 8. Just like in earlier versions of Windows it's fast and easy and the easiest way of finding files and programs on your PC.

Lesson 5 – The Settings Charm

In this lesson we are going to look more closely at another part of the Charms Bar, specifically the Settings Charm. We will also cover how to restart or shut down your Windows 8 PC.

Remember how we opened the Charms Bar in lesson 3.3?, there are several ways. You can use the hot corner in the top or bottom right of the screen, or if you have a touch screen you can swipe in from the right of the screen.

If you don't have a touch screen and you find the hot corner difficult to use, you can use the following keyboard combination to open the Charms Bar.

Press and hold the Windows key, then press and release the 'C' key, the Charms Bar will then open. You can then release the Windows key.

5.1 – Start screen settings Charm

If you open the Charms Bar while on the Start screen and then click on the Settings Charm, the sidebar shown in figure 5.2 will appear.

Figure 5.2 – The PC settings menu

This sidebar gives us access to some basic settings and also access to the Windows 8 built in help. There are a few settings that we can change under "Tiles", but we will cover them in lesson 43.3. In this lesson we will focus on the icons shown at the bottom of figure 5.2. These icons change basic settings on the PC. We'll take a look at what each one does in a little more detail now.

5.2 – The basic PC settings icons

The network icon lets you manage wired and wireless networks. Click or tap it to connect to a new network or to see the status of existing connections. We cover this in more detail in lesson 52.

This icon is the volume icon, letting you adjust the volume of your PCs sound effects. Simply click or tap it, then use the slider control to adjust to taste.

The sunshine icon here is for adjusting brightness, if your display supports this feature you can click or tap here and use the slider control to adjust the screen. Remember that setting the screen brighter will consume more battery power.

The icon here is supposed to look like a card with writing on. This is the Notifications icon. Notifications will appear on your computer screen when certain events happen, perhaps when an e-mail arrives for instance. By clicking on this icon, Windows gives you the option to hide notifications for a certain amount of time. This can be useful if you want to concentrate on something and don't want to be distracted.

The Keyboard icon allows you to change input language, if you have more than one language installed.

The Power icon is where you go to shut down or restart a Windows 8 PC. Figure 5.9 shows the options available when you click or tap on this icon.

Figure 5.9 – Power options

Selecting "Sleep" will put the PC into a low-power standby mode. If you're not going to use your PC for an hour or more, then putting it to sleep will save the status of your currently open applications and allow you to resume later. Waking the PC from sleep mode is much faster than starting it from cold, but sleep mode still consumes some power. It is advisable to save anything you are working on before using sleep mode.

Selecting Shut down or Restart will, as you probably guessed, either shut down the PC entirely or restart it. Sometimes it is necessary to restart your computer after installing new software, for instance. If there are Windows updates pending, you will see the option "Update and restart" in place of just "Restart".

5.3 – Account options

If you are used to earlier versions of Windows you may have noticed that the lock and log out options are not available from the power options. To perform these actions you must go back to the Start screen and click your account picture. In Windows 8.1 update 1, Microsoft also added a convenient short cut to the power options to the Start screen too. Figure 5.10 shows the menu that you can then access.

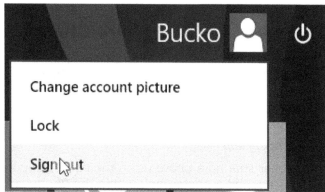

*Figure 5.10 – Accessing options for changing accounts and locking the PC.
Notice the power button in the top right of the picture*

The options shown in figure 5.10 are pretty self-explanatory. Clicking "Lock" will lock the PC and take you to the Lock screen, this is the screen you see when you first turn on your PC. Locking the PC won't close any of your open applications, but it will stop others from accessing your PC while you are away from it. Clicking on "Sign out" will sign you out of your PC entirely, closing down all the apps you have running.

If you have another user account on the PC, it will appear at the bottom of this menu. Clicking on this will switch to that account without signing you out of the PC. You will, of course, need to enter the account password to switch over to another account. We cover user accounts in full in lesson 36.

By clicking on the power button shown in the top right of figure 5.10, you can access the same power options that are shown in figure 5.9. This saves having to open the Charms Bar and is particularly convenient for keyboard and mouse users.

5.4 – Settings in other programs

Remember that the Charms Bar works with the tile you currently have open. So for instance if you open the Settings Charm while you are working with the Photos app, you will access settings for the Photos app. Keep this in mind, as the Settings Charm is the only way to change many settings in several of the tile applications.

Lesson 6 – The Share Charm

In this lesson we will be looking at the Share Charm. This is a context sensitive feature that does different things depending on which app is currently open. Not all apps support sharing but for those that do it can be a quick and convenient way of moving information between apps.

6.1 – Sharing in the Photos app

Figure 6.1 shows a user sharing a photo using the Photos app and the Share Charm. The user has opened a photograph within the Photos app and then opened the Charms Bar and clicked the Share Charm.

Figure 6.1 – Using the Share Charm in the Photos app

In figure 6.1 we can see the options to share this picture with the Mail app. On a machine that has more apps installed, there may be additional choices.

In figure 6.2, the user has clicked on the "Mail" button.

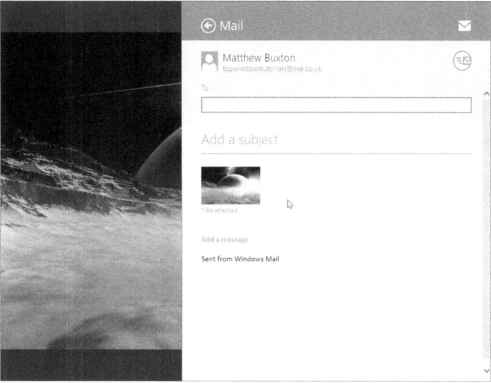

Figure 6.2 – Sharing a photo with the Mail app

In figure 6.2 we can see that Windows 8 has automatically attached the photo to an e-mail. All that remains is to enter your contacts e-mail address and click the send button and the photo will be e-mailed to them, as easy as that.

6.2 – Sharing in Internet Explorer

The Share Charm works in Internet Explorer too. Windows 8 actually includes two versions of Internet Explorer, there's a tile version and a desktop version. When using the tile version you can share any useful websites you come across using the Share Charm. Figure 6.3 shows this in action.

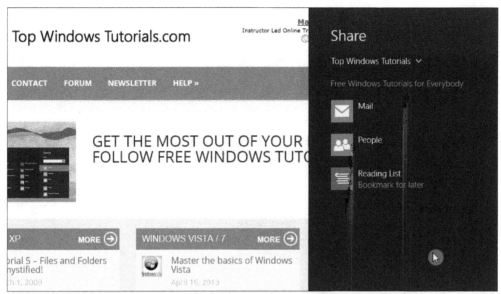

Figure 6.3 – Using the Share Charm in Internet Explorer

Notice that the sharing options in figure 6.3 are a little different to those in figure 6.1. This time we can e-mail the page, share it with people in the People app, or save it to our Reading List for later. The available sharing options will be different for different types of content. Figure 6.4 shows what happens if a web page is shared with the People app.

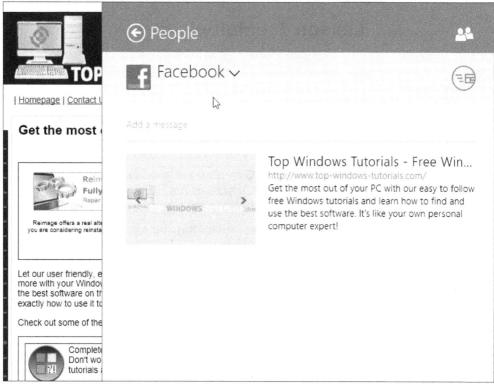

Figure 6.4 – Sharing a web page with the People app allows it to be posted directly to your social networks

By sharing the page with the People app, the link can now be posted directly to the users Facebook page or Twitter account. Your social networking accounts will need to be linked to Windows 8 first and we cover this in lesson 9.1.

That covers the basics of using the "Share" Charm in Windows 8. As Windows 8 matures, we can expect many more programs to start supporting sharing. Experiment using sharing in other apps too and discover the possibilities for yourself.

Lesson 7 – Multiple tiles

In this lesson we will be discussing ways of working with multiple Windows 8 tile applications at once. In Windows 8.1, Microsoft have improved multitasking with tile applications and now you can work with two or even three tiles at once (if your display is large enough). To use multiple tiles at once, we "insert" them into a part of the screen. If you are familiar with "snapping" tiles in Windows 8, you will find these new improvements easy to use.

To use multiple tiles, the Windows 8 PC must have a screen resolution of at least 1366x768. You can check your PCs screen resolution by searching for "screen resolution" and then clicking the icon that appears.

There are several ways of inserting tiles, including the right click method, dragging tiles or using a keyboard shortcut.

7.1 – Inserting with a right-click

To use this method, you must open a compatible application first, you cannot 'insert' the Start screen, but virtually all tile apps are compatible. You will also need two or more apps open. To use the right click method, open the task switcher that we demonstrated in lesson 3.1. Now, instead of clicking on an application to switch to it, right click instead, figure 7.1 shows the menu that will then appear.

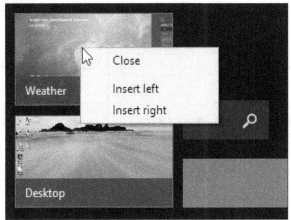

Figure 7.1 – Using a right click to insert a tile application

You can insert an application to the left or right of the screen. When you do, the application will appear on either the left or right hand half of the screen. Figure 7.2 shows an example of two tile applications running together.

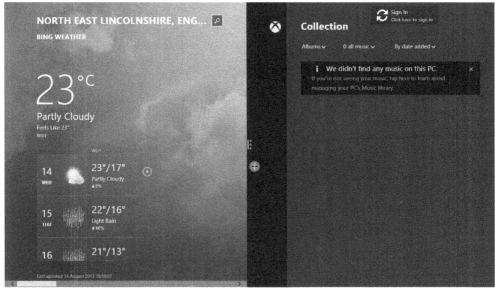

Figure 7.2 – The Weather app is inserted on the left

If your Windows 8 PC has a very high resolution display (1080p or greater) you can even insert a third application in the same manner.

7.2 – Resize control

The resize control, shown on the left here, is new in Windows 8.1. By dragging this control with your finger or the mouse, you can resize the apps you have running together. If you drag this control too far to the left or the right, the app will then disappear from the screen. If you let go of the control at this point, the app will simply close.

7.3 – Opening further apps

When running two or more apps together, the behaviour of newly opened apps changes a little. When you launch a new app, it will hover above the applications you already have open. Figure 7.4 illustrates this.

Figure 7.4 – Opening a new app while running two apps together

To position the app on your screen, drag it with your mouse pointer or finger and place it on the desired screen area. If you find dragging the app to be too awkward, you can move your mouse pointer to either edge of the new app's tile in the middle of the screen. The app will then tilt in that direction. If you click now, the app will then place itself in the appropriate half of the screen. If your screen resolution is too low to support running another app simultaneously, it will replace the app that is currently running on the selected screen area.

7.4 – Arranging apps by dragging

You can arrange applications using your mouse (or finger on a touchscreen), you do this in a similar way to closing them. To rearrange any application that is currently open on the screen, first move your mouse pointer to the top of the app then click and hold down the left mouse button. Now, drag the app down until it becomes a small tile, then simply drag it to the desired position on the screen and let go of your mouse button.

If you use this method to drag an app all the way over to the left, it will pop into the task switcher. Using this technique, you can remove the app from the screen without closing it. Figure 7.5 shows an example of dragging an app into the task switcher.

Figure 7.5 – Moving the Health and Fitness app from the left of the screen into the task switcher

Once you have done this, you can then drag another app from the task switcher over into the blank space. If there's no blank space on your screen and you drag an application from the task switcher, it will simply replace whichever application is currently running in that screen space. If you find dragging apps too awkward, simply click or tap the application in the task switcher and it will then hover above your currently open apps, ready to be positioned just like when we opened a new app from the Start screen in lesson 7.3.

7.5 – Arranging apps with the title bar

In Windows 8.1 Update 1, there's an even quicker way for keyboard and mouse users to arrange tiles. While working with any tile, move your mouse pointer to the top of the screen and the title bar will appear. Now, right click on the icon in the top left corner. See figure 7.6 for an example.

Figure 7.6 – Using the title bar shortcut to split an application left or right

You can now choose "Split Left" or "Split Right" to instantly split the application across your screen.

7.6 – Arranging apps with the keyboard

Another way you can arrange applications is with the keyboard. With two or more apps open on the screen, use the keyboard shortcut shown to select an app to work with.

When you press this keyboard combination, an app will be selected from the screen. Windows will make the selected app appear slightly smaller than usual. Keep the Windows key held down and keep pressing the dot or period key until the app you want to move is selected. Still keeping the Windows key held down, press the left or right arrow key to shuffle the app to the left or right of the screen.

7.7 – Using insert with the desktop

Remember that insert works on the desktop too. In this instance, the desktop is treated as a single tile app, so you cannot insert individual desktop apps using this technique. If for example you wanted the latest weather information available while you work with your desktop programs, firstly, open the Weather app. Now, go back to the Start screen and open the desktop. Next, open the hot corner task switcher (see lesson 3.1) and drag the weather app out, positioning it on either side of the desktop. It will then snap into place next to the desktop and can be resized using the resize control. Figure 7.8 shows the Music app inserted next to the desktop.

Figure 7.8 – Working on the desktop with a tile app inserted to the side of the screen

That is all you need to know to use multiple tiles in Windows 8. As you will probably agree, the Windows 8.1 improvements to tile multitasking add some much needed flexibility to the tile apps and are a big improvement on the multitasking seen in Windows 8 originally.

Chapter 2 – Getting Social

Social networking sites have made it really easy to stay in touch with friends and family around the world. Millions of people use sites like Facebook and Twitter to share photos, videos and memories with their friends and loved ones. The Windows 8 tiles have been designed to make using social networking easy. In this chapter we'll see how Windows 8 makes it easy and fast to manage your online interactions.

Lesson 8 – Mail

E-mail could be considered the oldest of the social networking tools available on the internet today. Pre-dating even the modern internet, e-mail isn't without its problems. Without special software it lacks any kind of security. Furthermore, support for sending files with e-mails is primitive compared to more modern alternatives. Nevertheless, e-mail is still widely used especially in workplaces where social networking sites may be frowned upon.

8.1 – Introducing Windows 8 Mail

After Windows 7 came with no e-mail software, Windows 8 now reverses that trend and comes with the mail application designed for the new tile interface. Figure 8.1 shows the Mail app open on a typical Windows 8 machine.

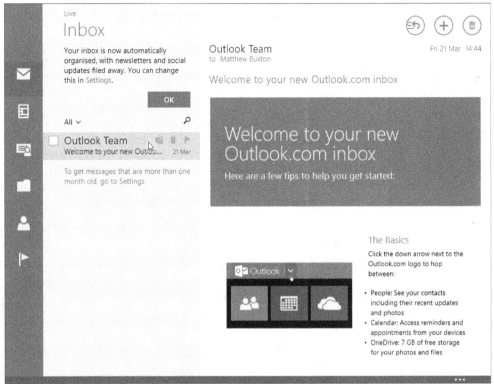

Figure 8.1 – The Windows Mail app

If you are using your Windows 8 PC with a Microsoft account, the Mail app will be linked to your Hotmail/Outlook e-mail. If not, you will be prompted to sign in to your Microsoft account the first time you use the Mail app. We also cover Microsoft accounts versus standard logins in lesson 36.2.

If this is the first time you have run the Windows 8 mail app, you may be asked if you want to add another account. Choose "No, thanks" for now, we will cover how to add other accounts later in this lesson.

In figure 8.1, we can see the various folders in the users Outlook.com account, as well as the icons on the left of the screen which represent various e-mail categories. These categories are a new addition to the Windows 8 mail app. Newsletters and social updates are placed into special folders that can be accessed by clicking the buttons on the left.

To open the inbox and read messages, simply click or tap on the inbox icon. The inbox icon is the envelope shaped icon near the top left. Since the mail application will open the inbox by default, we can see the contents of the users inbox in figure 8.1.

In the example shown in figure 8.1 the user has just one e-mail in the inbox folder. Messages are listed in date order with the most recent message listed first. The name of the sender is shown on the first line in big lettering and then below it the subject of the e-mail. For instance, the highlighted message is from "Outlook Team" and the subject is "Welcome to your new Outlook..". The contents of the message that is currently selected are shown on the right of the app. To highlight and read another message, simply click or tap it.

By default the e-mail app will only download two weeks worth of e-mails. If you are using your Windows 8 PC on a metered connection, such as a cellular modem, this setting will prevent too much unnecessary data being transferred. You can change this setting by opening the Charms Bar and using the Settings charm.

8.2 – Replying and composing

When an e-mail is selected, there are three icons the user can click. These icons are at the top right of the screen.

 Compose new message:- Click or tap this icon to start a fresh new message.

 Delete the message:- You will still be able to retrieve the message again by going into your deleted items folder.

 Reply to message:- Clicking or tapping this icon will open up a sub menu with three options for replying to the e-mail. The options are shown in figure 8.5.

Reply

Reply all

Forward

Figure 8.5 – Reply options for an e-mail

75

If you simply want to reply to the message, click on "Reply". Clicking on "Reply all" will reply to the sender and any other recipients too. Be careful when using this option, chain e-mails like those that send virus hoaxes often get forwarded to thousands of people like this. The original sender then harvests e-mail addresses for spamming.

Clicking on "Forward" will send the message directly to another user. You will be given the option of editing the message before sending it on to another contact.

Remember that many e-mails are sent by automated systems and from accounts that are not monitored. For instance, the message from "Outlook Team" that we can see in figure 8.1 is sent by a computer and any replies sent directly to this message would simply be discarded.

Figure 8.6 illustrates composing a new message within the Mail app.

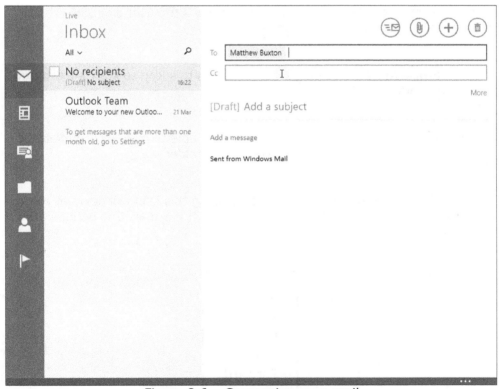

Figure 8.6 – Composing an e-mail

To send an e-mail, the first thing needed is the recipients e-mail address.

This can be typed in manually into the box near the top. Alternatively, start typing someone's name and Windows 8 will look them up automatically from the People app. In Windows 8, the People application replaces the address book type functionality you may have used in other e-mail software. We cover the People application in more detail in lesson 9. You can send an e-mail to multiple people too, just keep typing names into the "To" box.

The box below the "To" box is labelled "Cc". Cc is short for "Carbon copy". This means that anyone you add to this list will also receive the e-mail. By clicking on "More" you can also reveal a box labelled "Bcc". Bcc is short for "Blind carbon copy". Anyone you add to the Bcc list will also receive the e-mail, but they won't be able to see the e-mail addresses of any other recipient on the Bcc list. This is a great way to protect your friends privacy if you absolutely must send out an email to dozens of your contacts.

When you click on "More", the Priority box will also appear. If an e-mail is important, you can try marking it as high priority, but many e-mail programs (and users!) simply ignore this.

When you're done composing your message, click this icon to send it. Note that while most e-mails are received correctly, there are no guarantees. If your message is important and you don't receive a reply then be sure to send a follow up message or contact the recipient by another means. The e-mail system will sometimes send you a message to notify you if an e-mail account is invalid, but it does not send a message to confirm that an e-mail has been received.

8.3 – Adding new accounts

If you want to add another account to the Mail application, follow these steps. First of all, open the Charms Bar on the right of the screen (see lesson 3.3) and click on the Settings Charm. You should then see the option "Accounts", click on this, then choose "Add an account". You should then see the menu shown in figure 8.8.

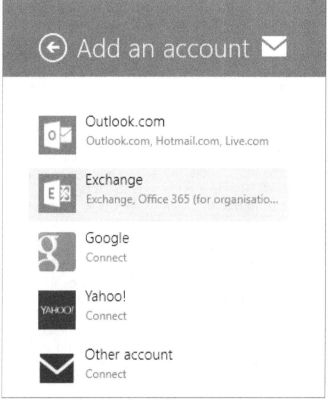

Figure 8.8 – Adding accounts

You can now choose "Outlook.com", "Exchange", "Google", "Yahoo" or "Other account". If you choose "Other account" you will need to manually configure the server settings as per your ISP or e-mail providers instructions. Figure 8.9 shows an example of adding a Google mail (G-Mail) account.

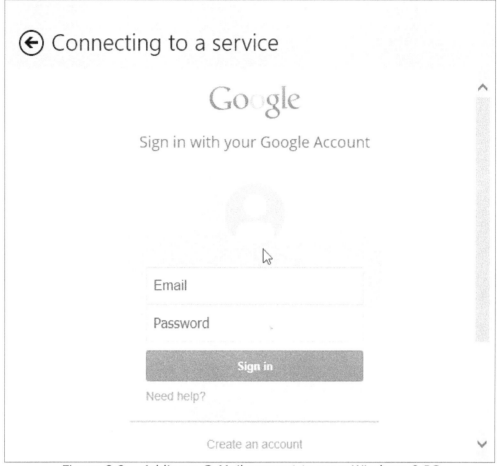

Figure 8.9 – Adding a G-Mail account to your Windows 8 PC

To add a G-Mail account, enter your Google Mail account details when prompted and your Google Mail will then be imported. When the import is complete, you can send and receive G-Mail from your Windows 8 PC.

8.4 – Moving messages

If you want to move a message to a different folder, first select the message you want to move and then right click with your mouse or swipe upwards from the bottom of the screen with your finger. You will then be able to select the "Move" icon and move the message to a different folder.

That concludes our tour of the Windows 8 Mail tile. The Mail tile is great for touch screen users, but not so hot for those of us using more traditional PCs. If you want a powerful e-mail solution tailored to desktop use, check out our Mozilla Thunderbird tutorials on top-windows-tutorials.com

Lesson 9 – The People app

Continuing our tour of the social aspects of Windows 8, in this lesson we will be focusing on the People app. The people app acts like an address book and a social networking hub in Windows 8. We saw this briefly in the last lesson when we used it to select a contact to e-mail. You can open the People app directly from the Start screen too, figure 9.1 shows the People app open.

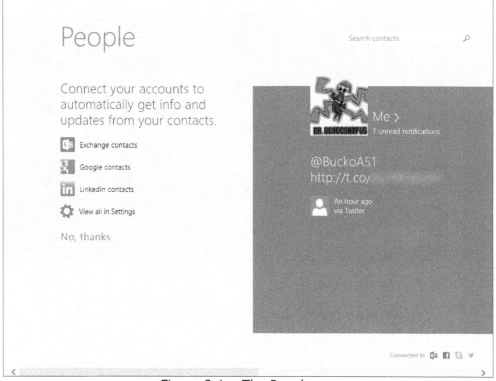

Figure 9.1 – The People app

When you first start the People app, you will be prompted to sign into your Microsoft account, if you are not signed in already. You will then see the screen shown in figure 9.1. At the left of the screen, we can see account types that can be linked. The People app will link your Microsoft account automatically, but of course many more of us use Twitter or Facebook to keep in touch with our friends and family. We will look at how to link accounts later in the lesson. On the right of the screen we can see the newest message sent to our currently linked accounts.

To start browsing contacts, scroll the screen to the right with your mouse or a finger. The screen will change to resemble the one shown in figure 9.2.

Figure 9.2 – Choose a letter to start browsing contacts

Click on a letter to start browsing your contacts. In figure 9.3, the user has clicked on the letter "A".

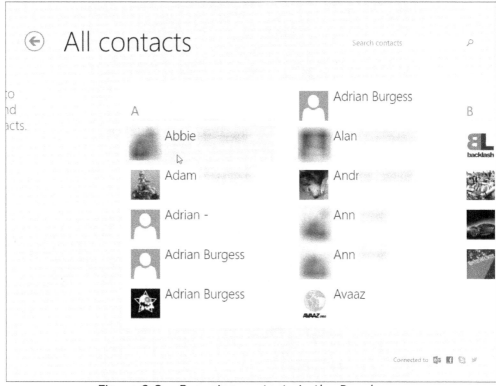

Figure 9.3 – Browsing contacts in the People app

We can see that the People app has a typical address book type layout. By default contacts are sorted in alphabetical order by first name. You can search through your contacts by simply scrolling through them. Alternatively, use the search box at the top of the screen to search for a contact.

9.1 – Linking social network accounts

In figure 9.1 the users account is already linked to Facebook and Twitter and so contacts from both those services have already been imported. To link accounts, open the Charms Bar then click on the Settings Charm. You should then see the options shown in figure 9.4.

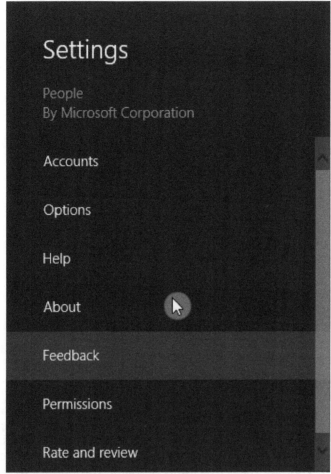

Figure 9.4 – Settings for the People app

From the options menu, click on "Accounts". The menu will then change to the one shown in figure 9.5.

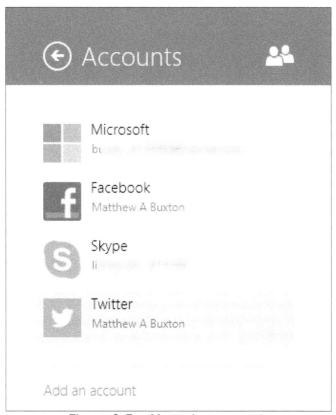

Figure 9.5 – Managing accounts

In figure 9.5 we can see that the current user has four accounts linked to his or her Windows 8 PC. To add another account, simply click on "Add an account" at the bottom. The menu shown in figure 9.6 will then appear.

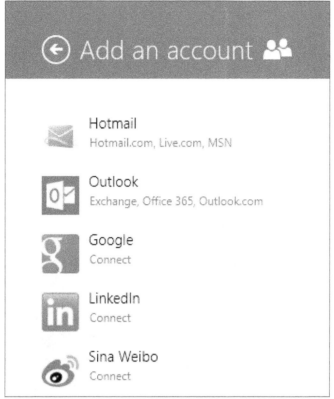

Figure 9.6 – Adding a new account to a Windows 8 machine

Figure 9.6 shows some of the various services that can be added to a Windows 8 PC. Facebook and Twitter are not shown because they are already linked in this instance (it's only possible to add one Twitter account per user). You can also add Google and LinkedIn accounts as well as Hotmail and Outlook, which covers both Outlook.com and Exchange servers (typically used in corporate environments). The Sina Weibo service is a blogging service that is popular in China.

From here, adding an account is as simple as clicking the account type you want to add then entering your user name and password for that account.

9.2 – Other People app options

There are a couple more options you might want to change according to taste. Did you notice that the People app sorts people in alphabetical order by first name? Traditionally address books are sorted by surname. To change this behaviour, open up the Settings Charm like before, but this time click on

"Options". The options shown in figure 9.7 will then appear.

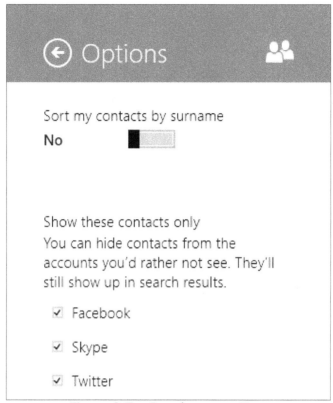

Figure 9.7 – People app options

The top option shown in figure 9.7 gives you the option to sort contacts by last name or surname, more like a traditional address book would do. Turn this off or on according to your personal preferences. Below this, the app gives the option of showing or hiding certain contacts. If you aren't interested in your Hotmail contacts for instance, you could hide them by deselecting "Hotmail". You can use this option to stop duplicate contacts appearing in the People app, but there is a better way to manage this that we will show you in part 9.5 of this lesson.

9.3 – Working with contacts

Clicking on a contact in the People app will show various information about that contact. Figure 9.8 shows an example of this.

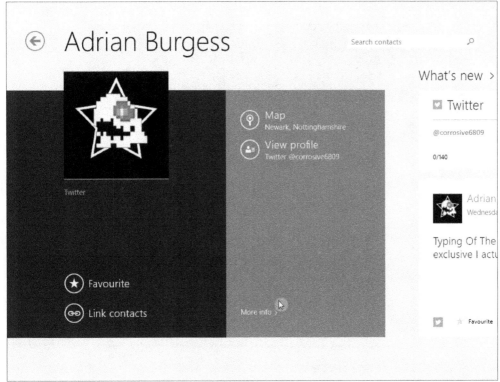

Figure 9.8 – Viewing a contact

In figure 9.8 we can see some basic details for the contact on the left. The picture is the users chosen avatar. Some users prefer to use a photograph of themselves for this, but many, like Adrian here, prefer to use an icon or drawing instead. Next to the picture, there are two icons you can tap or click. The icons are labelled "Map" and "View profile". We will come to those in a moment. Over on the right of the window, the column is labelled "What's new". Here you can view your friends recent Tweets, Facebook posts or posts to other social networks. Their newest posts are shown furthest to the left. Scroll the window along to the right to read further into the past.

To view your friends public profile, click on "View profile". For Facebook profiles, Windows will open Internet Explorer and automatically take you to Facebook to view the profile.

Savvy internet users tend to avoid filling out too much personal information on publicly viewable profiles, so you may need to fill in more personal information like address or phone numbers yourself. We will show you how to do this when we edit the contact later.

If you do have your contacts address or location stored in the People app, you can click or tap on "Map address". Windows will automatically insert the Bing Maps app onto the screen and show you your friends approximate location. We cover Bing Maps in lesson 16.

9.4 – Editing contacts

There are several other operations we can carry out with contacts. Right click or swipe your finger upwards from the bottom of the screen to reveal some extra icons. We will investigate each of these later, but for now, we're concentrating on the Edit icon.

If you want to edit a contact's details, first open the contact (as in figure 9.8) then right click or swipe upwards from the bottom of the screen and choose "Edit". You can now change details for your contact as necessary. Figure 9.10 shows an example of editing a contact.

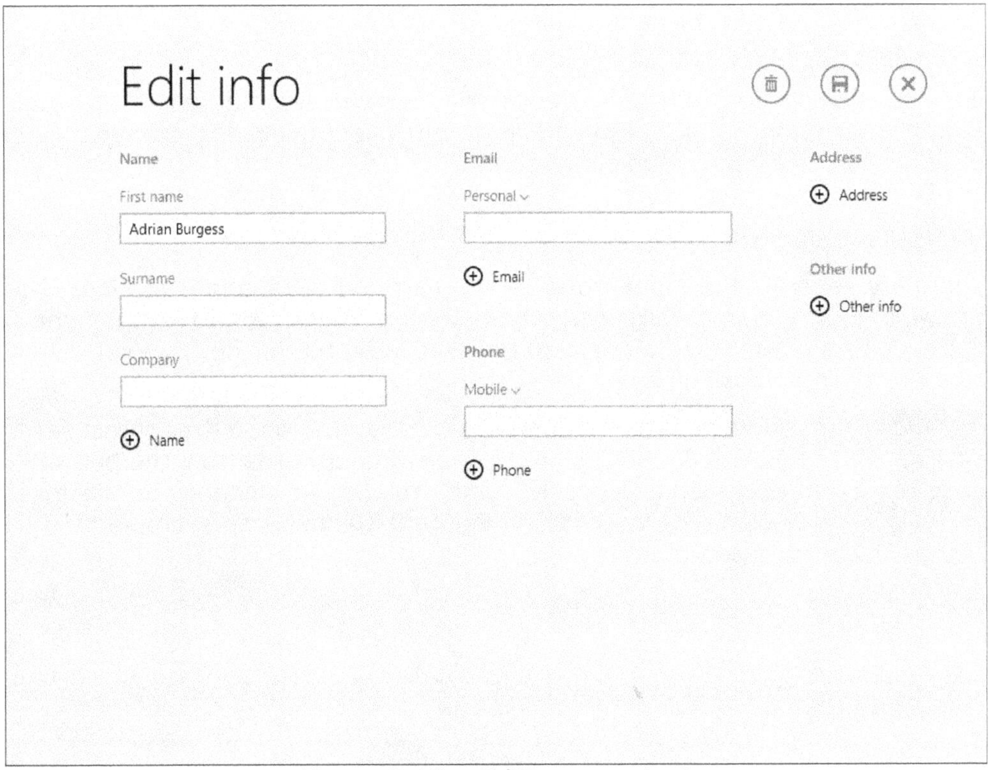

Figure 9.10 – Editing a contact

Simply click or tap on a text entry box and enter the relevant information, then click on the "Save" button near the top right hand corner of the screen (the button in the middle of the three) when you are done. Information you enter here will be stored in your account, it won't be available on the public internet.

9.5 – Linking contacts

Linking contacts is a good way to reduce clutter in the People app. Many of your friends may have more than one social networking account. After you import all your Twitter and Facebook contacts, for instance, you will probably have entries for Twitter accounts and Facebook accounts that belong to the same individuals. By linking these accounts, you reduce clutter and duplicate contacts in the People app. To get started linking accounts, click on the "Link contacts" button, as seen in figure 9.8.

In figure 9.11 we can see an example of linking a contact called "Adrian".

Figure 9.11 – Contact linking options

On the left of figure 9.11 we can see two accounts that are already linked. The People app has found a Messenger account that may also belong to Adrian. To link this Messenger account, simply click or tap on it. If the People app didn't identify the correct account, you can simply click or tap "Choose a contact". This will open up your full address book and allow you to choose any contact to link.

When you go back and browse contacts in the People app, linked contacts will appear as a single entry, reducing clutter in your address book.

9.6 – Other contact options

As well as linking contacts, you can also set a contact as a favourite by clicking the Favourite button shown in figure 9.8. Favourite contacts will appear first in your People app before the rest of your address book.

There are a few other options we can access from the app's menu. Right click or swipe up from the bottom of the screen to access them.

 By clicking "Pin to Start" the contact will appear on the Start screen, useful if you want to create a shortcut to an often used contact.

 Clicking on "Delete" will remove the contact from your address book entirely. Note this won't necessarily stop a contact from messaging you. If you need to block a user who is harassing you, you should log into the appropriate social network on the web and follow the steps there to block the user.

9.7 – What's new

The 'What's new' section of the People app gives you an easy and fun way to view Facebook, Twitter, Microsoft and other networks all in one place. This is very convenient, saving you the bother of opening up several apps or websites. To access What's new, right click on the People app and choose the "What's new" button from the top menu. Figure 9.14 shows the What's new section on a typical Windows 8 PC.

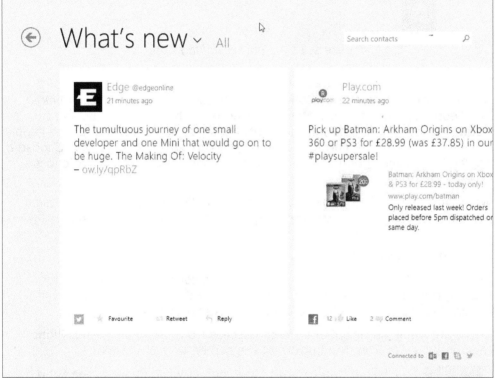

Figure 9.14 – Find out what's new across your social networks with 'What's new'

In figure 9.14 we can see a Twitter post and a Facebook post by two different users. To see more posts the user need only scroll the screen to the right. You can reply to Twitter posts by clicking the "Reply" link at the bottom of the post. You can leave comments on Facebook posts by clicking on the small "Comment" button under each Facebook post. You can also "Like" a post simply by clicking the icon under the post.

If you want to go directly to Facebook to view a post, first click on "Comment", then right click or swipe your finger up from the bottom of the screen. You should then see the "View on Facebook" icon. This will open Internet Explorer and take you directly to the Facebook website.

That's all we wanted to cover regarding the People app. As you can see, this is a great little app for staying in touch with your friends and family.

Lesson 10 – Photos

The final app we are looking at in this chapter is the Photos app. This app makes it easy to find all your photographs, no matter where they are on your PC. We're not sure why, but the Photos app seems to have lost a few features with Windows 8.1. Gone is the option to browse Facebook or Flickr photos and the app is now just for browsing pictures stored on your PC.

Figure 10.1 shows the Photos app open on a Windows 8 PC.

Figure 10.1 – The Photos app

Each tile on the app represents a picture or collection of pictures. In figure 10.1 we can see "Camera Roll" and "My Holiday". These are sub-folders in our pictures folder. We cover folders in lesson 20. To open a folder in the Pictures app, you simply click on it. Click on "Camera Roll" to browse photos taken with your devices built-in camera, for instance. In figure 10.2, the user has opened the Camera Roll folder and is viewing the pictures inside.

Figure 10.2 – Browsing a photo folder in the Photos app

When browsing a picture folder, use the back button (shown in the top left of figure 10.2) to go back to the app's main screen. You may need to click this button several times if you are exploring nested folders. Again, we cover folders in lesson 20 so don't worry if you don't understand that just yet.

10.1 – Browsing pictures

Click on any picture to open it. When viewing a picture like this, you can use the left and right arrow controls to browse to the previous and next pictures in the folder. Figure 10.3 illustrates this control.

Figure 10.3 – When viewing a picture full screen, move your mouse or finger to the left or right edge and click to move to another image

Clicking on the arrow circled in figure 10.3 will change to the next picture, allowing you to browse through your pictures like a flick-book.

To exit full-screen viewing mode and go back to the main photo app window, click or tap on the picture and a back pointing arrow icon will appear in the top left hand corner of the screen. Click or tap on this and you will be taken back to the list of photographs in the current folder.

10.2 – Picture browsing tools

When scrolling through your picture folders, right click or swipe up from the bottom of the screen to access a few other options.

 Clicking on "Select all" lets you select all the pictures currently on display. You might do this if you wanted to then share them to another app using the Share Charm, for instance.

97

Clicking on "New folder" will create a new folder within the current folder. You can create folders to help you organise your pictures. For instance, you could create a folder called "Holiday 2013" and then a sub-folder called "Beach" to store all your beach pictures from your 2013 holiday. We cover folders in more detail in lesson 20.

The Import button lets you add pictures from a mobile device to your pictures folder.

Slideshow simply shows each picture in order. To get back from the slideshow, right click or swipe from the bottom and then click on the back arrow.

10.3 – Fun with pictures

With an individual picture selected, there are a number of fun things you can do to help you personalise your Windows 8 PC. Right click or swipe up from the bottom of the screen to reveal some additional buttons. Some of the buttons that are now revealed will allow you to do quick, minor changes to the images themselves, such as rotating or cropping them. In figure 10.8 the user has opened the "Set as" menu.

Figure 10.8 – The "Set as" menu for a picture

The options on this menu perform the following operations.

Lock Screen:- This is one of my favourite new options for Windows 8. By selecting this option, the current picture will appear on your Lock screen. This is the screen you see each time you power on your PC or whenever you lock it. To do this in Windows 7 required third party software so it is great to see it here in Windows 8 where everyone can use it.

Photos Tile:- Sets the current picture to appear on the Photos tile on the Start screen. Note that this prevents the Photos app tile from cycling through your other pictures. If you want to change back to the default behaviour, make sure you are in the Photos app and then open the Charms Bar and click on the Settings Charm. Now click "Options" from the menu and change the "Shuffle photos on the Photos tile" control from Off to On.

That's all you really need to know to use the Photos app. As you can see it is a quick, easy and fun way of browsing photos on your PC.

Chapter 3 – More Tile Apps

In this chapter we'll round off our tour of the new tile applications. Windows 8 bundles a lot of new software to take advantage of the new tile interface and most of it is very straightforward to use.

Lesson 11 – The App Store

In this lesson, we are going to learn about the App Store in Windows 8. The App Store is an app in itself of course, so you could call it the 'App Store app'. For simplicity's sake we will stick with App Store. The App Store is the only way to get new tile software for your Windows 8 PC. You can find both tile and desktop software in the App Store, but while desktop software can be downloaded or purchased from websites or retailers all around the world, tile software can only be obtained through the Windows App Store tile.

To open the store, simply click the tile on the Start screen, figure 11.1 shows the Store tile running on a Windows 8 PC.

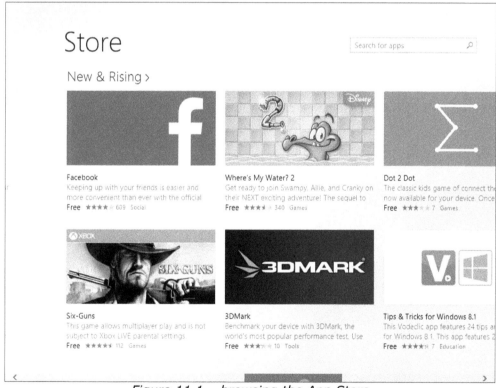

Figure 11.1 – browsing the App Store

The store is split into several categories. Scroll to the right using your mouse or a finger on a touch screen to browse the main categories. For instance, in figure 11.1 you can see "New & Rising". Click or tap this heading to view more apps in that category. Notice how each app has a star rating with it. These are based on user reviews, so generally the more stars an app has the more satisfied the users are with it. We'll show you how to leave a rating for an app you use later in this lesson.

11.1 – Free and paid apps

When you see an app you are interested in, simply click or tap on its tile. The app store will now open a new screen showing you more details about the app you selected. Many apps are entirely free to download, while some have a fee. Figure 11.2 shows an example of a paid app.

Figure 11.2 – Viewing an app. This app requires you to pay a fee to unlock it, though you can get a free trial version too

If you want to buy an app like this, you will need some way to pay for it. When you click on "Buy", the button label will change to read "Confirm" just to make sure you didn't click by accident. If you click on "Confirm", you will be asked to sign into your Microsoft account if you are not already signed in, or to confirm your password if you are. You will then be taken to the Payment and Billing screen **unless you have credit in your Microsoft account already**, in which case your account will instantly be debited. Figure 11.3 shows the Payment and Billing screen.

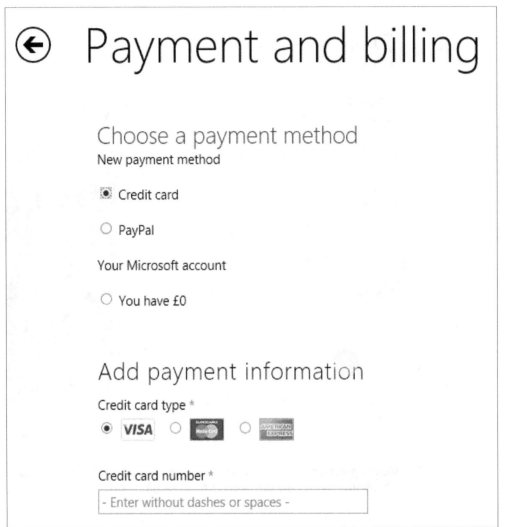

Figure 11.3 – Entering payment details

Usually, payment is made via a credit card, but in future it may also be possible to purchase store credit in the form of a top up card. If you use other Microsoft services such as Xbox Live, you can use credit from these services to buy Windows 8 apps too. Remember that apps you purchase will be available to download in the store on any other Windows 8 PCs you use without any additional charges, as long as you sign in with your Microsoft account.

Many paid-for programs also have a trial mode. In figure 11.2 you can see a "Try" button. In this case you can press this button to try out a demo of the game or app before you buy. The trial version will download in the background while you browse the store. Typically the trial version will be time limited or not have all the capabilities of the full version.

11.2 – Finding more in the store

While browsing the store, you can view more categories by right clicking in the store, or swiping your finger down from the top of the screen to open the menu shown in figure 11.4.

Figure 11.4 – Several more options and categories can be browsed from the App Store menu

Click or tap on any category to browse it. You can also move your mouse pointer or finger to the left or right edges of the screen and click the arrows that then appear to see more categories. To get back to the store home screen at any time, click on the "Home" button in the top left.

To access content you purchased in the past, but haven't yet download to the machine you are currently using, click on the "Your account" button.

You can also search the store easily, simply use the search box in the top right of the screen.

11.3 – Installing a new app

The process of installing a new app is really easy. For paid-for apps, the app will install after payment is taken. For free apps, simply click on "Install".

When you click to install an app it will download and install in the background. You do not need to wait in the App Store, you can carry on browsing for other apps or use your PC for any other task. When the process is complete, you will see a notification message like the one shown in figure 11.5.

Figure 11.5 – This app has finished installing

Once you see the notification you can then go back to the Start screen and click on the new tile to start the app. If you don't see a tile for your new app, try searching for it instead. You can then pin it to the Start screen if you wish.

11.4 – Rating an app

Once you have installed and used your new app, you may wish to leave a review and/or a rating for other users to see. To do this, open the menu shown in figure 11.4 and click on "Your apps". Windows will then list all the apps you have downloaded. Click on one you want to rate and then look for the link that reads "Rate this app" or "Write a review". To rate the app simply click on however many stars you think the program deserves. To write a more in-depth review use the"Write a review" link. Figure 11.6 shows an example of rating an app called "Where's My Water?".

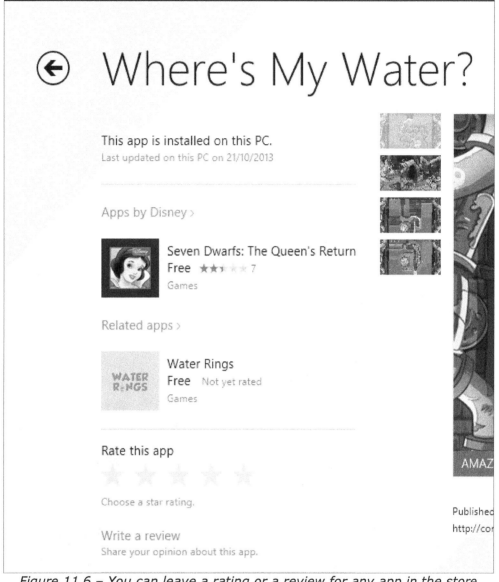

Figure 11.6 – You can leave a rating or a review for any app in the store

That's all there is to using the App Store in Windows 8. Now you can enjoy exploring and trying out new programs for your Windows 8 machine.

Lesson 12 – Music and Video

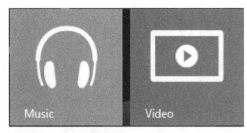

In this lesson we are going to look at two similar apps, namely Music and Video. Music and Video both have two purposes. Firstly, they can play files in your media library and secondly they can be used for purchasing new media files too. The Music app allows you to buy new music and the Video app allows you to buy or rent movies and TV shows. Figure 12.1 shows the Music app.

Figure 12.1 – The Music app

On the left of the program we can see three main categories, namely "Collection", "Radio" and "Explore". Clicking or tapping on "Collection" will list all the music currently on this PC. On a Windows 8 PC, music is stored in the Music folder. We will see how to navigate to folders and manipulate files in our File Explorer lessons, starting with lesson 20. Music and video that you store in the Music and Video folders (or in your libraries) will be available to the music and video tiles and to Windows Media Player, which we cover in lesson 57.

Windows 8 does not come with any music pre-installed. Later in the lesson we will show you how to buy music or listen for free. Alternatively, you can copy your own music collection from CD by using the techniques we discuss in lesson 58. In the example shown in Figure 12.2, the user has opened the "Collection" section of the Music app on a PC that has three music folders present.

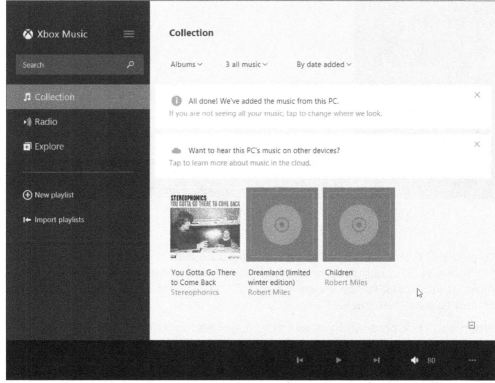

Figure 12.2 – Browsing music stored on a PC in the Music tile

12.1 – Playing music

To play an album, first click or tap on it from the list shown above. A screen listing all the tracks on the album will appear. See figure 12.3 for an example.

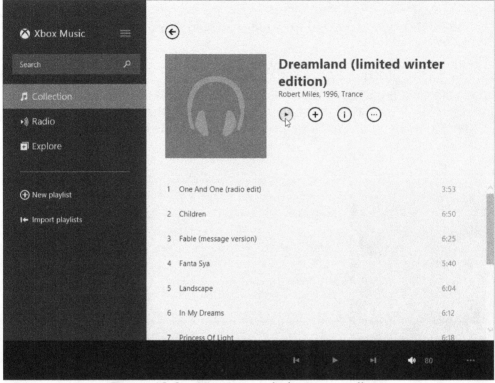

Figure 12.3 – Viewing and playing an album

To play the entire album, click on the Play button near the top of the screen (in figure 12.3, this button is directly under the mouse pointer). Alternatively, click or tap on an individual track in the bottom half of the screen to play that track.

When you click on an individual track, it will be highlighted and two new buttons will appear, figure 12.4 shows an example of this.

Figure 12.4 – Playing an individual track

Click on the triangle shaped play button to play the track now, or click on the Plus button to add the track to a playlist or to your Cloud Collection. We cover playlists later in this lesson. Cloud Collection songs are stored online meaning you can access them on any internet connected Windows 8 PC you use.

When playing music, you can use the buttons at the bottom of the app to control the playback. The buttons are shown in figure 12.5.

Figure 12.5 – Music playback controls

From left to right, the controls are as follows.

Previous:– Plays the previous track on the album or playlist. You can use the Previous and Next buttons to skip between tracks.

Play:– Use the play button to start playback or, if music is already playing, use this button to pause playback.

Next:– Plays the next track on the album or playlist.

Volume:– Click to adjust the music volume.

More options:– Click here to toggle repeat or shuffle. Turning on Repeat will cause your current album or playlist to repeat when finished, while shuffle will cause tracks to play in a random order on your current album or playlist.

12.2 – Creating playlists

A playlist is a list of songs created by the user. Many people create playlists for different moods or occasions. Have a house party coming up?, then create your own playlist for the event. Need some music to relax you after work?, create a playlist of your most soothing tunes to help you unwind. To get started, click on the "New playlist" button on the left of the screen (you can see it in figure 12.3). Windows will then prompt you to enter a name for your playlist. Once you have created the playlist, it will appear on the left under the "New playlist" button. Figure 12.6 shows an example of this.

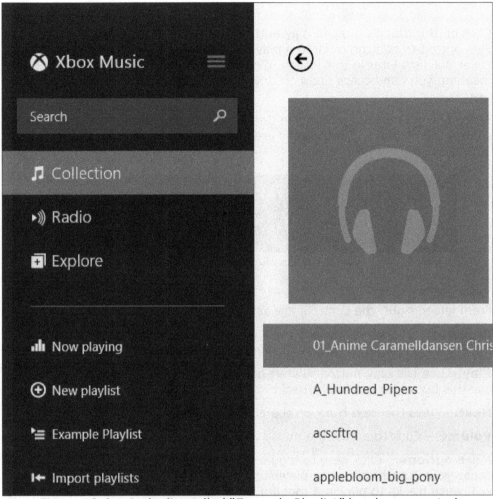

Figure 12.6 – A playlist called "Example Playlist" has been created

To add a track to the playlist, click on it so that it is selected (as in figure 12.4). Now, click the plus shaped button and a menu will appear, simply select your playlist from this menu to add the track to the playlist.

To play a playlist, select it from the left by clicking or tapping on it. It will then open just like with an album. Click on the play button to start playing the playlist. Note you must have at least two tracks on a playlist before the Music app will play it.

12.3 – Playing music outside the music folder

 The Music app can play music that isn't stored in the music folder or library. Perhaps you want to play some music from an external storage device, for instance. Although you could copy the music to your PC, it is possible to play it directly from the external drive too. To do this, first click on "Collection" on the left of the screen. Now swipe upwards with your finger or right click on a blank area of the screen. A menu should appear with the "Open file" icon as shown above. Click on this icon and you can browse to any location on your PC and open any music files.

12.4 – Radio

The music app in Windows 8.1 has a new feature called "Radio". To use the feature, click or tap on Radio on the left hand side of the screen, then click on "Start a station". You will then be prompted to enter an artists name. Enter the name of your favourite popular artist and (assuming the artist is available) the program will then play tracks from that artist, or artists in a similar genre. To use this feature, you require an active internet connection.

12.5 – Browsing music to buy

The music app also allows you to browse music to buy. Click on "Explore" on the left of the screen to get started. This will take you to the music store front page, where you can browse popular albums. Click on an album to view details about it, just like we did when accessing albums stored locally on the PC.

You can also search for albums and artists too. Use the search box in the top left of the screen. Figure 12.8 shows an example of a search for "Nero", a popular British electronic music trio.

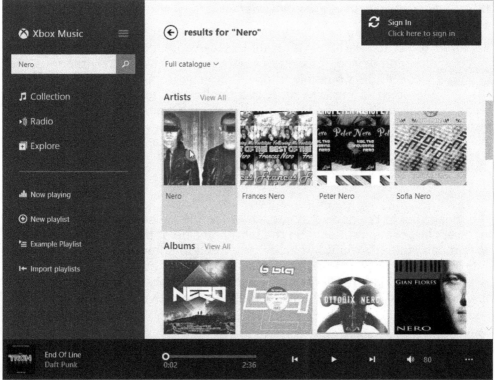

Figure 12.8 – Searching in the music app

If you find an artist you can click on them to browse their available tracks and albums, as well as related artists. Figure 12.9 shows an example of this.

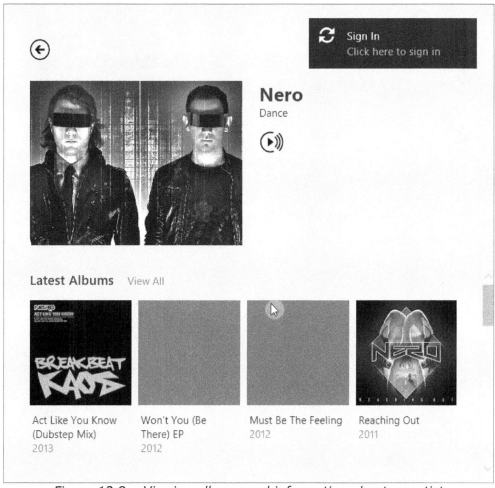

Figure 12.9 – Viewing albums and information about an artist

Sometimes the Windows Music store will label a single or an EP as an album. Click on an album cover image to open a full track list. In figure 12.10, the user has opened the "Won't You (Be There) EP".

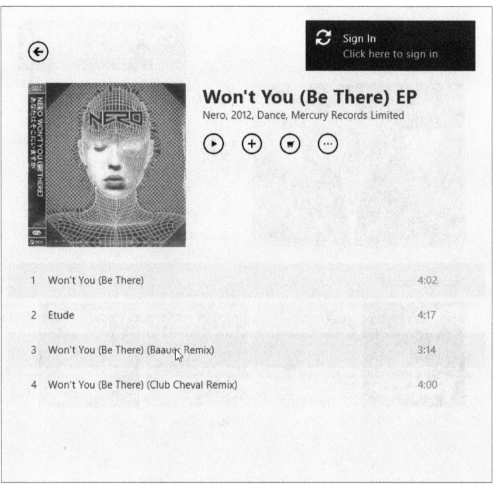

Figure 12.10 – Viewing an album

If you want to buy the album, click on the shopping cart button near the top of the screen. You will need to sign into your Microsoft account if you are not signed in already.

Microsoft now also offer music streaming services via the Music app in most regions. You can buy an unlimited music pass, that allows you to listen to as much music as you want for a monthly fee. Even without an unlimited pass, customers in many regions can still stream several hours of music a month for free. If music streaming is available in your region clicking on play will play the entire album. If music streaming is not available in your region, playing the album will usually play a preview of each track.

12.6 – The Video app

The Video app works in a similar way to the Music app. Figure 12.11 shows the Video app open on a Windows 8 PC.

Figure 12.11 – The Video app

In the video app, local files are listed on the left, while content that is available to view or purchase from the internet is listed on the right. To view a locally stored video file, just click on it. You can then control playback with the buttons at the bottom of the screen. Figure 12.12 shows the video playback buttons.

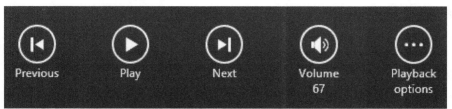

Figure 12.12 – Video playback controls

The buttons function in a very similar way to the Music app. Clicking on the Playback options button allows you to turn Repeat on or off.

To go back from playing a video to the video app main screen, click or tap the back arrow in the top left hand corner of the screen. If you don't see the arrow, move your mouse or finger over the screen and it will appear. You can also click or tap the screen in the middle to pause or resume playback, or drag the 'Q' shaped button along the time-line to skip to a specific part of the video.

While browsing video you can also right click or swipe your finger in from the bottom of the screen to access the "Open file" control. This will allow you to browse to video stored anywhere on your PC. This is useful for playing video on an external storage device, for instance.

12.7 – Browsing video to buy

Using the video app's built-in video store is easy. Use your mouse or finger to scroll the app to the right. You can then see various movies and video files that are available to buy or stream for free in the video store. You can search for titles using the search button in the top right of the app. Figure 12.13 shows a section from a search result for the movie "Iron Man 3".

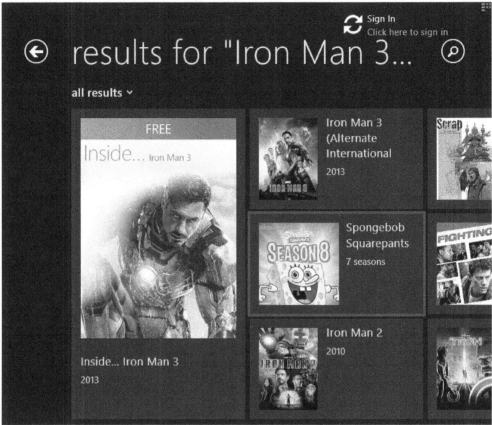

Figure 12.13 – Searching for a movie will often find trailers and documentaries too

Click on a tile to see the options for viewing the media. Some videos will be available to buy or rent, while others are free to watch. In figure 12.14, the user has clicked the tile for the film "Iron Man 3 (Alternate International)".

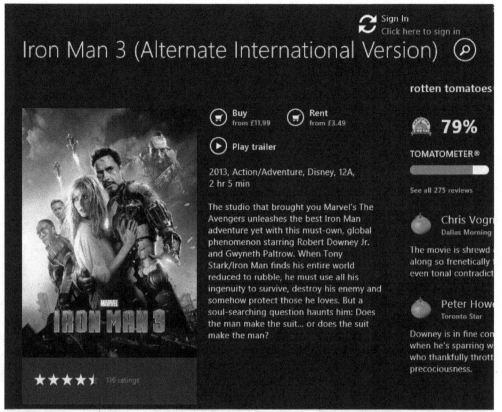

Figure 12.14 – Viewing a movie description and viewing options

12.8 – Viewing options

The movie in figure 12.14 can be bought or rented. Some files will only be available for rental, while others might only be available to purchase. Many movies also have a preview trailer, that you can watch for free by clicking the "Play trailer" button. By clicking on "Buy" or "Rent" you will be taken to the Viewing Options window. An example of this is shown in figure 12.15.

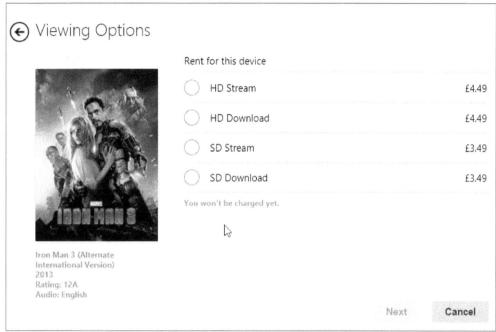

Figure 12.15 – Viewing Options

In figure 12.15 there is the option of SD Stream and SD Download. In this context, SD stands for "Standard Definition" and HD stands for "High Definition". High definition movies are better quality, but have larger file-sizes and therefore need faster internet connections to stream.

What is the difference between stream and download? If you select stream, the video will start right away and download as you view it. When you choose this option, you need a fast internet connection and must remain connected to the internet throughout viewing. If you choose download, you must wait for the entire movie to download through your internet connection before you can watch it. You may want to download a movie if, for instance, you want to watch it on a long train or air journey where an internet connection may not be available. If you download a rental movie, it will automatically delete itself after the rental period has expired.

That concludes our tour of the Music and Video tiles, be sure to check our Windows Media Player tutorials later in the guide too, as well as our guides to media libraries.

Lesson 13 – The News and Sport apps

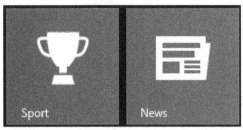

In this lesson we will be investigating two simple information apps, namely News, and Sport. The News and Sport apps bring content from the web to your Windows 8 PC in the form of a convenient app. Other information apps you download from the App Store will usually behave in a similar fashion to these two apps, so it's worthwhile mastering them even if you only use them occasionally.

13.1 – News

On the Start screen the News tile will scroll headlines across its surface. Clicking the tile will, of course, open the app. Figure 13.1 shows the app running.

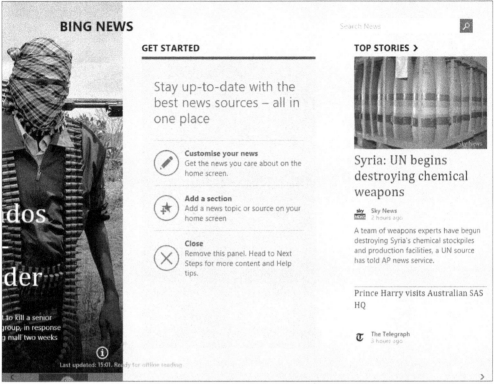

Figure 13.1 – Browsing news in the News app

The News app is designed to look good on tablet devices just like other tile apps and it is fun and easy to use. In figure 13.1 the user is scrolling along the news using the mouse. Stories are divided into categories, such as World, Science and Technology and Entertainment. When a headline or picture catches your eye, simply click or tap on it to read the story. Figure 13.2 shows a story open in the News app.

Sky News - Sunday, 6 October 2013

Glastonbury Tickets Sell Out In Record Time

Organisers Emily and Michael Eavis said they were "blown away" by the response.

In a statement, they said: "We're sorry that many of you missed out on a ticket.

"We genuinely try to make the ticket system as fair as it can be, but when demand outstrips supply, it is an unfortunate inevitability that some people will be left disappointed."

Sales got off to a shaky start on Sunday morning with technical issues affecting the first half an hour of sales.

The remaining 120,000 tickets for next year's event went on sale at 9am, with more than a million people pre-registered to buy the biggest festival ticket of the summer.

Weight of demand appeared to have slowed things down temporarily and official ticket agent See Tickets tweeted its apologies for a "difficult half hour".

The system stabilised at around 9.30am, with Emily Eavis thanking fans for their patience.

The £210 tickets were selling at a rate of 3,000 a minute, according to See Tickets, and by 10am 80,000 had already been sold.

Page 1 of 2

Figure 13.2 – Reading a story in the News app

To change pages in a story, move your mouse or finger to the middle edge of the screen. A navigation control will then appear allowing you to flip the pages. When you are done, click on the arrow in the top left of the screen to go back.

Like most other Windows 8 apps, you can search in the News app too, simply type your query into the search box on the top right hand side of the screen (see figure 13.1).

13.2 – News sources

The News application pulls in articles from various sources based on your geographic location. To see where the news is coming from, right click or swipe your finger from the top of the screen and then choose "Sources". Figure 13.3 shows a snippet from the resulting screen.

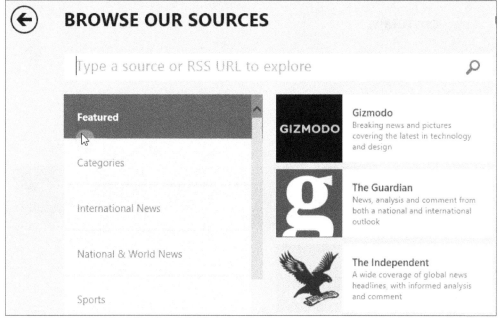

Figure 13.3 – Browsing news sources

Click on a category on the left to see which web sites and media outlets are providing news for that category. Click on one of the icons on the right to see all the news from that particular source.

13.3 – Customise your news

You can tailor the news app to your reading preferences by using the "Customise your news" button. To find this button, make sure you are in the main News app screen (as shown in figure 13.1) then scroll all the way to the left. You should then see the "Customise your news" button. You can also see this button in Figure 13.1. Figure 13.4 shows a screenshot of the Customise screen that opens when you click this button.

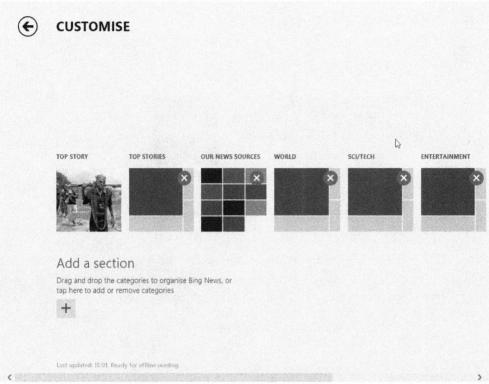

Figure 13.4 – Customising News

You can now organise the News app according to your tastes. If you're not interested in entertainment news, for instance, you can remove it from your News app by clicking the red cross above entertainment.

You can also add a new section too. Click on the plus shaped button under "Add a section" and a search box will then appear. In figure 13.5, the user is adding a section for gaming news.

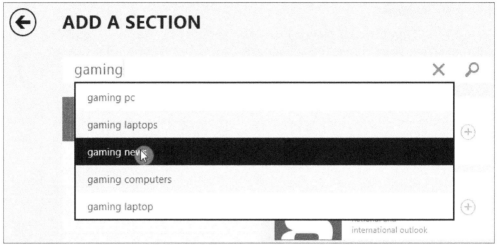

Figure 13.5 – Adding a section to the News app

You can search for any terms in the search box, but you can only add sections for the topics that Windows finds. Click on a search term to be taken to the search results. Figure 13.6 shows the search results for the "gaming news" topic.

Figure 13.6 – Click the plus button to add the topic

To add the topic, make sure to click the plus button (shown under the mouse pointer in figure 13.6).

When you add a topic, the News app will then search for relevant news related to the subjects and present it on the front page of the News app. You can add as many topics as you like.

13.4 – News videos

New on the Windows 8.1 News app is the videos feature. To access this, right click or swipe your finger down from the top of the screen, and choose "video".

Now you can watch several top news videos. To watch a video just click on it, the video will then open and play. The playback controls are then the same as using the Video app that we covered in the previous lesson.

13.5 – Sport

The Sport app works in a very similar way to the News app. Figure 13.7 shows the Sport app open on a Windows 8 PC.

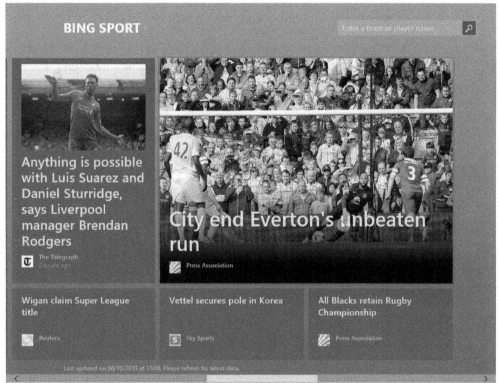

Figure 13.7 – The Sport app

Just like the News app, the main application shows you the headlines from the world of sport in an attractive, tablet PC friendly format which is great for browsing on all kinds of screens. Scroll along with the mouse or your finger and click on a story to read it.

There are several other options you can access by right clicking or by swiping your finger down from the top of the screen. Figure 13.8 shows the extra buttons you can access.

Figure 13.8 – Choosing a category for the Sport app

Use the buttons to choose a category to get information about a specific sport. For instance if you follow Formula 1, click the Formula 1 button to get news exclusively about Grand Prix racing.

Don't forget you can also search for teams or player names by using the search box available in the top right of the screen. If the Sport app finds your team or player, you will get all the fixtures and information about them.

13.6 – Favourite Sports

You can also access news about specific sports from the Sport app's main page. Scroll to the right until you find the favourite sports section. Figure 13.9 shows a picture of this.

Figure 13.9 – Favourite sports

You can easily customise the Favourite Sports section. To remove a sport, right click on it, then click the X icon that appears. To add a new sport, click the + button near the bottom right of the screen. A list of sports will then appear. Scroll through the list until you find the sport you're interested in, then click on the + icon to add it. You can add as many sports as you like. When you are done, click on the back button in the top left of the screen. News about your favourite sports will appear on the front page of the Sport app and can also appear on the live tile on the Start screen too.

You can also click or tap on any sport in the list of favourite sports to jump directly to news and fixtures about that sport.

13.7 – Favourite Teams

To the left of the favourite sports section on the main page of the Sport app is Favourite Teams. This feature lets fans keep up to date with the sports news that matters to them the most. By default this section is empty, but by clicking on the + icon, a search box will appear. You can search for your favourite team now. Unfortunately we found that only major teams were supported by this feature. If, for instance, you follow a football club in a lower division or league, you're likely to be disappointed.

If your team was found, click on "Add". A tile for your team will then appear under Favourite Teams. You can then click on your teams tile to see all the results and fixtures for that team.

That's all you need to know to use the News and Sport apps. While these apps are simple, they are useful for lots of users and they put the most relevant information from the web right at your fingertips.

Lesson 14 – Travel, Finance, Weather

In this lesson we're going to look at thee more information applications that come with Windows 8. As you might imagine, using these applications is similar to using the apps we looked at in the previous lesson.

14.1 – Travel

The Travel app is very straightforward to use. Figure 14.1 shows the app running.

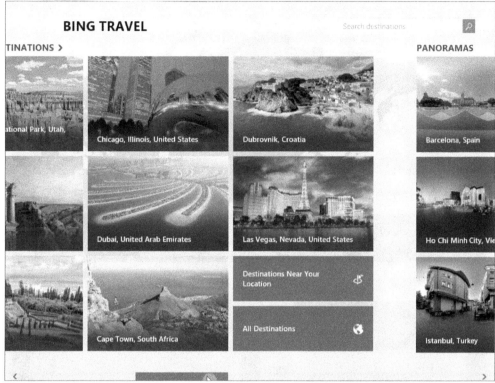

Figure 14.1 – Browsing locations in the Travel app

In the Travel app, each of the larger picture tiles represent a destination. Click on a destination to learn more about it. By right clicking or swiping your finger down from the top of the screen, you can access several other options, as shown in figure 14.2.

Figure 14.2 – Other options for the Travel app

Choose either "Destinations", "Flights", or "Hotels", to browse information in those categories. Choosing hotels, for instance, allows you to search for a hotel in any city to see if they have a room. Figure 14.3 below shows how this works.

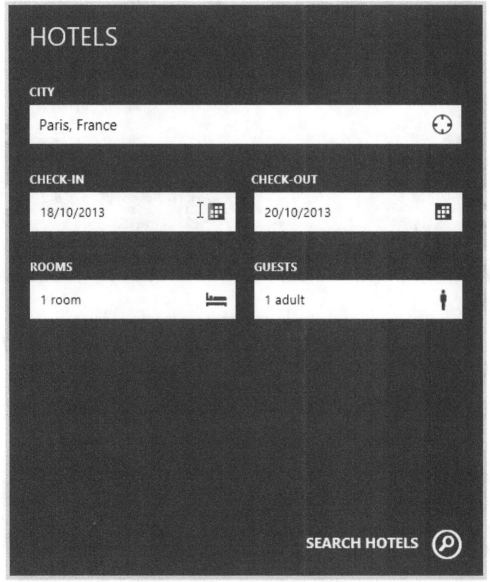

Figure 14.3 – Searching for a hotel

Enter a city name, or use the target shaped icon to choose your current location (if available). Choose a check in and check out date in the appropriate boxes (tap or click them to display a calendar) and then finally choose the number of rooms and guests before clicking "Search Hotels". The travel app will now present you with a list of hotels that can provide you with a room. Click on any of the results in the list to see more details. To make a booking you will be redirected to a third party service on the web.

Finally, clicking on "Best of the Web" on the menu shown in figure 14.2 will bring you a selection of the best travel news and information sites from the internet directly into the Travel app.

14.2 – Finance

The Finance app is very similar to the News and Sport apps. Figure 14.4 shows the app running.

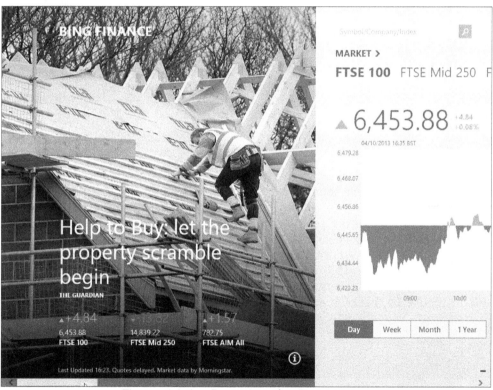

Figure 14.4 – Browsing the Finance app

The Finance app puts financial news at your fingertips. Just as with the other information apps, you can scroll along to the right to see all the information. You can check the various financial indices if you're that way inclined, or read a financial news story by clicking or tapping on the tile.

If you have a particular stock you want to watch, scroll along to the Watchlist. You can then click on the plus icon to search for the company you want to watch. This works exactly like adding a favourite sport or team in the Sport app.

By right clicking or swiping down from the top of the screen with your finger, you can access various other options. Figure 14.5 shows these options.

Figure 14.5 – Extra options for the Finance app

We're not going to cover each option exhaustively, since exploring and using them is as easy as it is in the other information apps.

The currencies feature is particularly useful. If you are wondering where the currency converter has gone in Windows 8.1, it's now moved to tools. Click the button next to tools (the button with a triangle on it) and you will be able to select "Currency converter" as well as several other tools. The currency converter is easy to use, simply enter the amount of currency in the box on the far left, choose the currency to convert from below it, then you can see instantly what it is worth in other currencies over on the right of the screen. If you don't see the currency you want to work with, use the plus button to add it. Figure 14.6 shows an example of the currency converter in action.

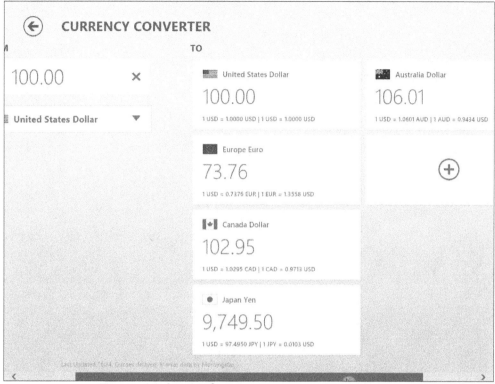

Figure 14.6 – Performing a currency conversion

In figure 14.6 the user has entered 100 and selected "United States Dollar". Over on the right we can see what the US Dollar is worth in Euros, Canadian Dollars, Japanese Yen and Australian Dollars. To add another currency, simply click on the plus button below the Australia Dollar tile.

That is all we wanted to show you in the Finance app. If you are interested in this app please explore the other features yourself. As you have probably guessed, the other features in this app work in a very similar fashion to those demonstrated in the other information apps.

14.3 – Weather

To finish this lesson we will take a look at the Weather app. Figure 14.7 shows the app open on a Windows 8 PC.

Figure 14.7 – The Weather app

The default location is shown at the top left of the Weather app. You can scroll to the right to see all the available weather data.

By right clicking or swiping your finger down from the top of the screen, you can access another menu. Figure 14.8 shows this menu.

Figure 14.8 – The Weather app menu

Again, we wont cover every option here, so feel free to go and experiment yourself.

Home:- Click or tap any time on the "Home" button to go back to the Weather home screen.

Places:- Click or tap here to either add a new place or view all the places that you are monitoring. Figure 14.9 shows an example of this.

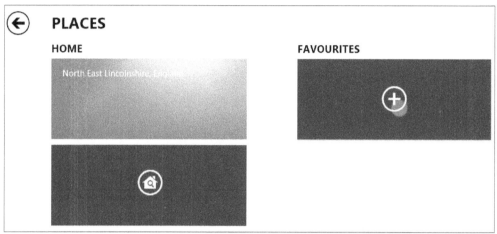

Figure 14.9 – Managing places in the Weather app

On the left, we can see our home location is North East Lincolnshire in this example. By clicking on the tile in the bottom left, we can change the home location if necessary.

Under Favourites, you can click on the Plus icon to add a new town or city. Windows will open a search box where you can type the name of the place you want to add.

When you add a location to Favourites, you can access it quickly from the Weather home screen by scrolling all the way to the right and clicking on "My Places". You will then be taken to the list of your locations and you can simply click or tap the tile for the location you want to view.

Of course, you can view weather data for any location at any time by using the search box in the top right hand corner of the app.

Weather Maps:- Choose this option to see a map containing weather data for your region. You can watch how cloud cover, temperature and precipitation is predicted to change over the next few hours. This data is also available from the Weather home screen.

World Weather:- This button takes you to the World Weather feature that we explore in the next section.

14.4 – World weather

If you fancy seeing what the weather is like elsewhere in the world, you can use the fun "World weather" feature. Go back to the Weather home screen and bring up the menu shown in figure 14.8, then select "World weather". Figure 14.10 shows the World weather feature in action.

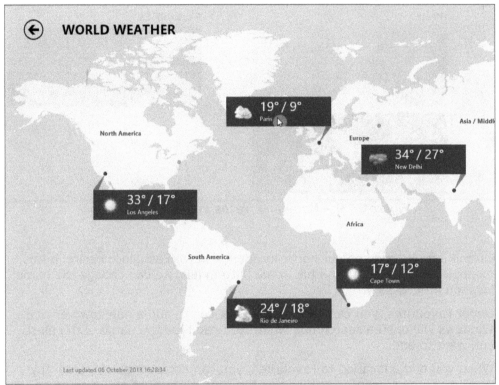

Figure 14.10 – The World weather feature

Using World weather, you can scroll round the map with your mouse or a finger and see the weather in various major cities around the world. Since I am in England, this usually shows me how much warmer and dryer other places are.

That is all you need to know to start using these three information apps. Windows 8 puts lots of information at your fingertips, saving you the bother of having to trawl the web.

Lesson 15 – Maps

Windows 8 ships with a simple map application called, unimaginatively, "Maps". In this lesson we will explore this app. The app is a simple, fun little application that has some basic route planning, but lacks turn by turn navigation and advanced features that more advanced mapping software has. Figure 15.1 shows the application open on a Windows 8 PC.

Figure 15.1 – The Maps app

If you have location services enabled, the Maps app will find your approximate location and open the map there. Use the plus and minus buttons at the right of the screen to zoom in and out of the map. Use the mouse or your finger on the touch screen to drag the map around the world.

15.1 – Map options

As with most tile apps, the Maps app has several more options available via its menu. Right click or swipe your finger up from the bottom of the screen to reveal the menu. The options on the menu are as follows.

Add a pin to the map so that you can find a location again quickly and easily. We will explore this option in a little more detail later in the lesson.

Click on this option and choose "Aerial view" to get an aerial photograph view of the map. You can even zoom in to see individual buildings and roads, though there isn't a street view option.

Uses the location services/GPS in your PC (if available) to move the map to your current location.

Click this button and then simply enter two locations to find driving directions between them. You will then be able to see the route map on the Maps application and also browse the route here. You can use the Share Charm on the Charms Bar to share the route information either with an e-mail contact or a person in the People app.

Use this button to search the map. You can search various categories such as "Eat + Drink" and "See + do".

15.2 – Pins and favourites

The Windows 8.1 Map app also lets you save places as "favourites" so you can quickly find them again. You can save your home location, for instance. Open the programs menu again but this time look at the top for the Favourites button (as shown on the left here). Click the button to manage your favourite locations. The screen shown in figure 15.8 will then appear.

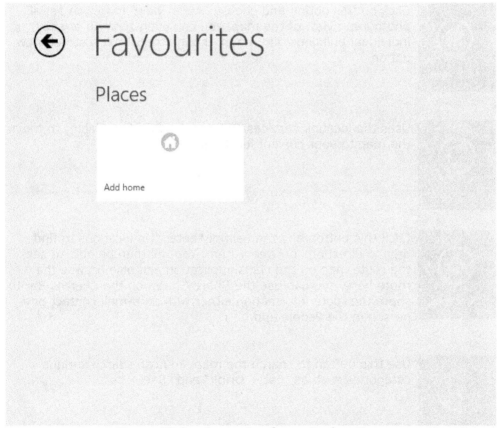

Figure 15.8 – Accessing favourite locations

Initially your favourite locations will be empty. You can click or tap the "Add home" tile and add your home location if you want to. A search box will appear allowing you to search for your home location and pin it as a favourite.

To add further locations to your favourites, use the "Add a pin" button on the applications menu. When you click this button, an orange pin will appear on the map. Click on the pin and hold your mouse button down or drag with your finger to place the pin. Once placed, you can click or tap on the pin to get directions, see what's nearby, add the location to your favourites or simply remove the pin. Figure 15.8 shows an example of this.

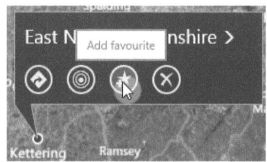

Figure 15.9 – Pinning a location on the map allows you to add it to your favourites

That's really all there is to the Maps application. As time goes on we expect many more feature rich mapping and navigation applications to appear in the App Store.

Lesson 16 – OneDrive

Cloud computing services have really started to take off in recent years. If you are unfamiliar with the term, it simply refers to using the resources (usually storage) of other computers on the internet. Rather than store your files locally, why not take advantage of services like OneDrive (previously known as SkyDrive) and store and back them up remotely, using your internet connection? Windows 8.1 has improved OneDrive integration even further, making it an even more convenient storage and backup service for Windows 8 users.

Figure 16.1 shows the OneDrive app open on a Windows 8 PC. To use OneDrive on a Windows 8.1 PC, you need to sign in with a Microsoft account.

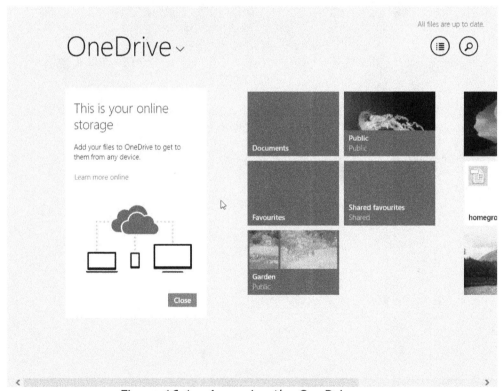

Figure 16.1 – Accessing the OneDrive app

Like most of the tile apps, OneDrive is straightforward to use. In figure 16.1

we can see five folders (the blue rectangles with writing on them). These are folders on the users OneDrive. To open a folder, simply click on it. In figure 16.2, the user has opened the "Garden" folder.

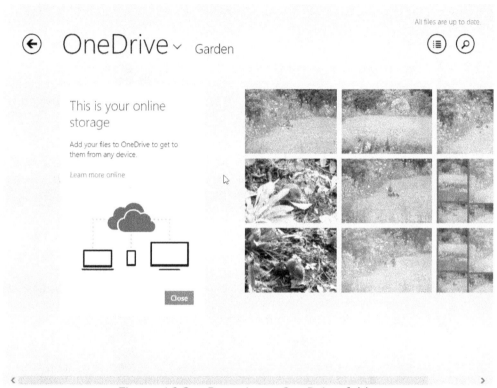

Figure 16.2 – Browsing a OneDrive folder

In figure 16.2 we can see some pictures inside the Garden folder. These are pictures that were placed onto this OneDrive account over two years ago, when the service was originally demonstrated on Top-Windows-Tutorials.com. To view a picture, simply click on it. Viewing a picture on OneDrive works just like it does with the Photos app (see lesson 10).

16.1 – Working with OneDrive

Again, just like with other tile apps, right click with your mouse or swipe your finger up from the bottom of the screen to reveal an extra menu. The buttons on this menu perform the following functions.

Selects all the files in the current folder. Using this button you can select an entire folder to download, for instance.

Creates a new folder inside your OneDrive. Creating folders is a great way to keep your OneDrive more organised. You can create them to store any kind of file. In figure 16.1 you can see several folders, such as "Documents", "Favourites" and "Garden".

Uploads files to OneDrive from your computer. Before clicking this button, make sure to open the folder you want to upload to. Then click this button and then browse to any location on your PC. Figure 16.7 shows an example of uploading a file.

Synchronises the contents of the OneDrive folder on your PC with the contents of your OneDrive on the internet. Windows will perform this operation periodically anyway, but if a newly added file has not downloaded to your PC yet, clicking this button should trigger it to download immediately.

When you click on the Add files button, you will see a screen similar to the one shown in figure 16.7.

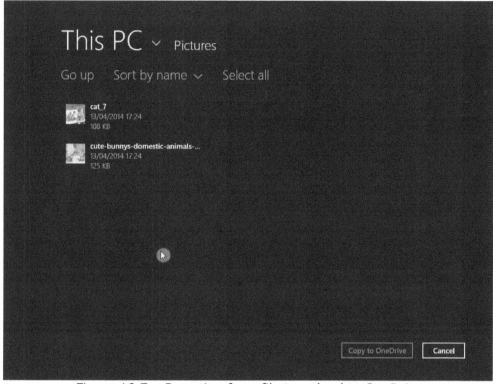

Figure 16.7 – Browsing for a file to upload to OneDrive

Choose the file or files to upload (you can click or tap several at once if desired) then click the "Copy to OneDrive" button. The file will then be uploaded to your OneDrive. Not only does this create a backup of your file, it also means that it can be accessed anywhere you have an internet connection. Files stored in your OneDrive can also be used with Microsoft's other online services, such as the online version of Office, Office 365. Of course, you can easily access this file from any of your Windows 8 PCs or even a Windows phone or other mobile device with the appropriate OneDrive app.

 These buttons change the viewing mode in the OneDrive app. If you don't like how the content is laid out in the app, click these buttons to change it.

When you have one or more files selected in your OneDrive, you will also see the following buttons.

Removes the selected files from your OneDrive.

Creates a copy of the selected files. To use this button, select the files you wish to copy, then click the button shown here. Now, navigate to the folder you want the copied files to be stored in and choose the Paste button on the toolbar.

Works the same way as Copy above, but moves the files rather than creating a copy of them.

Renames the selected files. You will be prompted to enter a new name for each file selected.

Downloads and saves the currently selected files to your computer. This does not remove them from OneDrive, it simply creates another copy on your computer.

Clicking this button will download the selected file and give you the choice of which program or app to use to open it. For instance if you had installed a graphics package on your PC and wanted to open a picture from OneDrive directly into it, you could use this button.

Simply deselects all selected files.

16.2 – OneDrive on the desktop

Windows 8.1 has full integration with OneDrive on the desktop. We will be covering the desktop in detail in the next chapter. Figure 16.16 shows a OneDrive folder open in File Explorer on the desktop.

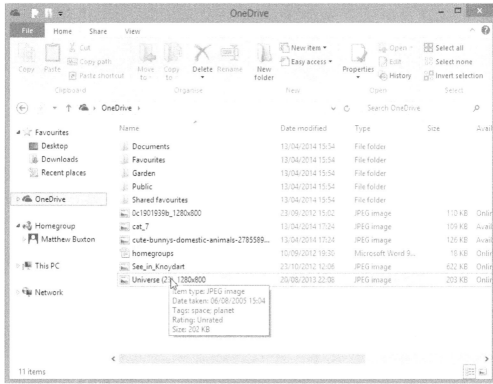

Figure 16.16 – Browsing the OneDrive with File Explorer on the desktop

Users with traditional desktop or laptop PCs almost universally prefer to work on the desktop rather than with the touch-centric tiles, so having the convenience of OneDrive on the desktop too is a huge bonus for many users.

That concludes our tour of some of the most useful Windows 8 tile apps. In the next chapter our tutorials will focus on the desktop and learning how to manipulate files and folders easily.

Chapter 4 – Back to the Desktop

While the new tile applications work to an acceptable level with a keyboard and mouse, there's just no getting away from the fact that they simply aren't optimal for non-touch screens. When you want to get some work done, or access the huge library of desktop applications and productivity software, it's time to go back to the desktop. The desktop in Windows 8 works almost identically to Windows 7 and mastering the desktop is absolutely key to getting the most out of your PC.

Lesson 17 – Introduction to the desktop

It's time for a quick tour of the Windows 8 desktop. The desktop has changed a little, but it should still be at least somewhat familiar to those of you who have used Windows before. To access the desktop in Windows 8, click on the Desktop tile on the Start screen.

17.1 – Desktop elements

Let us take a look at the elements of the desktop, figure 17.1 shows them.

Figure 17.1 – The standard Windows 8 desktop

Figure 17.1 shows the standard Windows 8 desktop you will see on a clean (new) installation of the operating system. We will now go over the basic elements shown in the picture.

Start button:- The Start button makes a welcome return in Windows 8.1. To open the Start screen from the desktop, simply click on the Start button here. Alternatively, press the Windows key to access the Start screen at any time, or use the Charms Bar (see lesson 3.3).

Taskbar:- The area at the bottom to the left of the notification area is called the taskbar. The taskbar works just like it did in Windows 7, but a little differently to both Windows XP and Windows Vista. On the bottom left of the screen you may have noticed some icons. If you are familiar with Windows Vista or earlier versions of Windows you will know that the taskbar is where you can see programs that are already running. If you've visited the desktop on your own Windows 8 machine, you might be wondering why there appear to be programs already running. Well, these programs are not actually running at all. Unlike earlier versions of Windows, programs can be "pinned" on the taskbar. This means that they will stay on the taskbar for easy access even when they are not running. By default we get File Explorer and Internet Explorer.

It is important to understand that icons on the taskbar do not necessarily represent programs that are running. You can click on the icons pinned to the taskbar to start the program running. When a program is running, it will have a border around its taskbar icon, see figure 17.2 for an example.

Figure 17.2 – Internet Explorer running on the taskbar, next to File Explorer which is "pinned" but not running

If you hover your mouse pointer over a running taskbar icon, Windows will show you a preview window.

Figure 17.3 – Hover your mouse pointer over a program running on the taskbar to see a preview of the window

You can click on the preview window to go directly to the application.

17.2 – Notification area

Notification Area or System Tray:- The official Microsoft name for this part of the desktop is the notification area, but lots of users refer to it as the System Tray. The notification area works the same in Windows 8 as it did in Windows 7. To see your notification area icons, you click the small up pointing arrow. See figure 17.4 for more details.

Figure 17.4 – The new notification area/System Tray is opened with a click on this small arrow icon

If you are not sure what the notification area is for, do not worry, we cover it in more detail in lesson 30.

To the right of the arrow icon highlighted in figure 17.4, there are three other icons. These icons are also counted as part of the notification area, though you might think otherwise at first glance. The flag shaped icon is the Action Center. This notifies you about potential problems on your PC, such as security alerts. Next to that is the network icon, this can be used for connecting quickly to networks, both wired and wireless. Then there's the volume icon, a quick click of this accesses a sliding control which can adjust the volume level for all sounds on your computer.

Date and time:- To the right of the notification area (see figure 17.1) is the date and time display. This is self explanatory. You can click on the date and time display down here to adjust your computers clock if it is not showing the correct time.

Show Desktop button:- Clicking in the very bottom right hand corner of the Windows 8 desktop will activate the Show Desktop button. This button hides all of your open windows so that you can see the desktop. Clicking it again will reveal the windows again.

Recycle Bin:- This lonely looking icon in the top left hand corner of the desktop is the Recycle Bin. Files and folders you delete are (usually!) placed in this folder before being removed entirely. We cover this in more detail in lesson 27.

Note:- The picture of the flower in the background on our desktop is called the desktop background or wallpaper. This picture can be changed to any image you like and we show you how in lesson 48. Many of our videos and lessons were compiled using a pre-release version of Windows 8.1 and the standard desktop background may change for the release version. Because of this, don't be alarmed if your desktop background looks different.

If you have never used Windows before, you might be confused as to what all these different components do. This lesson was really to give you an overview of the desktop components and not what they do, so move along to the next lesson where we look at how windows work on the Windows 8 desktop.

Lesson 18 – Windows on the Windows 8 Desktop

As you might imagine, windows are an important concept to master in Windows 8. Virtually every program you run on the Windows 8 desktop will create a window of some kind, the only exception being certain game and multimedia titles which take over the whole screen. Windows 8 comes with the same handy features for managing windows that Windows 7 introduced, which we will delve into in this lesson.

18.1 – A Windows 8 desktop window

The majority of desktop windows you will work with in Windows 8 have a common set of controls at the top. Take a look at figure 18.1.

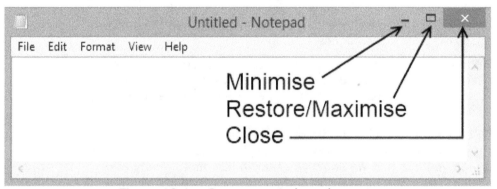

Figure 18.1 – Common window elements

At the top left of the window is the programs icon (which you will see on the taskbar when the program is running). The name of the window (which is usually the programs name) is shown in the top middle area. Directly below that, many programs have menus which can be accessed by clicking on them. In figure 18.1 you may be able to make out "File", "Edit", "Format", "View" and "Help".

On the top right of the window we have the common window controls. Clicking Minimise hides the window and shrinks the application down to the taskbar. Unlike previous versions of Windows, items on the taskbar are now represented by icons. To maximise the window again, click on the programs icon on the taskbar.

Clicking Close will close down the application completely.

The middle button (labelled Restore/Maximise in figure 18.1) changes depending on what state the window is in. When a window is maximised, that is, sized to fill all the available space on your monitor, this button is called "Restore". Clicking on Restore will make the window slightly smaller. Why would you want to do this?, simply because it makes it easier to resize and move the window, as we will see in a moment.

If the window is not maximised then clicking on the middle button will maximise it, expanding it to fill up all available space on your desktop.

18.2 – Moving and resizing

When a window is not maximised, it is easy to move and resize it. To move a window, simply click with your left mouse button on the title bar and hold your left mouse button down (or press with your finger on a touch screen). Now, drag the window to wherever you want it. When the window is in place, let go of your mouse button.

To resize a window, firstly move your mouse pointer to the edge of the window. When the pointer is in the correct place, it will turn into two oppositely pointing arrows. Click your left mouse button and hold it down, then drag with the mouse and let go. Your window will now snap to the new size. You can resize from any side, and from the corners too, which allows you to adjust the width and height at the same time. Figure 18.2 shows a mouse pointer ready to resize a window.

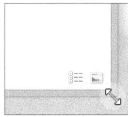

Figure 18.2 – When your mouse pointer looks like two arrows, you are ready to resize your window

18.3 – Ways to work with windows

Windows 7 introduced some great new tools to make working with Windows easier and more productive and Windows 8 has these same tools too. As you start becoming more confident with the desktop, you will start working with more and more open windows at once. The following features can help you manage and organise your desktop windows.

Desktop Peek:- In lesson 17, we touched on how the taskbar had been overhauled for Windows 7. Instead of window names, as seen in Windows Vista and earlier versions, we now get icons. When a program opens multiple windows, the icons stack on top of each other. To help you find the correct window, you can use Desktop Peek. Hover your mouse pointer over icons on the taskbar and you will see a preview of their window. Figure 18.3 illustrates this.

Figure 18.3 – Using Desktop Peek to preview windows from the taskbar

Hover your mouse pointer over one of the previews and Windows will turn all the other windows on the desktop transparent, allowing you to focus on the window you are previewing. To open or select one of the windows you are peeking at, simply click on the preview with your mouse.

Desktop Peek works with Internet Explorer too. If you use tabbed browsing (we cover this in lesson 54.1), you will see previews of your open tabs. This doesn't work in all third party web browsers yet, however.

Desktop Snap:- If you are used to working with multiple windows, you will know that windows can often become cluttered on your desktop. Windows 8 gives you a great tool to help with this called Desktop Snap. Take any window and then move it off to the edge of your screen on either side. When you have moved it far enough you will then see a transparent frame appear. Let go of the mouse button now and the window will snap to exactly half of the screen width.

Desktop Shake:- Shake is a feature introduced in Windows 7, possibly born out of frustration. If you are working with a desktop with a lot of open windows, all piled on top of one another in a chaotic fashion, simply grab the window you want to work with from the chaos and then by holding down your mouse button (just like when you move a window) shake it quite vigorously. Now the other windows on your desktop are minimised and you will be left with just the window you were shaking. You can also shake the window again to reverse the effect.

So, hopefully you will have discovered that working with windows on the Windows 8 desktop is easy and dare we say even fun? Many users find that Desktop mode suits how they work with their PCs much better than the tiles, which are really optimised for touch devices. If you're firmly in the desktop user camp, our next lesson will look at some of the ways you can make Windows 8 more desktop friendly.

Lesson 19 – Tweaking Windows 8 for desktop systems

If you're using Windows 8 on a machine without a touch screen, such as a traditional desktop or laptop device, you may feel that the tiles and the Windows store apps are a bad fit for how you want to use your PC. Few, if any of us want to sit at a desk and strain our arms to touch a touch screen. The big, bold finger friendly tile apps simply waste screen space when you're using a PC at your desk. Luckily, with a few tweaks, Windows 8 can behave exactly like Windows 7, making the operating system extremely flexible. Many users believe that Microsoft should have included these tweaks by default, but regardless, a few minutes of tweaking and (optionally) a few dollars spent and Windows 8 becomes arguably the best desktop operating system ever released.

19.1 – Secret Start button shortcuts

If you have migrated from Windows 8 to Windows 8.1, you probably noticed that the Start button has made a comeback. However, you may not have realised that there's a hidden menu on the Start button that you can access by right clicking on it. Figure 19.1 shows this menu.

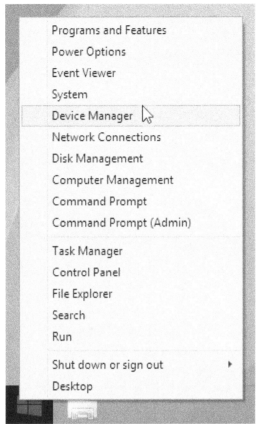

Figure 19.1 – The right-click Start button menu

As you can see, this menu gives you access to several handy shortcuts, including the Task Manger (see lesson 65), the Control Panel, File Explorer and the Shutdown and sign out options.

19.2 – Basic desktop PC tweaks

Microsoft made some concessions to disappointed desktop users in Windows 8.1 and added some new options to help tweak the OS for desktop use. To access these options, go to the desktop and right click on a blank area on the taskbar (see figure 17.1). Now, from the menu that will appear, choose "Properties". A taskbar and navigation properties window will then appear. The window has several tabs at the top, click on the "Navigation" tab. Figure 19.2 shows the resulting window.

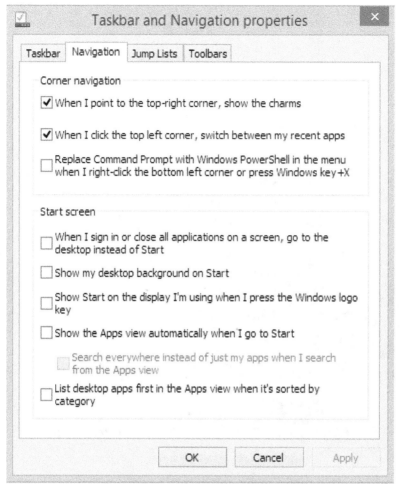

Figure 19.2 – Navigation properties

At the top of the window, under "Corner navigation" there are two options for disabling the hot corners. Turn the first option off to disable the Charms Bar hot-corner (as seen in lesson 3.3) and the second option to disable the task switcher (as seen in lesson 3.1).

In the second half of the window, we can see "Start screen" options. By selecting the first option in this section, "When I sign in or close all applications on a screen, go to the desktop instead of Start", you can change the behaviour of your PC so that you are sent to the desktop when you first start the machine, rather than the Start screen. As of Windows 8.1 Update 1, this is the default setting for PCs that do not have a touch screen. Keep in mind of course, you will still need to open the Start screen to launch programs. You can slightly tweak the behaviour of the Start screen by selecting the last two options in the list. For instance, you may want to make the Start screen go directly to Apps view. We covered the Apps view in lesson 4.3, Microsoft introduced Apps view to make the Start screen behave more like the old Start menu, however many users still feel it doesn't go far enough.

19.3 – Alternative ways to access apps

If you only use a handful of programs on your PC, you can either pin them to the taskbar or manually create shortcuts on your desktop. We mentioned pinning to the taskbar in lesson 17.1. You can pin any app that is currently running simply by right clicking on its taskbar icon and choosing "Pin this program to taskbar".

You can also pin an app that's not running, or create a shortcut to it on the desktop. To do this, firstly locate your program on the Start screen. You could do this by browsing or simply by searching for the app. Once you have located your program, right click on it. In figure 19.3 the user has located the third-party program Evernote and right clicked on its icon.

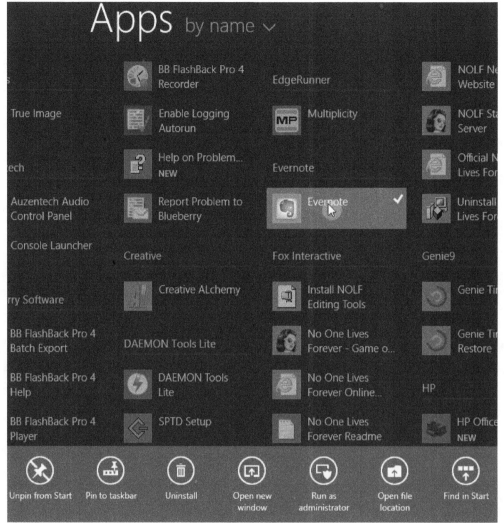

Figure 19.3 – Right click on a program on the Start screen to reveal these extra options

To pin the program to the taskbar, simply click "Pin to taskbar". Creating a desktop shortcut is a little more long winded. Firstly, click on "Open file location". This will send you back to the desktop and open a File Explorer window. Figure 19.4 shows an example of this.

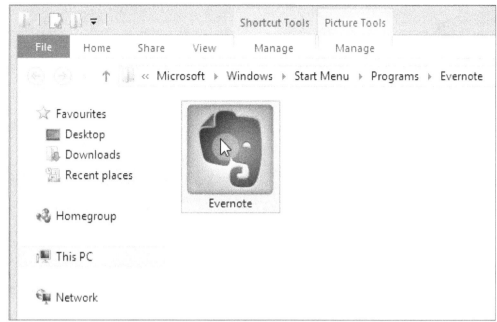

Figure 19.4 – Selecting "Open file location" from the Start screen will open a window like this

To create a shortcut to the program on the desktop, right click on the icon shown in the Explorer window and from the context menu choose Send to->Desktop (create shortcut). Figure 19.5 illustrates this menu option.

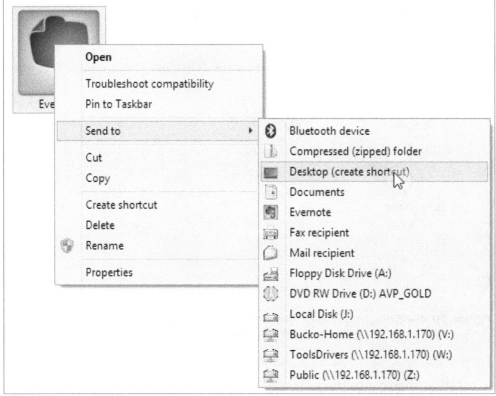

Figure 19.5 – Creating a desktop shortcut

The programs shortcut will then appear on the desktop for easy launching. Remember, if you add too many icons to your desktop it will become cluttered and you might as well just use the Start screen to search and launch your apps. This is especially true considering you cannot automatically search through desktop icons like you can with items on the Start screen.

19.4 – Changing default programs

One design decision that frequently annoyed desktop users in Windows 8 was the default applications Microsoft configured for handling media files. As of Windows 8.1 Update 1 however, Microsoft have addressed this criticism. When working with File Explorer, if you double click to open a media file (picture, music or video), it will open on the desktop rather than with the tile program. If you need to change these settings for any reason, it is easy to do so. While working on the desktop, navigate to any media file in File

Explorer, now, right click on the file and choose "Open with" from the context menu. A sub-menu listing various options will then open, at the bottom of this menu is the option to "Choose default program...". Click this option and the window shown in figure 19.6 will then open.

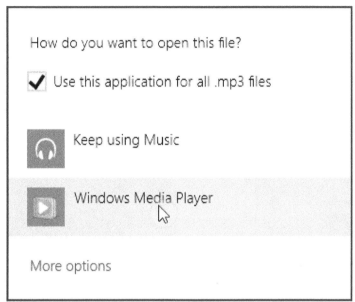

Figure 19.6 – Setting default applications for opening files

In this example, by selecting Windows Media Player and making sure the "Use this application for all .mp3 files" option is selected, the user can change the default double click behaviour for all mp3 files. Now, when an mp3 music file is double clicked, it will open in the desktop friendly Windows Media Player rather than the Music tile. We cover Windows Media Player in Chapter 10.

You can use this technique to set the default program for any type of file on your PC. If you install third-party media playback software, you can select it from this menu too. Of course, you can always switch back to the default behaviour by using the same technique.

19.5 – Restoring the Start menu and other third-party tweaks

Now we have Windows 8 behaving much more like a traditional desktop OS. For many users this will be entirely satisfactory. There's no getting away from the fact that the old Start menu, found in all versions of Windows from

95 to Windows 7, was simply better for keyboard and mouse users than the new Start screen. We will now take a brief look at two Start menu replacements that you can download and install. If you don't know how to install new software, see lesson 46.

Figure 19.7 shows a Windows 8 PC running Classic Shell. This is a free Start menu replacement that is very popular.

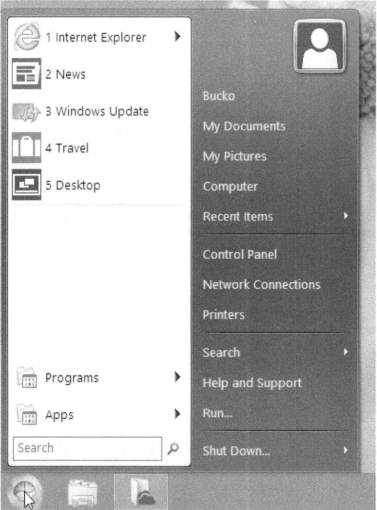

Figure 19.7 – The Classic Shell Start menu replacement

You can click the Classic Shell Start button to open the Start menu, then search for your apps or simply click them to launch them. Classic Shell is an easy solution to get your Start menu back. You can download it by visiting this website:- http://www.classicshell.net/

Figure 19.8 shows a PC running Start8. This is widely regarded as the best Start menu replacement.

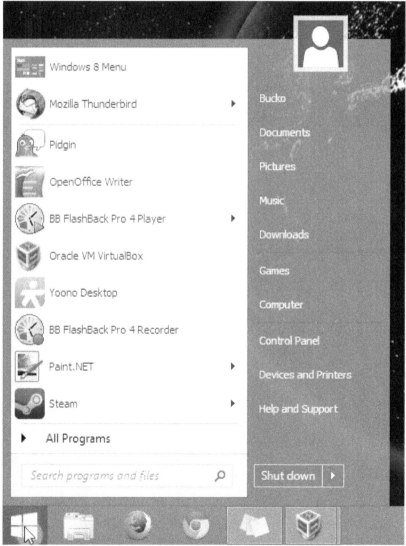

Figure 19.8 – The Start8 Start menu replacement

This Start menu more closely resembles Windows 7's Start menu and is fully compatible with Stardock Software's Windowblinds app, which allows you to completely skin and customise the desktop. Start8 is our favourite Windows 8 Start menu replacement and costs just four dollars ninety nine. You can find out more by visiting this website:-
http://www.stardock.com/products/start8/

19.5.1 - ModernMix

ModenMix isn't a Start menu replacement, but it might be useful to some Windows 8 users. ModernMix can take Windows tile apps and run them in a desktop window. Figure 19.9 shows a PC running this utility.

Figure 19.9 – Running tiles on the desktop with ModernMix

As you can see, the Windows Store is running in a desktop window, rather than full-screen. When using ModernMix you can change any tile application between normal Windows 8 behaviour and desktop mode. ModernMix is also

available from Stardock Software for four dollars ninety nine. You can find out more by visiting this site:-
http://www.stardock.com/products/modernmix/

ModernMix is certainly useful in some situations. Perhaps you have a favourite Windows 8 game that you want to play on the desktop, or maybe you want to use the music streaming services in the Music app (see lesson 12.4) while you work on the desktop. Keep in mind though, rather than running Windows tiles like this, it is usually possible to find an alternative app that does the same job but is properly optimised for the desktop interface.

That concludes this lesson on tweaking Windows 8 for traditional desktop and laptop systems. Hopefully any concerns you had about adapting to Windows 8 are now laid to rest.

Lesson 20 – Exploring File Explorer

 Computers run programs that manipulate information. In our ultra connected internet age, desktop and laptop computers in homes crunch through data and information at a rate that would have humbled the supercomputers of the past. Never before has it been easier and quicker to manipulate your pictures, videos and music files. In the next few lessons, we will show you how you can work with files and folders on the desktop. The program you will be using to do this is called File Explorer. File Explorer was known as Windows Explorer in previous versions of Windows and it has had a bit of an upgrade for Windows 8. Once mastered, File Explorer makes working with files as easy as organising a filing cabinet, easier in fact, since it does all the lifting and refiling for you!

20.1 – Your personal folders

Your personal folder contains four sub-folders by default. The folders are "Documents", "Music", "Pictures" and "Videos". You can access these folders from File Explorer or from the Start screen. To access your Documents folder, for instance, open the Start screen and then search for "documents" and click the first icon that appears in the results. You can also go to the desktop and start File Explorer from the taskbar and then click on the "Documents" icon in the window. Your Documents folder will then be open in File Explorer and look something like figure 20.1.

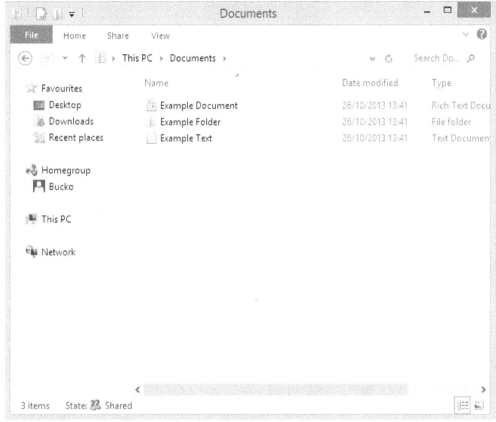

Figure 20.1 – A users Documents folder open in File Explorer

On a clean installation of Windows 8, the Documents folder will be empty. The items shown in figure 20.1 have been added just as an example.

In the left of the File Explorer window, we can jump quickly to several folders. Figure 20.2 shows the left hand column (or Navigation pane to give it its correct name) in more detail.

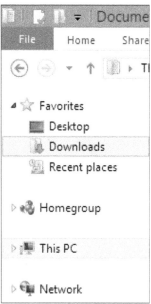

Figure 20.2 – The Navigation pane

Using the Navigation pane in File Explorer, we can jump to several folders. There's the Downloads folder, where files that you download from the web are stored. Recent Places, which, as you might expect, takes you to folders you recently opened. You can also jump directly to Homegroup and Network, which take you to resources on the network you're currently connected to, if they are available. "This PC" is the new name for Computer, we cover that in lesson 28.

Notice the small arrows or triangles next to the icons in the Navigation pane. These appear when you hover your mouse pointer over this area. You can click these arrows to expand that particular folder or location. For instance, clicking on the arrow next to "This PC" will show you the folders or locations that are available directly from "This PC". Figure 20.3 illustrates this.

Figure 20.3 – Expanding out "This PC" in the Navigation pane

The contents you will see under "This PC" will vary depending on what drives you have in your PC and what compatible devices there are on your network. We cover "This PC" in more detail in lesson 28.

To open folders in the Navigation pane, single click on them. File Explorer will then open the folder and show the contents in the main area on the right. To open files or folders in the main working area of File Explorer, we double click on them. So to see the contents of the folder "Example Folder" shown in figure 20.1 for example, we would double click on it.

20.2 – The individual elements of a File Explorer window

Figure 20.4 shows the basic controls from the top of a typical File Explorer window.

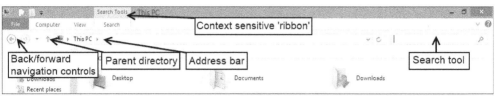

Figure 20.4 – Elements of a File Explorer window

Back/forward navigation controls:- As you browse through folders, you can use the back button (the arrow pointing to the left) to go back to the folder you were previously viewing. Similarly, the forward button (the arrow pointing to the right) will take you forward again.

Parent directory:- This control is new in Windows 8, if you can't make it out easily in the picture, it just looks like an up-pointing arrow. The button will take you to the parent directory, so for instance if you were in the "Videos" folder inside the "Documents" folder, clicking this arrow would take you back up to Documents.

Address bar:- The Address bar shows the address of the file on your computer. This is often referred to as the file path. Expert users can even type the address or path of a file directly into the address bar.

Search tool:- If you need to search through the contents of a folder, enter your search query here. Note that searching like this will only search through the contents of the current folder and its sub-folders, not through the entire computer.

Context sensitive ribbon:- The new ribbon replaces the toolbar in the new File Explorer. Tabs appear at the very top of the window as you work with files and folders in File Explorer. These tabs will change based on the content you are working with. Figure 20.5 shows an example of the tab that will appear when working with music in your music folder.

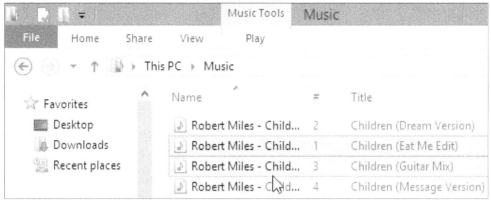

Figure 20.5 – Tabs on the ribbon interface will change as you work with different content

20.3 – Introducing the ribbon

In figure 20.5 the ribbon interface was hidden, but by clicking the tabs at the top of the window at any time you can open the ribbon. Figure 20.6 shows what happens when the "Music Tools" tab is clicked.

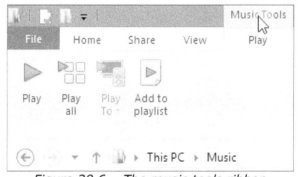

Figure 20.6 – The music tools ribbon

From the Music Tools ribbon you can play all music in the current folder. By clicking once on a media file, the option to play the currently selected file will become available. You can always access the different categories on the ribbon by using the menu bar below the tabs too. We will be seeing more of the ribbon in later lessons. Remember that at any point you can use the minimise/maximise ribbon control near the top right of the Explorer window to show or hide the ribbon. Figure 20.7 shows this control.

Figure 20.7 – The minimise/maximise ribbon control is circled

20.4 – Breadcrumbs

If you want to find your way back along a path, then leaving a trail of breadcrumbs might work, provided there's nothing around to eat them. Since birds and other animals don't eat digital breadcrumbs, you can rely on them for finding your way back down the path and off in other directions. Take a look at figure 20.8, it shows an example of using the breadcrumbs feature to navigate around the personal folders.

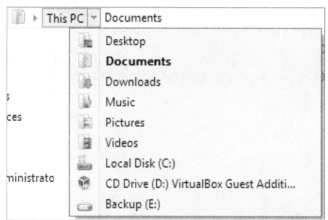

Figure 20.8 – Using breadcrumbs to navigate around folders in the path

In figure 20.8 we have opened the breadcrumbs menu at "This PC". The menu is showing us all the other folders we could navigate to from there. Rather than having to navigate back to the folder we can simply use the breadcrumbs here to quickly jump off to somewhere else.

Breadcrumbs are an advanced user feature so don't worry if you don't quite understand them yet. Do not be afraid to experiment for yourself, it is not possible to break anything playing with this feature.

20.5 – Folder views

Computers view all data as strings of binary numbers, but people are much more visual than that. Fortunately, there are several ways we can represent content in File Explorer. To change viewing mode, click on the "View" tab. This will open the ribbon and allow you to choose a viewing mode. Refer to figure 20.9 for a list of all the different folder view modes.

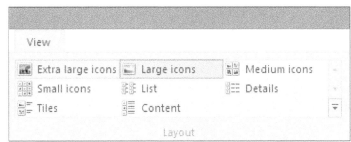

Figure 20.9 – Folder viewing modes available on the ribbon under the "View" tab

So what do all those viewing options do? Take a look at the following pictures for an example. These screenshots were taken from within a picture folder, other content will look different, of course.

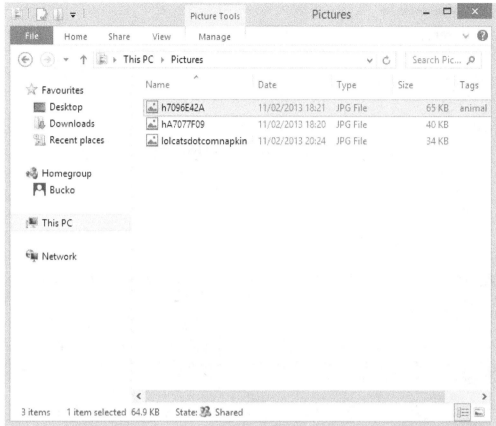

Figure 20.10.1 – Details view, the power users favourite

Details view is used most often when working with large numbers of files. You can easily see important information such as file types and sizes. We'll be looking at details view in more detail in the next lesson.

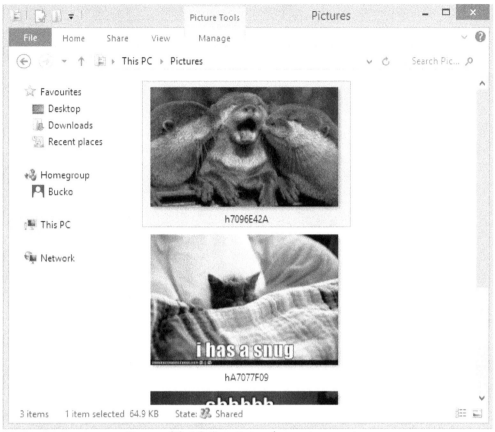

Figure 20.10.2 – Extra large icons view

An icon is a visual representation of a file or folder on your computer. In File Explorer, we can choose four different sizes of icon. Picture files will display as a thumb nail preview as seen in figure 20.10.2 if the icon size is large enough.

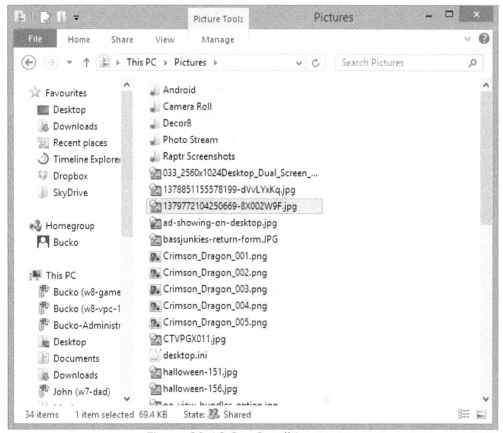

Figure 20.10.3 – Small icons view

In small icons view, the icons become too small to show a thumbnail picture preview and so simply revert to this small representation of a picture. Small icons view and list view, which we look at next, are very similar. You can only see the difference between these views when you have a folder with several files, hence the screenshots here are from a more crowded Windows 8 picture folder.

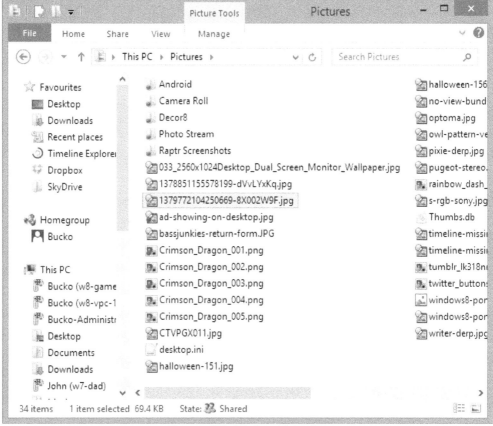

Figure 20.10.4 – List view

List view is similar to small icons view but lays things out slightly differently.

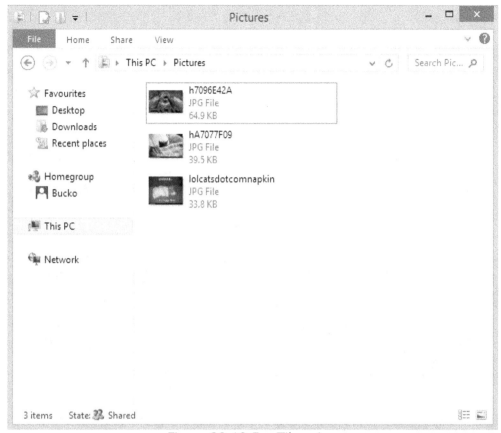

Figure 20.10.5 – Tiles view

Tiles view is similar to medium icons view except some information about the files is placed on the right next to the icon.

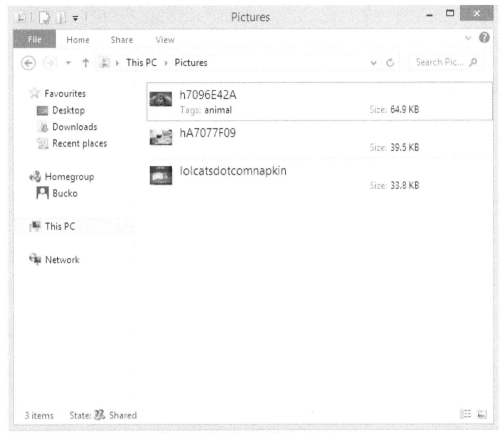

Figure 20.10.6 – Content view

Content view aims to strike a balance between details view and icon view. Files are arranged in a list with their file sizes shown on the right.

That concludes this introduction to File Explorer. You should now be reasonably confident navigating between folders on your PC. If not, be sure to practise all the techniques we showed in this lesson and learn at your own pace.

Lesson 21 – Advanced File Explorer techniques

 Continuing our tour of File Explorer, in this lesson we will look at some more techniques for viewing and managing files on your computer.

21.1 – Delving into details view

Recall how in lesson 20.5 we showed you the different folder views. Back then we said that details view was the view that power users used the most. Details view lets you find out all kinds of information about files on your computer. Figure 21.1 shows a folder open in details view in File Explorer.

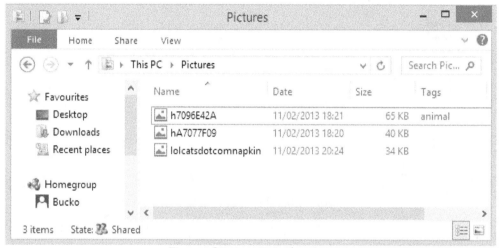

Figure 21.1 – Details view

In figure 21.1, we can see the date that the files were modified, the size of the files in Kilobytes (KB) and any tags that are applied (we cover tags in lesson 31.1). Right clicking on a column heading in details view enables us to add a new column, figure 21.2 demonstrates this.

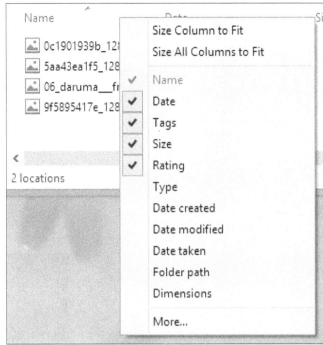

Figure 21.2 – Customising details view by adding more columns of information

After right clicking on a column heading, adding or removing new columns is just a matter of clicking on them from the menu. By clicking on "More..." at the bottom of the menu you can choose from hundreds of different types of meta-data (data about data). Not all meta data is relevant to all kinds of files, for example a picture of your back garden isn't usually going to have an "Album Artist" and your favourite music file is unlikely to have "Dimensions", at least not the kind that can be measured in inches or centimetres.

You can also sort your list of files by any of the columns you currently have displayed in details view. Simply click on the column to sort by that criteria, click again on the same column to reverse the sorting order (i.e. change from sorting from high to low or A to Z to low to high or Z to A).

21.2 – Preview pane

When you want to open a file in File Explorer, you double click on it. If you are sifting through a lot of files at once however, you might find it more convenient to use the Preview pane. To enable or disable the Preview pane, first click on the View tab on the ribbon. Figure 21.3 shows the Preview pane opened, the icon circled is the icon you will need to click to open the Preview pane.

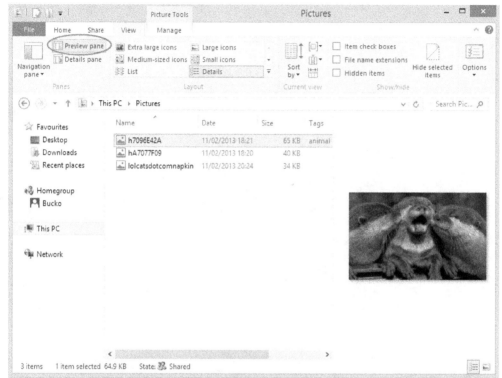

Figure 21.3 – A File Explorer window with the Preview pane enabled. Notice how the selected file appears in the preview on the right

21.3 – Details pane

The Details pane can activated by clicking the icon below "Preview pane". The Details pane gives us a huge amount of information about the currently selected file. Figure 21.4 shows an example of the Details pane.

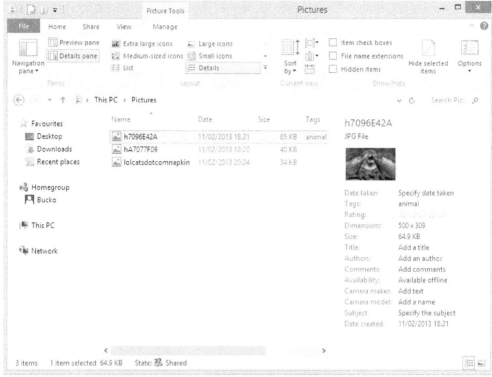

Figure 21.4 – Viewing the Details pane

Not only can you view these details using the Details pane, you can edit some of them too. Click on the text next to "Tags", "Title" or "Authors" for instance, to edit that information.

21.4 – Navigation pane

The Navigation pane is the list of items on the left hand side of the File Explorer window. You can see it clearly in all the previous screen shots. You can also toggle the Navigation pane off or on from the View tab on the ribbon. There are several useful functions you can carry out on the Navigation pane.

At the very top of the pane are the Favourite folders. If you find you are often using the same folder, you can add it to your favourites. Right click on "Favourites" next to the little star icon at the top and then choose "Add current location to Favourites".

The other short-cuts in the Navigation pane will take you to various places which we will be covering in later lessons. The Homegroup folders are shared folders on your network. Homegroups are covered in lesson 56. There are also short-cuts to "This PC" (previously known as "Computer"), which lets you explore all the drives attached to your local computer (we cover that in lesson 28) and if your computer is on a network, the network short-cut will let you browse available network storage locations.

As you have seen, there are lots of ways to work with your data in Windows 8. Don't feel you have to learn and master every possible way to display your data, experiment and use the views that work best for you and the way you work. As with most things in computing, the best way to learn is by trying for yourself, so don't be afraid to have a go.

Lesson 22 – Working with Files and Folders

In this lesson we will be building on some of the skills we developed in the previous lesson by taking a more detailed look at folders and files. For those of you who have used Windows before, much of the material here may be familiar. If this is your first time using Windows then, as always, we encourage you to learn at your own pace and experiment when reviewing the material presented here.

22.1 – Working with folders

We've seen several folders in the last few lessons that Windows 8 places on your computer by default. You are not limited to these folders however and creating new folders of your own is really easy. Figure 22.1 shows File Explorer open at a users personal folder.

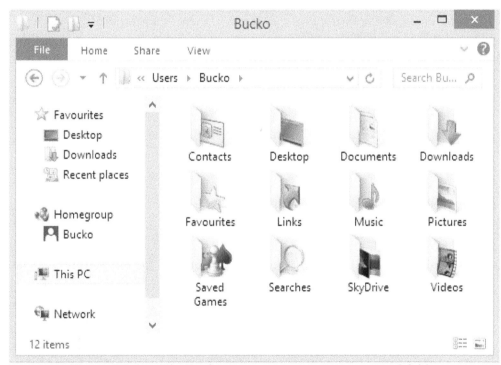

Figure 22.1 – File Explorer open on a users personal folder

Although the folders you can see in the picture are named "Documents"

"Music", "Videos" and so on, you can still copy any kind of information into these folders and that holds true for all folders on a Windows PC. Opening any folder is as simple as double clicking on it.

22.2 – Making your own folders

Just like with a real world filing cabinet, you can create your own folders inside your computer too. Unlike a typical office filing cabinet however, on your Windows 8 PC you can create a new folder wherever you like (except in protected locations such as operating system folders). You can nest new folders inside another folder, and folders inside these folders too. In fact you can nest folders almost without limits. You can create a new folder in several ways. One way is to open the "Home" tab on the ribbon and then click "New Folder". Figure 22.2 shows an example of this, the New folder button is circled.

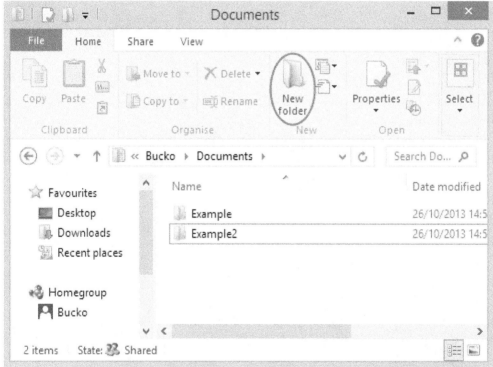

Figure 22.2 – Creating a new folder using the ribbon

Once you click the New Folder button, the new folder will appear instantly, all you need to do is type in a name for the folder using the keyboard. If you don't have a physical keyboard attached, Windows will open the on-screen keyboard for you.

Creating folders is great for organising files on your computer. You can create sub-folders for different projects, different events that you photographed or filmed perhaps, different albums or artists in your music collection or any way you choose.

22.3 – The context menu in File Explorer

Just like in previous versions of Windows, it is a good idea to get used to using the context menu. The context menu is very handy when working with files. To open the context menu in File Explorer, simply right click on a file or folder (see the Appendix – Using touch gestures at the end of the book if you are using a touch only machine). Figure 22.3 shows the resulting menu.

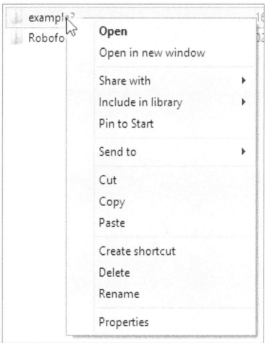

Figure 22.3 – Right click on a file or folder to open a context menu containing some common tasks

Context menus vary slightly between machines, and new software that you install may add extra options to the menu. Most of the options you can see in figure 22.3 will be covered in later lessons. In this lesson we will show you some of the most common tasks you can perform with files and folders from the context menu. Notice you can also pin a folder to the Start screen from here, by using the "Pin to Start" option. Very useful if you want to add a commonly used folder to your Start screen.

22.4 – Send to

Hovering your mouse pointer over the "Send to" option opens up another sub-menu. Figure 22.4 shows this menu.

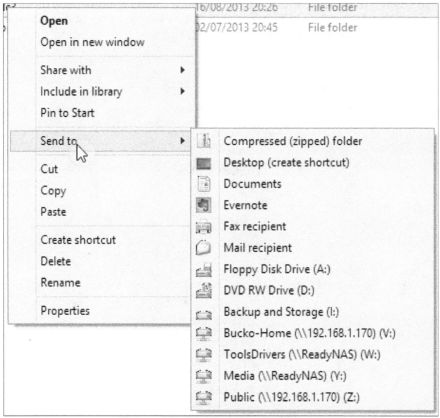

Figure 22.4 – The Send to menu

From this menu we can send the file or folder to various places or programs on our PC. What do each of these options do? We will take a look at each one now.

Compressed (zipped) folder:- This option creates a zip file with the files and folders we currently have selected. You can think of a zipped folder as being a compressed collection of files and folders. If you have dozens of files you want to transport across the internet, compressing them into a zipped folder can make them much easier to manage. Note that sending files or folders to a compressed (zipped) folder will not damage them in any way, nor will it remove them from their original locations. Accessing files inside a compressed or zipped folder is slower than accessing them in a normal folder.

Desktop (create shortcut):- This creates a shortcut to the file or folder on the desktop. The shortcut icon will appear on the same area as the Recycle Bin icon.

Documents:- Sends the currently selected file or folder to the Documents folder. If the file or folder is already in the Documents folder, it will create a copy.

Evernote:- This option has been added by a third-party program and will not appear on a standard Windows 8 machine.

Fax recipient:- Sends the currently selected document or folder to the Fax machine. This option will only work correctly if you have configured your Fax or Fax/Modem correctly. See the documentation that accompanied your hardware for more information.

Mail recipient:- Sends the currently selected files or folders to your e-mail program where they can then be forwarded across the internet to friends or associates. Avoid sending excessive or large files through e-mail as this may cause problems with many popular e-mail services.

Floppy Disk Drive:- If your computer still has an old fashioned floppy disk drive, choosing this option will copy the files (space permitting) to the floppy disk in drive A. It is a little surprising to see the venerable floppy disk still featured on the Send to menu in these days of gigabyte sized USB drives physically no bigger than your thumb!

The other options on the menu will send the file to the various drives on your PC. Of course, your PC will certainly have different drives to ours and so the remaining options will be different.

22.5 – Cut, copy and paste

Directly below the Send to options on the context menu are the Cut and Copy options. Mastering the art of cut, copy and paste is one of the best things you can do to make yourself more productive on your Windows PC. Cut is used for moving files or folders, whereas copy is used (unsurprisingly) to copy them. Take a look at figure 22.5.

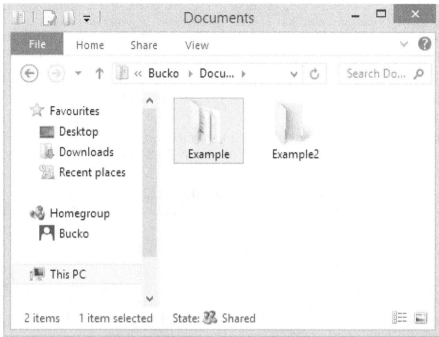

Figure 22.5 – Folders in a File Explorer window

If you wanted to move the folder named "example2", shown in figure 22.5 so that it was nested inside the folder named "example", you could do this by using the context menu. Right click on the "example2" folder and choose "Cut" from the context menu. Now, open the folder you want to move the file or folder into, in this case the folder called "example". Now right click on an empty space in the File Explorer window and choose "Paste" from the context menu. The "example2" folder will then appear. If we had chosen "Copy" instead of "Cut" then the folder would not have been removed from its original location.

> **Ctrl** The Cut, Copy and Paste functions are also available on the ribbon under the "Home" tab. Furthermore, you can use the Control (Ctrl) and C keyboard shortcut for copy and the Control and V keyboard shortcut for paste.

You can also move files and folders by dragging them. Dragging is done by clicking with your left mouse button on an icon and then holding down your left button. Now, as you move your mouse the icon will move too. You can now simply drop the icon wherever you want it. We explore this in more detail in lesson 23.1.

22.6 – When file names collide

Windows needs to tell files apart just the same as you do, so you cannot have two files with the same name in the same folder.

If you try and put a file with the same name as an existing one into the same folder, Windows will show you information about both files and ask you to confirm that you want to replace the original file.

If you try and put a folder with the same name as an existing one into the same folder, the contents of the folders will be merged. Any files which exist inside both folders will be overwritten. If a file is in the source folder but not in the destination folder, it will be moved to the destination. If a file is in the destination folder but not the source folder, it will be left alone. Figure 22.7 shows two folders. Notice how there's a file called "File3" in both folders.

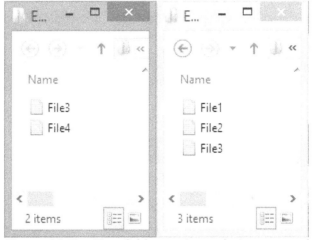

Figure 22.7 – Two folders prior to being merged

Now, consider figure 22.8, here the contents of the two folders have been merged together.

Figure 22.8 – The merged contents of two folders, shading has been added to File3 for illustration purposes

In the example illustrated, File1 and File2 are unchanged. File3 (coloured red or shaded darker in figure 22.8) was overwritten, because it existed in both the source and the destination folders. File4 was moved in from its original location, because it existed in the source folder but NOT in the destination. We will explore file name collisions more in lesson 23.2.

22.7 – Renaming or deleting files and folders

Renaming any type of file or folder can be done easily from the context menu. Simply right click on the file or folder you want to work with then choose "Rename" from the context menu. Now, type a new name and press Enter. If you prefer, you can select the file and click "Rename" from the Home tab on the ribbon too, both methods work exactly the same.

Eventually you will want to remove a file or folder from your PC. You can do this easily from the context menu, simply right click on a file and choose "Delete". Files and folders that are deleted are usually (but not always) sent to the Recycle Bin. You should see the Recycle Bin on your desktop, you can open it with a double click. To take a file out of the Recycle Bin, right click on it and choose "Restore". We take a more detailed look at the Recycle Bin in lesson 27.

You can also delete files or folders by clicking on them once and then clicking the Delete button on the Home tab of the ribbon or by pressing the Delete key on your keyboard.

That concludes this lesson. By now you are becoming quite competent at working with files and folders on your PC, the next lesson will show you some advanced techniques for dealing with large numbers of files. Remember, practise makes perfect so don't be afraid to try out the techniques we have reviewed here.

Lesson 23 – Working with multiple Files and Folders

In the last lesson, we saw how to use the context menu or the ribbon to copy and move files on our hard drive. In this lesson, we will review and build on those skills as we work with multiple files.

23.1 – Dragging and dropping

This is a somewhat difficult concept to explain with just words and pictures. You can move, or drag an icon by clicking on it with your left mouse button, then, keeping your mouse button held down, move your mouse. The file or folder will now follow your mouse cursor. Figure 23.1 shows an example of a folder being dragged into another folder.

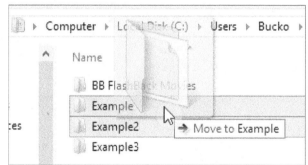

Figure 23.1 – Dragging a folder into another folder will move it

23.2 – File name collisions revisited

We already learned that we can't have two files or folders with the same name in the same folder. If there is a file name collision when copying or moving a file, you will see the window shown in figure 23.2.

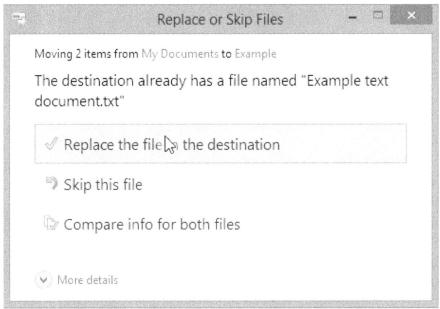

Figure 23.2 – Windows needs your permission to replace this file

The choice is pretty easy here, click on "Replace the file" to overwrite the conflicting file or folders or "Skip this file" to leave the files as they are. If you click on "Compare info for both files" you can check things like date stamps to help you decide which file to keep.

If there is a file name collision during a folder merge, you will then see the window shown in figure 23.3.

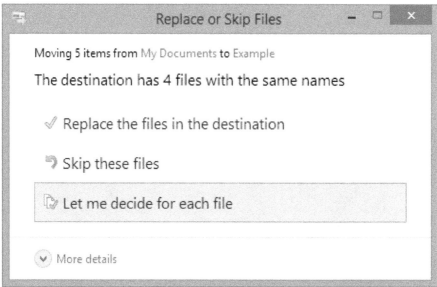

Figure 23.3 – A file collision when merging a folder

You now have the option to "Let me decide for each file". Figure 23.4 shows what happens if you choose this option.

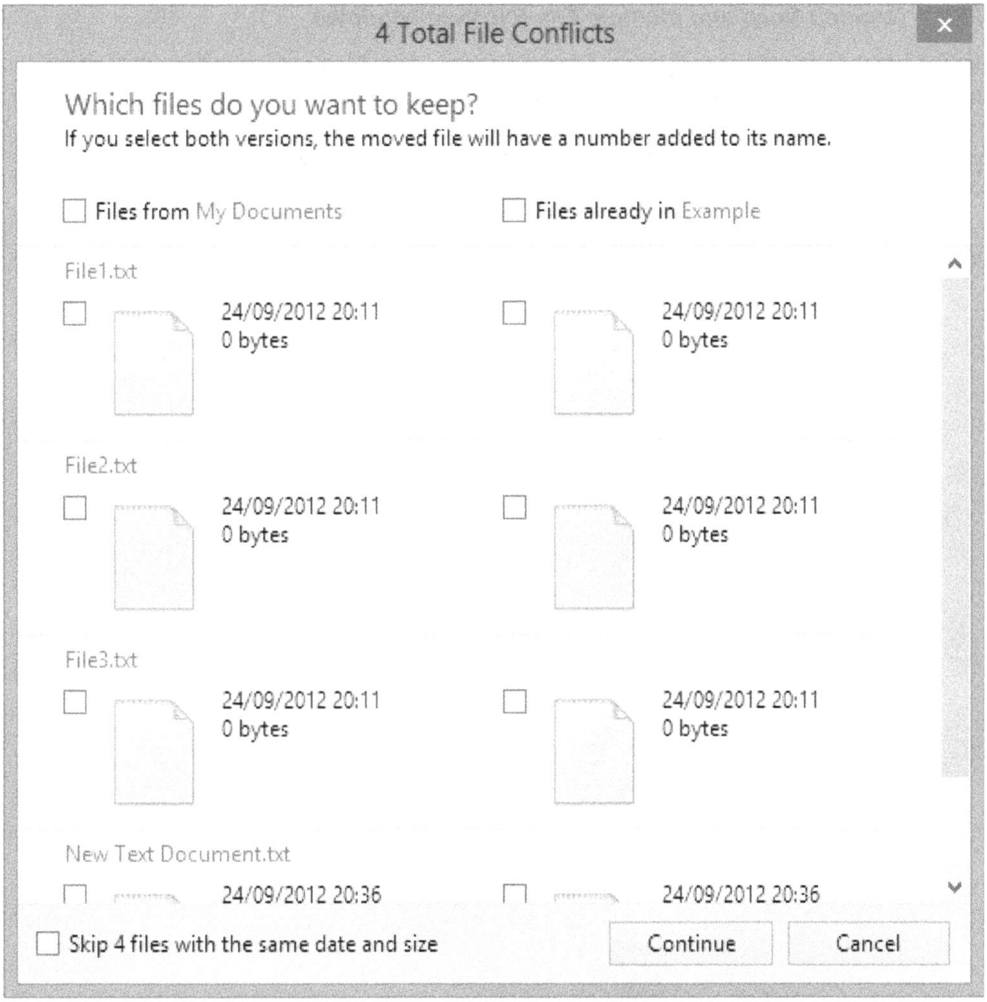

Figure 23.4 – Resolving file conflicts manually

Files in the source directory are shown on the left, while files in the destination directory are shown on the right. Windows gives us information about when the file was last modified, you can use this information to determine which is the most recent copy of a document. Tick or check the files you want to keep. If you choose to keep both conflicting files, then the file in the source directory will have a number appended to its file name. This renaming by numbering enables you to keep both versions of a file if you are unsure which is the correct one.

23.3 – Desktop Snap and multiple File Explorer windows

It is possible to drag and drop files between File Explorer windows. A neat way of setting this up is to use Desktop Snap. When working, copying and moving files between two folders, you can use Snap to size File Explorer windows to exactly half the screen width. To do this, you need to drag the window to the edge of the screen until a transparent frame appears (remember, to drag a window you click and hold on its title bar as you move your mouse). See figure 23.5 for an example.

Figure 23.5 – Using Snap to resize a File Explorer window, wait for the transparent box to appear before letting go of the mouse button

Once you have snapped one window to one side of the screen, repeat the process with the other window, moving it to the opposite side of the screen. If you don't have another File Explorer window, the easiest way to open one is to right click on the folder you want to work with and choose "Open in new window". Figure 23.6 shows this.

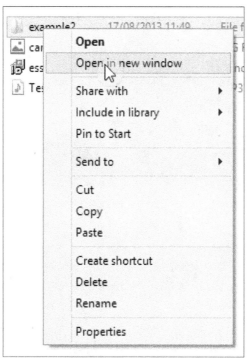

Figure 23.6 – Right click on a folder and choose "Open in new window" to open up a whole new File Explorer window

Now you can drag the new window to the other side of the screen and use Snap to snap it into position. Figure 23.7 shows a screen shot of a desktop configured like this.

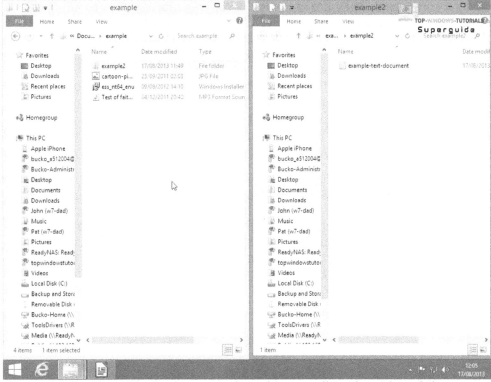

Figure 23.7 – Two File Explorer windows 'Snapped' to the sides of the screen

With your windows configured like this, it is easy to drag and drop files between them (of course, the windows could be sized or positioned however you like, but this configuration is particularly convenient for working with two folders at once).

To move files between the two folders, all you need to do is drag the file across from one window to the other. Files can be moved back in exactly the same way.

Remember when using this technique that dragging a file from one window to another can either move or copy the file, depending on the storage device you are working with. Files are moved if you drag them between two folders on the same storage device. If you drag a file or folder from one storage device to another, the files are copied instead.

To demonstrate this, consider an external USB stick/thumb drive. USB stick drives (also known as thumb drives or pen drives) are portable storage devices which can be attached to the common USB connectors on most modern computers. They are very useful for transporting files to and from work, school or college, for example. When we drag a file from our computers hard drive onto a device like this, it is copied, rather than moved. Why is this? It is not usually worth making lots of copies of a file over the same drive since it just wastes space. When you are working with a removable drive on the other hand, perhaps for backup or transporting files, it would not be a good idea to remove the originals from your computer, especially considering how easy it is to lose a USB stick drive!

23.4 – Working with multiple files at once

So far we have been working with individual files and folders, but what if we wanted to copy or move dozens of files at once? Fortunately for us, we do not have to do them one at a time. There are several ways we can select more than one file or folder at once. One of the easiest ways is to lasso them. To do this, click in an empty space in the File Explorer window and hold down your mouse button, just like you do when you drag an icon or window. You will see a square start to appear, Figure 23.8 illustrates this.

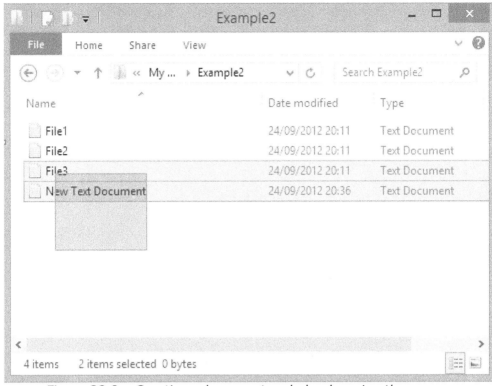

Figure 23.8 – Creating a lasso rectangle by dragging the mouse

Drag the lasso rectangle over the files you want to select and then let go. Now all of the files that were within the boundary of the lasso will be selected.

23.5 – Keyboard short cuts for working with multiple files

There are also some handy keyboard short cuts for selecting multiple files.

| Shift | The Shift keys (sometimes represented as a small up pointing arrow) are located at the far right and far left of the second row of keys from the bottom on a standard keyboard. Using Shift, |

you can select a range of files from a list. For example, to select File1, File2 and File3 in figure 23.8, first click on "File1", then hold down shift and click on "File3".

| Ctrl | The Control or Ctrl keys are located at the far right and far left of the bottom row of keys on a standard keyboard. This key can be used to select and deselect individual files. Simply hold down Control |

while you click on files and folders to individually select and deselect them. Any files you click while holding down Control will stay selected once you let go of the key.

You can also use the Home tab on the ribbon to select multiple files and folders. The file selection tools are on the far right of the Home tab. Figure 23.9 shows the options that are available.

Figure 23.9 – File and folder selection tools on the ribbon

When you have multiple files selected, you can work with them just like you do with an individual file. That means you can use the context menu or the ribbon to Cut, Copy or Send to, or you can drag and drop them. When working with a large number of files, selecting several at once is a huge time-saver, so be sure to practise and master this technique.

That concludes this lesson. Now you have a solid understanding of how to manipulate files on your computer. In the next lesson we look at Libraries, a file organisation feature that was introduced in Windows 7 and improved even further for Windows 8.

Lesson 24 – Libraries

Modern computer users are storing more and more information on their machines. Digital cameras have made it super easy to take thousands of pictures. The internet has made it cheap and easy to purchase huge music collections and even video collections too. Libraries were introduced in Windows 7 to help manage users rapidly expanding file collections. Power users will often rave about Libraries, but regular users frequently find them confusing. In Windows 8.1, the libraries have been hidden away, meaning that regular users may rarely encounter them. If you only have one hard drive on your PC, then you can skip this lesson if you like. Otherwise, read on for some handy tips for organising bigger media collections.

24.1 – Activating libraries

If you want to use libraries in Windows 8.1, you will need to enable them in the Navigation pane. To do this, open a File Explorer window and click on the View tab, then click on the Options button on the right of the ribbon. A folder options window will then appear, as shown in figure 24.1.

Figure 24.1 – Restoring libraries to the Navigation pane

Make sure the "Show libraries" option is selected and then click on "OK". You will now be able to see a shortcut to your libraries in the Navigation pane.

24.2 – Working with libraries

When you access a library in File Explorer, or anywhere in Windows, it appears just like a regular folder. This is probably why beginners often find the concept to be confusing. Libraries can, in fact, show data from several locations on your computer. This can be useful on machines with two or more hard drives. On a machine like this, media files may be spread over different hard drives and in different folders. If you want to browse all your photographs or music together, you can put them in the same library even if they are not in the same folder. Figure 24.2 shows a Music library on a Windows 8 machine. The user has already added some music files to his computer and this can be seen in the example.

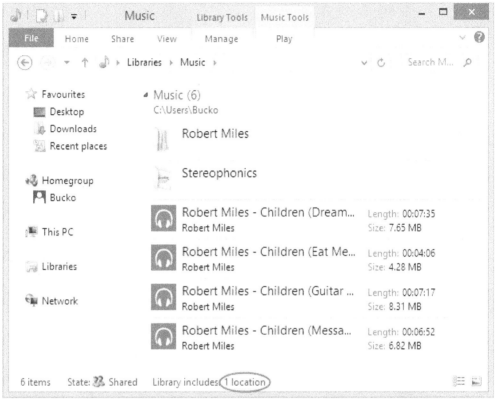

Figure 24.2 – File Explorer in a Music library on a Windows 8 machine. Note the text circled showing how one location is included

In Windows 8.1, libraries only contain one location by default. In Windows 8, there were two locations for each of the libraries. For the Music library, this would be the users own music folder and the public music folder. If you have upgraded your Windows 8 machine to Windows 8.1, then your libraries should still include those two locations.

To see which locations are included in a library, click on the Library Tools tab on the ribbon, then click on "Manage Library".

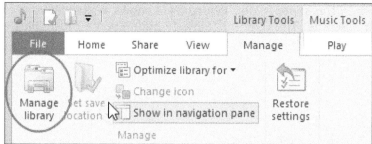

Figure 24.3 – Use the ribbon under "Library Tools" to access the Manage library button

The window shown in figure 24.4 will then open.

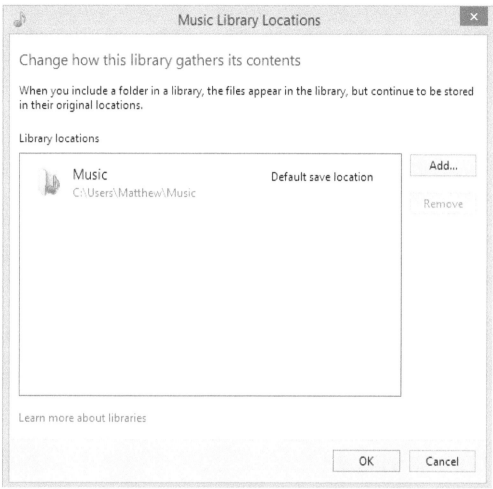

Figure 24.4 – The Music library contains just one folder by default, not very useful

In figure 24.4 we can see that the library contains just one folder. Like this, it isn't very useful. To add a location, click on the "Add..." button. You can then browse to any folder on any storage location on your PC (well, almost any location, there are some exceptions that we will discuss in a moment). When you have located the folder you want to include in your library, click on "Include folder". Figure 24.5 shows a Music library with content added from a secondary hard drive.

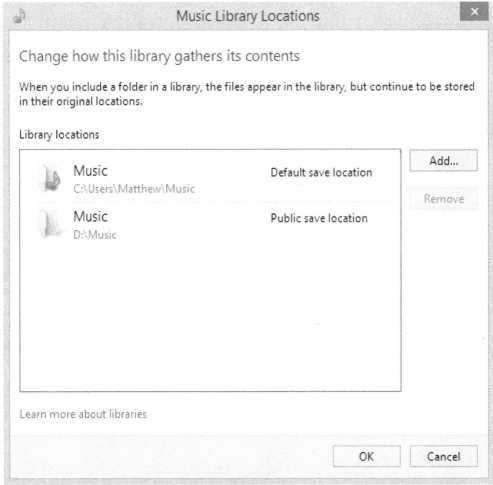

Figure 24.5 – A Music library with two locations added

Now, when the user browses to their Music library, they will in actual fact be getting a combined view of the "Music" folder at 'C:\Users\Matthew\Music' and the folder at 'D:\Music'. So in effect the library will show the content in both of these folders. If you're not sure what that means, you can take a refresher on file paths in our prerequisite skills section, either on your Superguide DVD/Download or in the PC basics section on Top-Windows-Tutorials.com.

Figure 24.6 shows the newly configured library open in File Explorer.

Figure 24.6 – Browsing a library with two locations included in File Explorer

Music folders you add to your music library like this will also be available instantly in the music libraries in the Music tile and in Windows Media Player.

Notice in figure 24.5 that the top folder is marked as the "Default save location". What does this mean? Since we can work with our libraries like any other folder, if we were to copy or move a file into this library from somewhere else, the file would actually be placed into the My Music folder.

The second folder is marked as the "Public save location". The idea of the public save location was to make it easier for users to share files. Public sections of a library can be accessed by all users of the PC, while the regular private sections are only accessible to the user who is currently logged in. Public save locations are rarely used and Microsoft may phase them out entirely in the future.

You can add several more locations to your libraries if you want to. As well as folders on local hard drives, it is possible to add network storage locations or even a removable hard drive. As mentioned earlier, there are some restrictions on what kind of locations can be added to Libraries. Unfortunately, USB thumb or stick drives are not supported and you can only add network locations that are indexed and available off-line (this basically means their contents are mirrored on your computers hard drive). For more information about what files and folders can be included, open the Manage

Library window again (figure 24.5) and click on the "Learn more about libraries" link at the bottom of the window. A Windows Help and Support window will open, from here, click "What types of locations are supported in libraries?".

24.3 – Sorting data in libraries

When working with libraries in File Explorer, they behave almost exactly the same as regular folders. Figure 24.7 shows a typical Music library with several folders added to it.

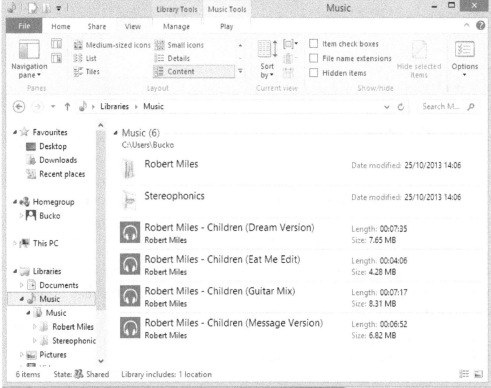

Figure 24.7 – A Music library with two folders

Notice that the File Explorer window shown in figure 24.7 is showing us the path to the folders included in the library (C:\Users\Bucko). To view your libraries like this, you will need to use the "Group by" button on the View tab of the ribbon. Figure 24.8 shows where this button is.

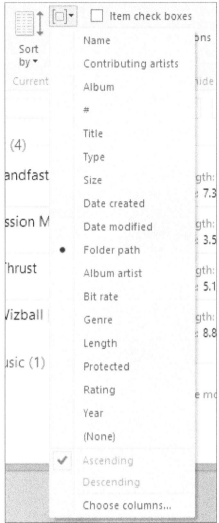

Figure 24.8 – Choosing a different grouping for a library folder

You can also use the "Sort by" button, which is to the left of the "Group by" button to sort the files different ways. If you don't see these buttons, try making your File Explorer window wider using the window sizing techniques we covered in lesson 18.2. Windows 8 gives you dozens of ways to view the data in your libraries and folders, there are far too many possibilities for us to cover here, so experiment and find the views that work best for you.

24.4 – Pictures library

The Pictures library behaves in much the same way as the Music library. Figure 24.9 shows a typical Pictures library.

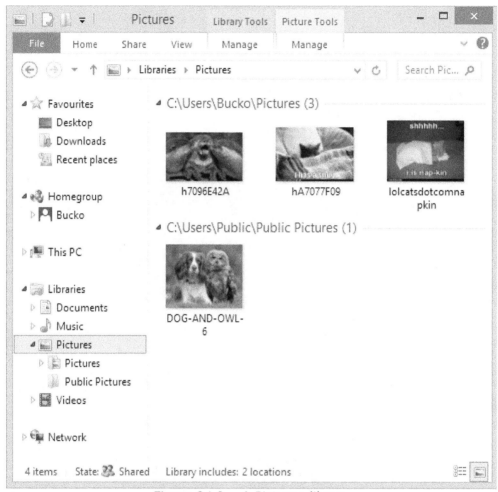

Figure 24.9 – A Pictures library

The Pictures library shown in figure 24.9 has two locations, the users personal pictures folder and the public pictures folder. This was the default configuration for libraries in Windows 8, so many Windows 8.1 machines will have libraries configured like this too. Again, the data can be sorted by using the Group by and Sort by controls on the ribbon. Of course, we can also use the folder views, Preview pane and Details pane with all our libraries just like we did with regular folders in lesson 20.

Just like music added to the music library, any picture folders you add to your pictures library will instantly be available in the Pictures tile.

24.5 – Open file/folder location

When working with libraries, you can instantly go to the actual file or folder location by using the "Open file location" or "Open folder location" on the context menu. Figure 24.10 shows an example of this.

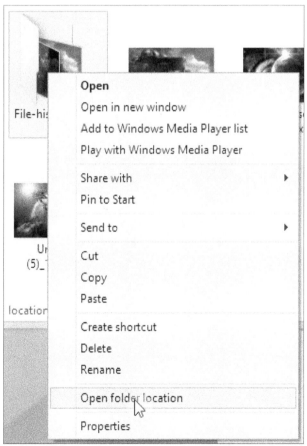

Figure 24.10 – Use this context menu option to jump directly to a folders location on your computer

Certain operations can only be carried out when you open the folders true location in File Explorer and not when viewing the file or folder in library view.

That concludes our lesson on libraries. For those of us with powerful PCs with multiple hard drives, libraries are a great feature of Windows 8 that help keep your files organised and grouped together.

Chapter 5 – Deeper Into Folders

In this chapter we will continue to build your Windows 8 desktop skills by looking at some advanced folder and file operations. You have come a long way since the start of the course and you are rapidly turning into a Windows 8 expert! Remember, read, watch and review the material at your own pace. As we delve into these more complex subjects you might find you need to refresh your memory from earlier chapters. Learning to use an operating system well is not a race, so take your time.

Lesson 25 – Folder properties

Folders on a Windows 8 machine have unique attributes, or properties associated with them. In this lesson we will delve into these properties and explore some of the attributes we can change.

25.1 – Accessing folder properties

To access the folder properties for any given folder, simply right click on the folder and choose "Properties" from down at the bottom of the context menu. Figure 25.1 illustrates this.

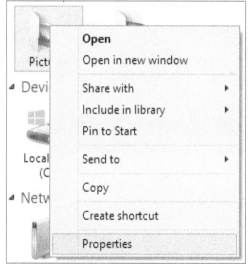

Figure 25.1 – Accessing folder properties

You can also access folder properties by opening the Home tab on the ribbon and clicking on "Properties". Once you do this, you will see the folder Properties window, figure 25.2 shows this window.

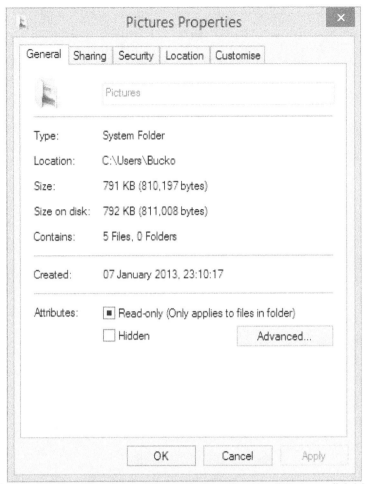

Figure 25.2 – The Properties window for the "Pictures" folder

By default the folder Properties window will open on the "General" tab. This tab shows us some general information about the folder, such as the size it takes up and how many files it contains. Notice that we can see values for "Size" and "Size on disk". "Size" refers to the total size of all the files, "Size on disk" is the actual amount of storage space these files take up. Size on disk is always a little bigger due to the way files are stored on a hard drive.

Under "Attributes" at the bottom of the window there is a box labelled "Read-only". If you cannot delete a file or folder then sometimes deselecting this box will help.

Notice the tabs labelled "Sharing" and "Security". These tabs let you set permissions for other users to access your folders either locally or over the network (the local network not the internet). We discuss Homegroups and how to share folders on a home network using Homegroups in lesson 56. Discussing security permissions is an advanced topic that you will probably never have to deal with unless you are a systems administrator. On some systems, these tabs may not appear, so don't be alarmed if you don't see them.

Special folders such as "Pictures" and "Music" have a location tab. These folders are actually links to other folders. See figure 25.3.

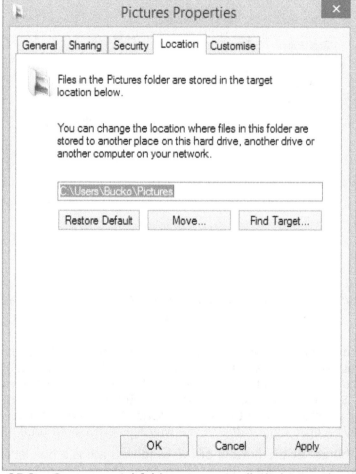

Figure 25.3 – Some special folders are actually links to other folders

In figure 25.3 we can see that actually, the pictures folder points to "C:\users\Bucko\Pictures". The default location should be suitable for most users, but if necessary it is possible to change the location of your personal folders by clicking on "Move...". This is occasionally useful if you want to move your pictures or music folder to a larger, secondary hard drive for example. However, since certain badly written third party software may have issues with systems that have been reconfigured like this, we would advise against it. If you need to add more storage space to your personal folders, you can always use libraries, as shown in lesson 24.

25.2 – Customise tab

The bulk of this lesson will focus on the options available in this tab. Note that if you do not see this tab when you open the folder properties window, you are probably working with the folder in a library and not from the folders true location. To go to any file or folders true path or location, right click on the file or folder and choose Open file/folder location. See lesson 24.5 for an example of this.

Figure 25.4 shows the folder Properties window open on the Customise tab.

Figure 25.4 – A folder Properties window open on the customise tab

At the top of the window, we are asked "What kind of folder do you want?" Windows 8 knows about several different types of content and the makers of Windows 8 realised that the best way to view pictures in a folder might not necessarily be the best way to view music, for example. Use the drop down box under "Optimize this folder for:" to tell Windows what type of content is stored in the folder. We can choose from "General Items", "Documents", "Pictures", "Music" and "Videos". When you choose one, Windows will open this folder in a viewing mode suitable for that kind of content.

In lesson 20.5 we demonstrated the different folder viewing modes. It is possible to specify what kind of folder view is used for each type of content. For example, you can have large icons view for pictures and details view for documents, we will show you how in the next lesson.

If the box labelled "Also apply this template to all subfolders" is selected, then any folders inside the current folder will also be switched to pictures view, or whatever view was selected in the drop down box.

25.3 – Folder pictures and folder icons

In the bottom of the window shown in figure 25.4 is a button labelled "Change Icon...". Using this option we can change the icon for the folder to any icon we choose.

If you don't see this option on your folder, try going to the location tab (see figure 25.3) then clicking on the "Find Target..." button. This should open up a new File Explorer window with your folder in it. Now, right click on the folder and choose "Properties" again. This time you should be able to see the "Change Icon..." option on the customise tab.

Above that option is the option to change the folder picture. You can use any picture on your PC as the folder picture. Click on "Choose File" and then browse to your pictures. Choose the picture by clicking on it and then click "Open". Back on the folder properties window, click "Apply". The picture will then be added to the folder in File Explorer. If you don't see the picture right away, click on the Refresh button (the curly shaped arrow next to the address bar in File Explorer).

Figure 25.5 – A folder with a custom picture applied to it

Changing folder icons is also easy. Click on the "Change Icon..." button as shown in figure 25.4. The standard Windows icon library will then appear, this is shown in figure 25.6.

Figure 25.6 – Browsing for an icon

Browse through the icon gallery here and pick out any icon you like, then click "OK". This will return you to the folder Properties window. Click on "Apply". You should now see your new icon in File Explorer, if you do not, click on Refresh. Note that Windows will not allow you to apply folder pictures and/or change icons on certain pre-created folders. If you create the folder yourself however, you can always change the icon or the picture.

If you want to remove your custom icon, simply access the icon gallery and click the "Restore Defaults" button that can be seen in figure 25.6. To remove a custom folder picture, access the customise tab of the folder Properties window (figure 25.4) and click on "Restore Default" under "Folder pictures".

That concludes this lesson on folder properties. Changing and customising your folders can be useful and fun. Go ahead and experiment for yourself, you can always undo any changes you make by using the "Restore Default" buttons shown in the previous figures. In the next lesson we look at advanced folder customisation, don't worry, it's not as hard as it sounds!

Lesson 26 – Folder options

Since we have been exploring folders in the past few lessons, now might be a good time to look at some advanced folder customisation options.

26.1 – Folder options window

We can access the Folder Options window from the Control Panel or, more conveniently, from a File Explorer window. To access the options through File Explorer, open the ribbon and select the View tab, then click on the Options button on the right. Figure 26.1 illustrates this.

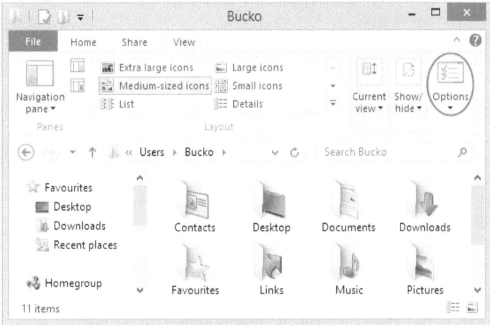

Figure 26.1 – Accessing Folder Options from File Explorer

Figure 26.2 shows the Folder Options window which appears when you click the Options button on the ribbon.

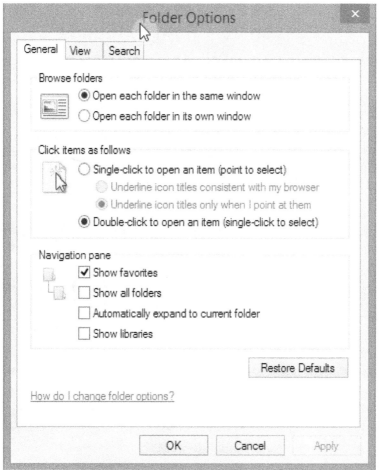

Figure 26.2 – The Folder Options window

26.2 – General folder options

In figure 26.2, there are three categories of options. We will take a look at what each of these options does.

Browse folders:- In lesson 23.3 we demonstrated how to work with multiple File Explorer windows. We opened a new File Explorer window by right clicking on a folder and choosing "Open in new window". By choosing the "Open each folder in its own window" option, you will change the behaviour of File Explorer so that every time you double click on a folder, a new Explorer window will open.

With this option enabled, the desktop can become cluttered very quickly, but some users do prefer to work this way.

Click items as follows:- For users who struggle with the timing on double clicks, these options can be very helpful. Choose "Single click to open an item (point to select)" and now you only need to click once on an icon to open it. This does make dragging icons a little more tricky and you may find you accidentally open them when trying to drag, but a lot of users prefer this method rather than the dratted double click.

In the sub options, "Underline icon titles only when I point at them" is fairly self-explanatory. However, you might be wondering what "Underline icon titles consistent with my browser" means. Basically it means that all icon titles (the text below the icons) will be underlined, just like links are underlined in Internet Explorer.

Navigation pane:- Recall that the Navigation pane is the left hand column on a File Explorer window. We covered the favourites in lesson 21.4, you can turn them off here if you don't use them. Choosing the "Show all folders" option changes the layout of the Navigation pane so that more icons are displayed. With show all folders selected, you will see the Libraries become stacked under "Desktop" for instance. If you prefer a more compact less cluttered view, keep this option turned off.

The "Automatically expand to current folder" option is best demonstrated with pictures. Figure 26.3 shows a File Explorer window with this option turned off.

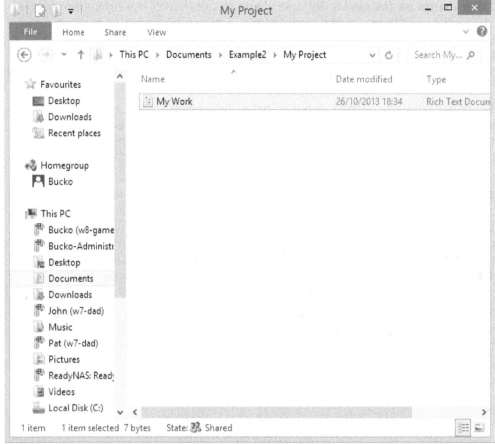

Figure 26.3 – File Explorer window with the "Automatically expand to current folder" option turned off

Notice that although the address bar shows that the current folder is "This PC\Documents\Example2\My Project", the Navigation pane is still pointing at just "Documents". Now, figure 26.4 shows an Explorer window with the "Automatically expand to current folder" option turned on.

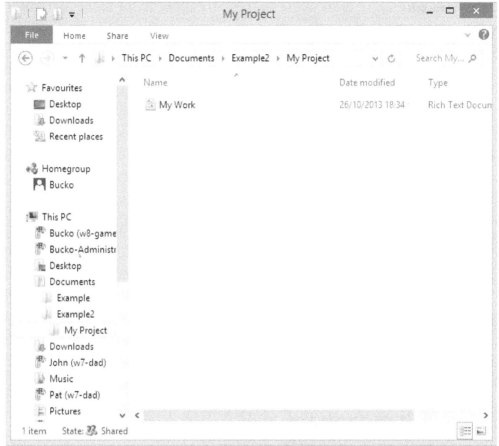

Figure 26.4 - File Explorer window with the "Automatically expand to current folder" option turned on

In figure 26.4 you can see that the Navigation pane now matches the address or path shown in the address bar. With the Automatically expand to current folder option enabled, the Navigation pane will always match the address bar like this.

Finally, the "Show libraries" option was covered in lesson 24.1.

When changing options in the Folder Options window, don't forget that you can always revert back to the default options by clicking "Restore Defaults" and then clicking on "Apply".

26.3 – View tab

You can access the "View" tab in the Folder Options window by clicking on it once. Figure 26.5 shows the Folder Options window open on the "View" tab.

Figure 26.5 – The "View" tab of the Folder Options window

There are two main sections to this tab, they are "Folder Views" and "Advanced settings".

The Folder Views options contains just two buttons. By clicking "Apply to folders" it is possible to set the current viewing mode across all folders of the same type. What does this mean? Consider this example, File Explorer is viewing a music folder and the viewing mode has been changed to details view (changing folder viewing modes was covered in lesson 20.5). Now, the user opens the Folder Options window (just like we did at the start of the lesson) and then navigates to the View tab. The user wants all the music folders to open up in details view, so he/she clicks the "Apply to Folders" button. From now on, all music folders will be shown in details view whenever they are opened up.

Clicking on the "Reset Folders" button restores all the folders to their default view.

The Advanced Settings in the bottom half of this tab contain all kinds of tweaks and customizations you can do to File Explorer. Rather than try to cover every minor option in excruciating detail, the best way to learn is by experimenting. You cannot damage your computer by changing these options and you can always revert back by clicking on "Restore Defaults".

There are a couple of important options that are found under the advanced options that we do want to look at in detail however.

26.4 – Hidden files and folders

On a Windows 8 computer, there are several folders that are used exclusively by the operating system. These folders contain files that are used by Windows when it loads and when it runs. Because tampering with these files can potentially be disastrous, by default Windows will hide them from view, so you cannot accidentally navigate into them. Occasionally, while troubleshooting your computer or if directed to do so by a technical support representative, you may need to access these folders. Please be careful if you do modify the contents of these folders however! One mistake and you might find your Windows installation starts acting in a very strange manner or even stops working altogether.

In Windows 8, you can also show or hide hidden files and folders from the View tab on the ribbon, figure 26.6 shows the location of this option.

Figure 26.6 – Show or hide hidden items quickly by using this option on the View tab of the ribbon

If you can't see the option to show hidden files on your ribbon, you may need to make your current File Explorer window a little wider.

Figure 26.7 shows the root (top level) folder on a Windows 8 hard drive with the "Show hidden files, folders and drives" option turned off.

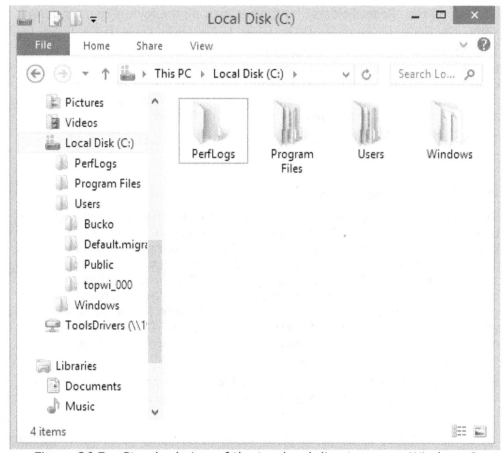

Figure 26.7 – Standard view of the top level directory on a Windows 8 system drive

Figure 26.8 shows the same folder, but with the "Show hidden files, folders and drives" option turned on.

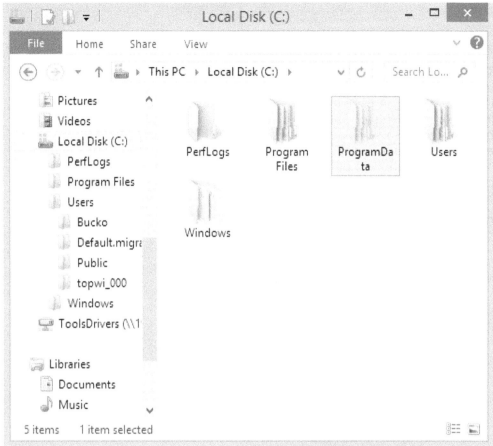

Figure 26.8 – View of the top level directory on a Windows 8 system drive, with the Show hidden files, folders and drives option turned on. Notice the extra ProgramData folder that has appeared

In figure 26.8 we can see an extra folder has appeared (it is highlighted in the picture). You may also have noticed that the folder appears fainter, or ghosted compared to the other folders, to indicate that it is normally hidden.

A related option to "Show hidden files, folders and drives" is "Hide protected operating system files". This option is only available on the View tab of the Folder Options window. If you deselect this option, you will see even more files and folders appear on your computer. Again these are important operating system files that you should never change or tamper with unless you are absolutely certain that you know what you are doing. We recommend leaving these files hidden while working normally with your computer.

26.5 – Hide extensions for known file types

This option causes a lot of confusion and even trips up seasoned Windows users. Most files on a Windows computer have a file extension at the end of their file names. A file extension is a period (dot) character followed by three letters or more (historically file extensions were limited to three characters, but in modern versions of Windows they can be longer). Typical file extensions include ".mp3" for mp3 files, ".avi" for video files and ".jpg" for Jpeg photograph files. By default, Windows hides this information from you, this was probably done to make working with files less confusing for beginners.

Consider figure 26.9. You can see several music files in File Explorer.

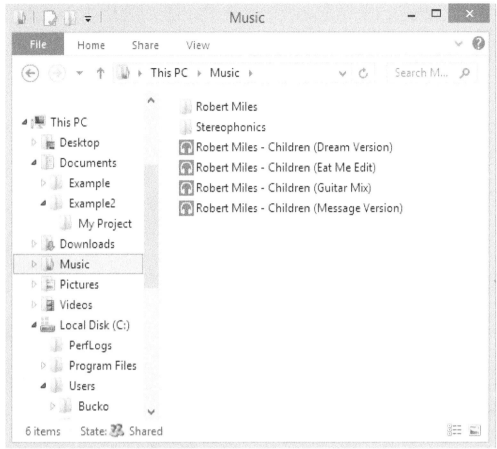

Figure 26.9 – Viewing music files with the "Hide extensions for known file types" option turned on

The top file is called "Robert Miles – Children (Dream Version)". The actual file name of this file is "Robert Miles – Children (Dream Version).mp3" but Windows is hiding the extra file extension information from us. Figure 26.10 shows another File Explorer window with the hide file extensions option turned **on** (the default setting).

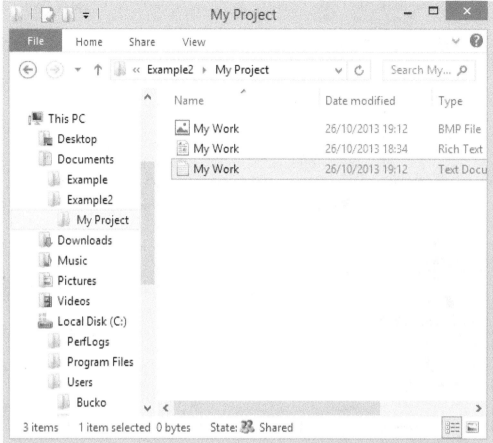

Figure 26.10 – Three files in the same folder with the same name? Not really, the file extensions are different, just Windows is hiding this information from us

The hide file extensions option can be particularly confusing with files of similar names. In figure 26.10 we have three files. "My Work.bmp", "My Work.rtf" and "My Work.txt". With the "Hide extensions for known file types" option turned **on** (the default setting) it appears as if we have three files in the same folder with the same name, something that we already told you is impossible! Figure 26.11 shows the same folder but with the "Hide extensions for known file types" option turned **off**.

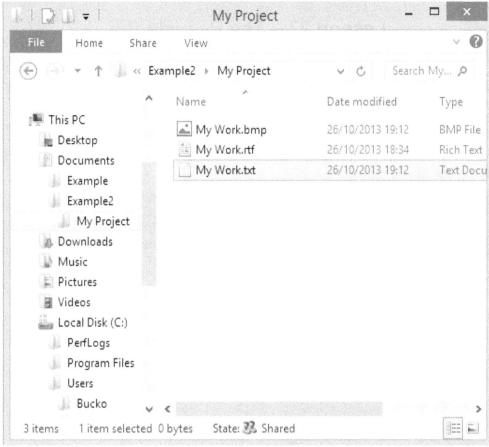

Figure 26.11 – Turning "Hide extensions for known file types" off reveals extra information about a file name

To avoid this kind of confusion, many users turn the "Hide extensions for known file types" option off. If you do turn it off, keep in mind that if you rename a file and accidentally remove its file extension, Windows wont know how to handle that file any more, unless you rename it again and put the file extension back. Even worse, if you remove the file extension and put the wrong one back, Windows may try to open the file with the wrong program.

That concludes this lesson on folder options. We are getting into some advanced Windows 8 operations and hope the information presented here was not too daunting. In the next lesson we will be looking at the Recycle Bin and how Windows handles the files you delete.

Lesson 27 – The Recycle Bin

Because it is easy to accidentally delete files and something of a chore to undelete them again, Microsoft introduced the Recycle Bin way back in Windows 95. Now, when you delete files from your PC, they (usually) end up in the Recycle Bin before being removed completely. In this lesson we will explore how the Recycle Bin works and how to recover files that have been sent there.

27.1 – Into the Recycle Bin

 The Recycle Bin is, by default, the only icon on your Windows 8 desktop. The icon shown here looks as if it has some crumpled paper inside it. This is to indicate that there are files or folders in the bin. To open the Recycle Bin, we simply double click on it. Figure 27.2 shows the Recycle Bin window.

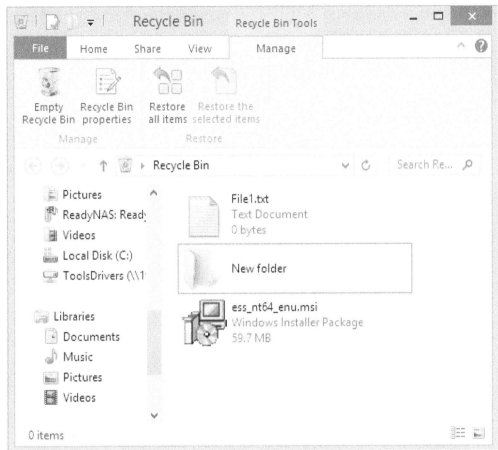

Figure 27.2 – The Recycle Bin opens in a standard File Explorer window

The Recycle Bin opens in a File Explorer window just like any other folder on your PC. The ribbon will automatically change to reflect the special tasks that can be carried out with the Recycle Bin. By clicking on "Empty the Recycle Bin", all the items in the window will be permanently deleted. By clicking on "Restore all items", all the items shown are put back into their original folders (i.e. the folders that they were placed in before they were deleted).

Notice that we said the files would be "permanently deleted" when "Empty the Recycle Bin" was clicked. This is not strictly true. There is still the possibility of recovering those files with some kind of undelete utility or data forensics tool kit. Emptying the Recycle Bin does not protect you from this. If you are working with particularly sensitive information you may need to use a third party file shredding utility. These work like their real-world counterparts and make sure that files cannot be recovered once the are removed from your computer.

Naturally, it is possible to work with individual files in the Recycle Bin as well as its entire contents. turn on the Details pane (from the View tab on the ribbon) and single click on an item in the Recycle Bin and you can see the original file path or address for the file or folder. Clicking on "Restore this item" will move the file back to its original location. See figure 27.3.

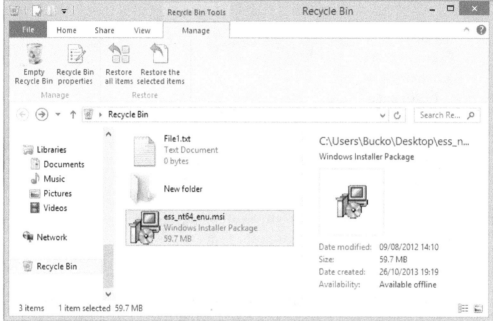

Figure 27.3 – Working with individual files in the Recycle Bin

In figure 27.3, we can see that if we click on "Restore the selected items", the "ess_nt64_enu.msi" file will be restored to "C:\Users\Bucko\Desktop". This is the address or path of the users desktop, so the icon would reappear on the desktop in this case.

To permanently delete a selected file, right click on it and choose "Delete" from the context menu. This will free up the space on your hard drive that the file was occupying.

27.2 – Sending files to the Recycle Bin

Most files that you delete will initially be sent to the Recycle Bin. Take a look at figure 27.4.

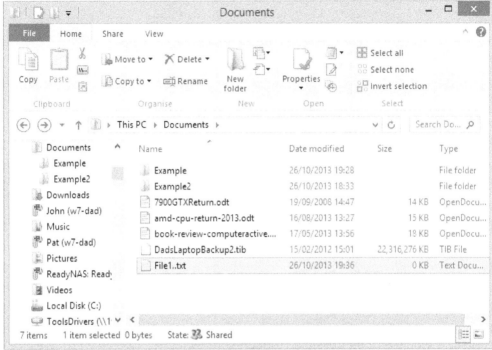

Figure 27.4 – A typical File Explorer window with the Home tab open on the ribbon

There are several ways to send the file "File1.txt" to the Recycle Bin. We can select it and then press the "Delete" key on the keyboard. We can use the Home tab on the ribbon and click "Delete". Alternatively, use the context menu by right clicking on the icon and then choosing "Delete". Whichever method you prefer, they all have the same end result, the file is removed from this folder and placed in the Recycle Bin. Once there, we can click on it and see where it came from and then restore it back to its original location if necessary.

27.3 – Files that are not sent to the Recycle Bin

While most files you delete are initially sent to the Recycle Bin, some are not. In figure 27.4 we can see a large file called "DadsLaptopBackup2.tib". This file is over 20 gigabytes in size. Files this large are normally just too big to fit in the Recycle Bin. We can still remove them by deleting them with any of the methods described previously. However, this time when you attempt to delete the file, the window shown in figure 27.5 will appear.

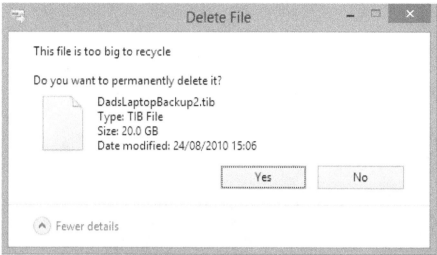

Figure 27.5 – This file is too big to fit in the Recycle Bin

If you click "Yes" then the file will be removed from your computer. Of course, it would still be possible (though somewhat inconvenient) to use special data recovery software to undelete it.

Certain other files are not sent to the Recycle Bin when deleted, to explain why we need to explore some technical information about how the Recycle Bin works.

27.4 – Recycle Bin folders

The Recycle Bin is a little like the library folders in that in actual fact it is an aggregate or combined view of several folders. Each drive on your computer, be it internal or external, can have its own Recycle Bin folder. This folder is normally a hidden folder called "$Recycle.Bin". When you open the Recycle Bin then the folder that opens shows the combined view of all the "$Recycle.Bin" folders on your PC.

If you connect to a storage device, perhaps a network drive or network folder that hasn't had a Recycle Bin configured, then any files that you delete will not be sent to the Recycle Bin, they will just be removed. Windows will warn you that the file will be permanently removed so make sure you pay attention to the messages and be extra careful.

So, with those two important exceptions, all files and folders you delete are sent to your Recycle Bin first. Note that you can also empty the Recycle Bin by right clicking on it and choosing "Empty Recycle Bin".

27.5 – Recycle Bin Properties

There are some advanced Recycle Bin preferences that can be changed by clicking "Recycle Bin properties" from the ribbon or by right clicking on the Recycle Bin and choosing "Properties". Figure 27.6 shows the Recycle Bin Properties window.

Figure 27.6 – A Recycle Bin Properties window

In the Recycle Bin Properties window there are several settings we can tweak. At the top of the window we can see the Recycle Bin Location. Recall that each drive has a Recycle Bin folder associated with it. From this list you can choose the Recycle Bin to work with. On the machine that figure 27.6

was taken from there is only one Recycle Bin but machines with several drives may have two or more.

Under "Settings for selected location" we can specify a maximum size. Remember the size specified is in megabytes, but the size shown under "Space Available" is in gigabytes. There are one thousand twenty four (1024) megabytes to a gigabyte, so the maximum size for this Recycle Bin is around the eight gigabyte mark. It is possible to increase or decrease that size by entering a new value in the Maximum size (MB): box, although for most users the default size is fine.

Below the Custom Size option is the option to disable the Recycle Bin altogether. If this option is chosen, files are removed immediately when deleted. We do not recommend that beginners enable this option, in fact we don't recommend that anyone does. Having the safety net of the Recycle Bin is always a good idea.

Finally there is an option called "Display delete confirmation dialogue". This option was turned on by default in previous versions of Windows, but Microsoft have decided to turn it off by default in Windows 8. If you select this option then Windows will put up a window asking "Are you sure you want to remove this file?" when you send a file to the Recycle Bin. You may prefer to turn this option on while you get used to your PC, to avoid accidentally sending any files to the Recycle Bin.

When you are done configuring the Recycle Bin Properties, click on "Apply" and then "OK".

That concludes this lesson on the Recycle Bin and this chapter! You are now quite the competent Windows 8 user, give yourself a pat on the back for getting this far. The next chapter focuses on exploring other elements of Windows 8 and improving your skills further.

Chapter 6 – Polishing Your Skills

We have come so far and learned so much about Windows 8 since the start of this course. In this chapter we will be rounding off our tour of the various desktop operating system elements.

Lesson 28 – This PC

"This PC" is the new Windows 8.1 name for "Computer" (also known as "My Computer" in Windows XP). From "This PC", you can get access or browse to all of the storage devices attached to your PC. You can open This PC by searching for "This PC" on the Start screen and then clicking the icon that appears. Alternatively, click on "This PC" on the Navigation pane of any File Explorer window.

28.1 – Inside This PC

Figure 28.1 shows a typical "This PC" window.

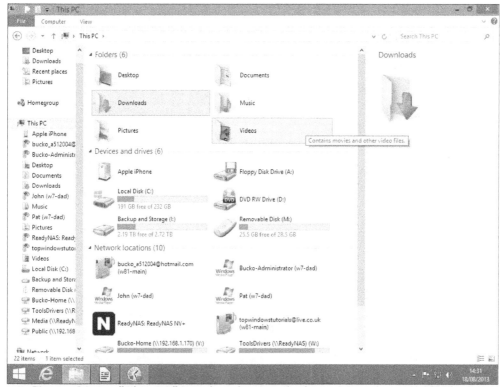

Figure 28.1 – "This PC" Window from a desktop PC with several drives

Figure 28.1 shows a desktop computer with two hard drives, a DVD recorder drive, a floppy drive and several other removable drives, as well as several network drives.

28.2 – Personal folders

In Windows 8.1, convenient shortcuts to your personal folders are always available at the top of the "This PC" window. Simply double click on any of the folders to open them in File Explorer.

28.3 – Devices and drives

In Windows 8.1, all storage devices that are attached locally to your PC are shown in the Devices and drives section. Previously, removable drives were in their own section.

There are several drives attached to the PC we can see in the picture. Every Windows 8 machine will have at least one hard drive. The machine in this example has two hard drives, Local Disk (C:) and Backup and Storage (I:). We can see at a glance how much space is free on each drive by looking at the blue bar or the values below it (C: drive has 191 gigabytes (GB) free out of 232GB, for example). To get some more detailed information about a hard drive, right click on the drives icon and from the context menu choose "Properties", or click once on the drive icon and choose "Properties" from the Computer tab on the ribbon. The drive Properties window will then open, figure 28.4 shows this window.

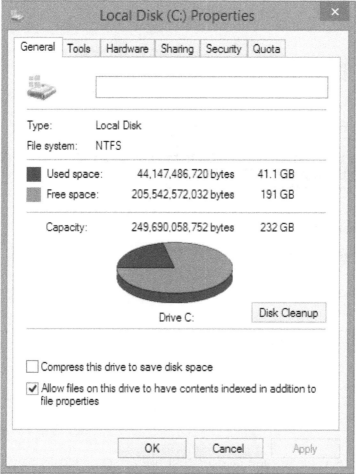

Figure 28.4 – General drive properties

We can see in figure 28.4 a pie chart which represents space on the drive. There are also two options below the pie chart.

Compress this drive to save disk space:- When we talk about compressing data in computing it refers to the art of storing information more efficiently so that less space is consumed. By selecting this option to compress the drive, you might gain a little space on your hard drive but adversely it might degrade your computers performance. We recommend leaving this option disabled.

Allow files on this drive to have contents indexed in addition to file properties:- When this option is selected, Windows will add the contents of files such as Word documents into the search index. Then, when you perform a search you can quickly search inside text files too. The only reasons to turn this option off are to improve disk performance on an older computer or to prevent sensitive file information being left in the search index.

There are a few other drives we can see under Devices and drives too. Floppy Disk Drive (A:) is an old fashioned floppy disk drive. Windows 8 still supports floppy disks; although they are obsolete by modern standards, some PCs still have floppy drives.

Drive D: is a DVD rewriter drive. Everyone should be familiar with CDs and DVDs, the universally popular format for storing music and videos. If your Windows 8 computer has a DVD rewriter drive, you can use it to play DVD videos and also write your files to CD or DVD recordable discs.

Device M: is a portable USB stick drive or thumb drive. These are common portable storage devices that fit in your pocket and store gigabytes of information. They have virtually rendered the floppy disk obsolete.

Figure 28.5 – A SanDisk Cruzer USB stick drive. Actual length is around the length of an adult thumb, so these drives are often referred to as "thumb drives"

Finally, we can also see an Apple iPhone. Many smart phones, media players and similar devices can connect to the PC for backup or to share files. Consult the documentation that came with your device for details of how to do this.

28.3.1 – Hidden drives

By default, Windows 8.1 will hide removable storage devices that it detects have no media inserted into them. To change this behaviour, access the View tab on the Folder Options window (see lesson 26.3). Now, deselect the option "Hide empty drives". On the PC shown in our example, drives E:, F:, G: and H: are present, but not shown in Devices and drives. These drives are part of a memory card or storage card reader. Memory card readers accept storage cards that are commonly used in cameras, media players and even games consoles. Figure 28.6 shows a typical memory card reader.

Figure 28.6 – A typical memory card reader

Since the memory card reader was empty, Windows hid those drive letters as it would not be possible to access them.

To browse any of the attached drives, simply double click on them. If you double click on an empty drive, Windows will prompt you with "Please insert a disk into Removable Disk". Disk in this context can refer to a storage card too.

28.4 – Network Locations

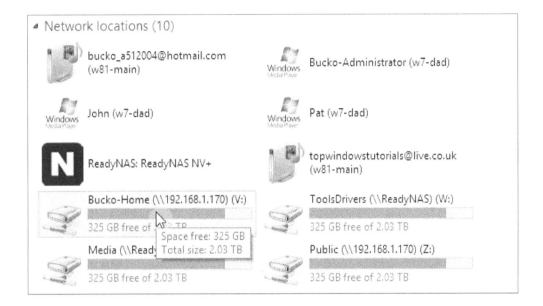

The last section we can see in figure 28.1 is called "Network Location". Storage devices here exist on your home network, rather than the public internet. Windows 8 can detect all kinds of network services. The top three rows of icons represent media devices on the same network as the PC. The Windows Media Player icons are libraries of shared music that other users in the house have on their PCs, for instance.

If you use network storage devices for backup or file storage, you can create shortcuts to your most commonly used network locations by mapping a drive letter to them. To do this, choose "Map network drive" from the ribbon. You can then either enter the network address manually or browse across your network for the correct location. The PC in our example has four such mapped drives, which point to various locations on the network.

28.5 – Other devices

What other devices might we find in This PC? Some portable devices, such as media players, personal digital assistants or smartphones install their own special software. These devices then appear below Network Connections in their own category. Usually working with them is as easy as working with other storage devices, but consult the owners manual that came with the hardware for more details.

That concludes our tour of "This PC" in Windows 8. Now you understand how to access storage devices on your PC you will be ready for our tutorials on system backup which we cover in lesson 32.

Lesson 29 – More about the taskbar

The taskbar saw some significant changes in Windows 7 and in Windows 8 there are a few neat improvements too. Once you get used to the new features, they can actually be very helpful. In this lesson we will look at jump lists and taskbar personalisation.

29.1 – Jump lists and the taskbar

Jump lists were one of the new features that appeared throughout Windows 7 and have persisted to Windows 8 too. On the taskbar they can be used to quickly jump to frequently used tasks in an application. To access the jump list for a program on the taskbar, simply right click on the programs taskbar icon, figure 29.1 shows Internet Explorer's jump list.

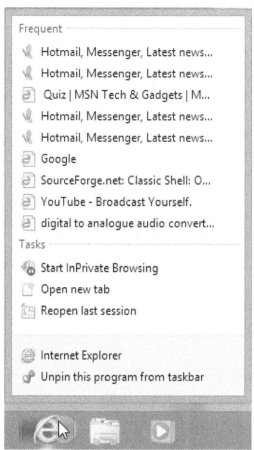

Figure 29.1 – Internet Explorer's jump list, accessed by right clicking on its icon

From Internet Explorer's jump list, we can go straight to one of our most frequently used websites. Under "Tasks" it is possible to switch to private surfing mode (InPrivate), that (supposedly at least) leaves behind no web history on the computer. We can also open a new tab, reopen our last browsing session or simply launch Internet Explorer as normal by choosing "Internet Explorer". We take a brief tour of Internet Explorer 11 in lesson 53.

Notice that Internet Explorer does not have to be running in order to access its jump list.

Any program pinned to the taskbar can have its own jump list. Usually for older (pre Windows 7) software the jump list simply includes the most recently opened documents or the most frequently opened files or folders.

Desktop programs that are Windows 7 or 8 aware can have their own custom jump lists. Figure 29.2 shows the jump list from Windows Media Player.

Figure 29.2 – Jump list from Windows Media Player

Just like the Internet Explorer 11 jump list, Windows Media Player lists the most frequently used media or play lists at the top and then additional tasks below them.

29.2 – Moving the taskbar

There are several customisations we can do with the taskbar, the most simple being moving and resizing it. Before you can move the taskbar, it needs to be unlocked. Right click on the taskbar and deselect the "Lock all taskbars" option, as shown in figure 29.3.

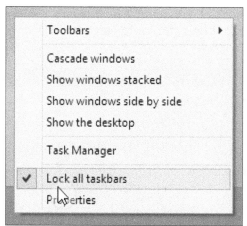

Figure 29.3 – Before the taskbar can be moved or resized it must be unlocked

When the taskbar is unlocked it can be moved to any screen edge. This is done by clicking and holding down the mouse button and then dragging the mouse towards one of the screen edges. The taskbar can also be resized in the same way we resized a window in lesson 18 by moving the mouse to the edge of the taskbar and dragging it upwards. A bigger taskbar is often useful on powerful machines with large monitors. When there are lots of programs open at once, a bigger taskbar gets less cluttered.

It is a good idea to lock the taskbar again when you are done moving and/or resizing it. If you do not, you are likely to accidentally move or resize it as you work with your PC.

29.3 – Adding toolbars to the taskbar

There are several optional toolbars that can be added to the taskbar. To add a toolbar, right click on the taskbar and choose "Toolbars". Figure 29.4 shows the available toolbars.

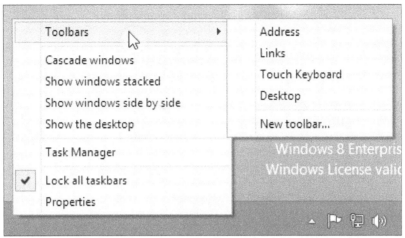

Figure 29.4 – Choosing a toolbar to add to the taskbar

Let's see what each of these toolbars does.

Address:- Enables the user to enter a web address or local address or path directly into the taskbar.

Links:- This toolbar enables you to quickly jump to your favourite internet links which you added to your "Favourites" in Internet Explorer (see lesson 54.2).

Touch Keyboard:- Adds a toolbar that gives quick access to the on-screen keyboard, useful for typing if you have a tablet PC with no keyboard connected.

Desktop:- Provides links to common locations on the computer and on the desktop.

New toolbar:- Creates a custom toolbar. Choosing "New toolbar..." opens up a file browser window. Simply browse to any folder on your PC and choose "Select Folder". The content from that folder will then be available from the taskbar.

29.4 – Other taskbar customisations

There are several other customisation options for the taskbar. To access them, right click on the taskbar and choose "Properties". Figure 29.5 shows the resulting window.

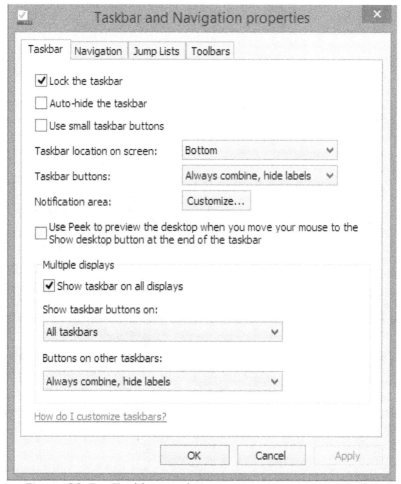

Figure 29.5 – Taskbar and Navigation properties Window

At the top of the Window there are several options. We already covered the "Lock the taskbar" option. "Auto-hide the taskbar" makes the taskbar automatically shrink down out of sight when it is not in use. To reveal it again, move the mouse pointer to the bottom of the screen (or the edge of the screen where the taskbar is positioned), the taskbar will then reappear. This option is useful on smaller monitors where screen space is at a premium.

Selecting "Use small taskbar buttons" reduces the size of program icons on your taskbar, figure 29.6 shows an example of this.

Figure 29.6 – Small icons Vs large icons on a Windows 8 taskbar

Using the "Taskbar location on screen:" menu, it is possible to reposition the taskbar automatically, rather than by dragging it.

Below this control is the "Taskbar buttons:" control, figure 29.7 shows the available options.

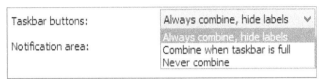

Figure 29.7 – Taskbar button options

Each option will change how the icons are displayed on your taskbar. We will take a detailed look at each option now.

Always combine, hide labels:- This is the default setting you have been using while working through this course. Icons will appear on your taskbar without labels. Windows from the same applications will stack on top of each other.

Combine when taskbar is full:- This makes the taskbar behave more like it did in previous versions of Windows. Icons for programs will be displayed next to a label indicating the window title. Figure 29.8 shows an example of this.

Figure 29.8 – A taskbar set to "Combine when taskbar is full" mode

Never combine:- Works the same as "Combine when taskbar is full", except that as the taskbar fills up, Windows won't combine related windows (e.g. multiple File Explorer windows) into groups.

Finally, it is possible to disable the desktop Peek button (the button at the end of the taskbar that we showed you way back in lesson 18) by deselecting the "Use Peek to preview the desktop" option.

When you are done making changes, be sure to click on "Apply" to make them take effect.

29.5 – Multi-monitor support

Windows 8 includes some great improvements for multi-monitor users. If you're doing any kind of work on your PC, two or even three monitors can be extremely useful. This book was written on a workstation with no less than three monitors, and the author is a strong advocate of the multi monitor desktop!

In figure 29.5 we can see a section at the bottom of the window called "Multiple displays". If "Show taskbar on all displays" is selected, then each monitor on your PC will get its own independent taskbar. In previous versions of Windows, there was only ever one taskbar, which users usually placed on their central display.

There are also several options for how the taskbar icons are positioned across your multiple taskbars. Figure 29.9 shows the available options.

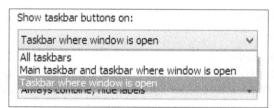

Figure 29.9 – Changing taskbar button options for multiple displays

On a system with three monitors (which we'll call A, B and C) the options would have the following effect.

All taskbars:- A window open on either monitor A, B or C would have a corresponding taskbar icon on all three taskbars.

Main taskbar and taskbar where window is open:- Assuming monitor B is the main monitor, a window open on monitor A would have an icon on the taskbar on monitor A and on monitor B, but not on monitor C. If the window was on monitor B, it would only have a taskbar icon on monitor B (since monitor B is where the main taskbar is positioned).

Taskbar where window is open:- A window open on monitor A would have a taskbar icon on monitor A's taskbar only.

Below the options for taskbar buttons is the option to change the types of

268

button shown on your secondary taskbars. This works in exactly the same way as with the primary taskbar (see figure 29.7).

Note – In Windows 8.1, Microsoft improved multi-monitor support for tiles too. When you open a tile on a multi-monitor system, you can freely drag it to any of your monitors. You can then open another tile and position it on a different monitor.

That concludes our tour of taskbar customisation. In the next lesson we will take a more detailed look at another component that changed significantly in Windows 7, the notification area or system tray as it is sometimes called.

Lesson 30 – The notification area

The notification area was significantly overhauled for Windows 7 and these improvements have persisted in Windows 8 too. The notification area is often called the system tray, though the official Microsoft name has always been "notification area". It was introduced as a place for programs which generally ran in the background and did not need a window permanently open. Software such as antivirus packages or automatic backup tools can place small notification icons in this area. From these icons users can see at a glance that the program is running normally, or the program can notify the user that it needs their attention.

30.1 – The new notification area versus the old

As computers became faster and equipped with more memory and other resources, many users started installing all kinds of programs that utilised the notification area. As a result, it became very cluttered. It is not uncommon for systems to have more than twenty of these little icons and it quickly becomes unmanageable.

Figure 30.1 – A cluttered notification area from a Windows XP machine

Windows 7 tackled this problem by redesigning the notification area. The most important or frequently used icons can still be present on the taskbar, while the rest are hidden away in a pop-up menu and only appear if they need your attention. Figure 30.2 shows the Windows 8 notification area.

Figure 30.2 – A Windows 8 notification area

In the picture we can see three notification icons that are permanently displayed. The flag shaped icon is the Action Center. This notifies you about potential problems on your PC, such as security alerts. Next to that is the network icon, this can be used for connecting quickly to networks, both wired and wireless. Then there is the volume icon, a quick click of this accesses a sliding control which can adjust the volume level for all sounds on your computer.

In figure 30.2 we can also see that by clicking the arrow icon, we get a pop-up menu showing us some other notification icons. On this system we can see an icon for safely removing USB and other removable drives (top left). It is always advisable to use this icon to let Windows know that you are going to remove a device before physically unplugging it. There are also three icons for third-party software the user has installed. To access additional settings for any application running in the notification area, simply open the pop-up menu and then click, double click or right click on the programs icon. These actions will access different options depending on the program.

30.2 – Customising the notification area

If you have an application that you access regularly from the notification area, you may want to make it appear permanently like the three default icons. To do this, first open the pop-up menu (as shown in figure 30.2) then choose "Customize...". Figure 30.3 shows the window which will then appear.

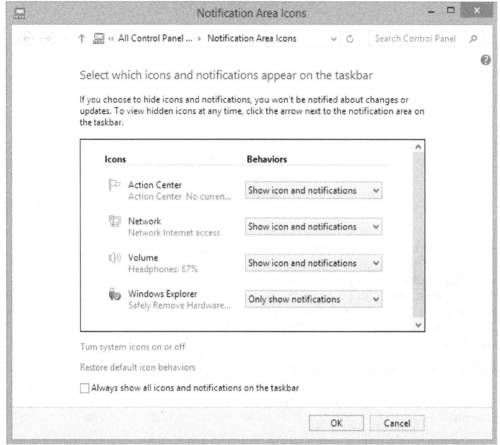

Figure 30.3 – Customisation options for the notification area

The list in figure 30.3 shows all the items in the notification area, including the default Windows 8 ones. From this list we can change the behaviour of each icon/program. Notice how "Windows Explorer – Safely Remove Hardware" is set to "Only show notifications". With this setting, the program icon will be hidden unless it needs to notify the user of anything.

The three default notification icons, Action Center, Network and Volume have their behaviours set to "Show icon and notifications". With this setting they will always appear in the notification area.

There is one other setting that we can choose, that is "Hide icon and notifications" With this setting, the icon will still appear in the pop-up menu (figure 30.2), however Windows will suppress any notification messages the program sends and the icon will remain in the hidden menu even when the program wants to notify you of something. We do not recommend using this setting with software such as antivirus packages that may need to inform you of possible security problems.

Finally, right at the bottom of the window is the option to "Always show all icons and notifications on the taskbar". This reverts back to the classic behaviour (pre Windows 7) described at the start of the lesson. If you don't have many notification area icons you might prefer to do this, but for most of us the new way is a big improvement.

That concludes this lesson on the Windows 8 notification area. Don't forget that although the notification area icons are hidden away neatly in Windows 8, they still represent programs that are running and therefore consuming computer resources. If you let too many of these programs run, you will start to slow your computer down, so be careful not to install too many. In the next lesson we will look at Windows 8's extensive in-built search options.

Lesson 31 – Search is everywhere

In Windows 8, as was the case with Windows Vista and Windows 7, search is built into almost everything. In lesson 4.1 we showed you how to search from the Start screen. It is also possible to search from File Explorer windows and in places such as the Control Panel. Windows 8 search is a powerful tool and learning how to use it correctly can make you super productive.

31.1 – Tags and other meta data

Meta data (data about data) enables you to add descriptive information to files to help you find them more quickly. Just like you might add coloured stickers to items you file in a filing cabinet, in Windows you can add tags to your data. Figure 31.1 shows the available meta data for a picture file.

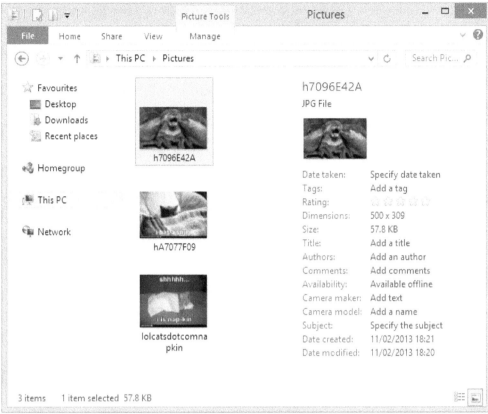

Figure 31.1 – Meta data for the top most image can be seen in the Details pane on the right

In figure 31.1 the user has opened the Details pane and clicked on an image. The meta data for the image is then shown on the right of the window. We can specify the date taken, a rating out of five and add a tag, as well as edit the title, authors, comments, subject and camera make and model. Tags are probably the most useful types of meta data to add to pictures. To add a tag, click on "Add a tag" and type a descriptive tag for this image, for example "animal", since this is a cute animal image. Press the Enter key to save a tag or press the right arrow key and enter another tag. Tags are separated with semicolons (;). You can add as many tags as you like, just press Enter when you are finished and make sure each tag has a semicolon separating it.

Once you have tagged an image, you can search for it from the Start screen, just like we did in lesson 4.1. Any images tagged "garden" for example, would show up if you search on the Start screen for "garden". You may need to change the search type to "Files" or perform a full search by clicking the magnifying glass icon before they show up however, see lesson 4.2 for more information. If you tag all your pictures with descriptive tags, you will be able to locate them much more quickly.

31.2 – Indexing options

Windows can find information on your PC more quickly by using a search index. Files that are indexed have a reference to them in a giant search index or catalogue that Windows 8 maintains. In this lesson we will take a look at the indexing options. You can access these options from the Control Panel or more simply by searching for "indexing options" from the Start screen under Settings and then clicking the icon that appears. Figure 31.2 shows the Indexing Options window.

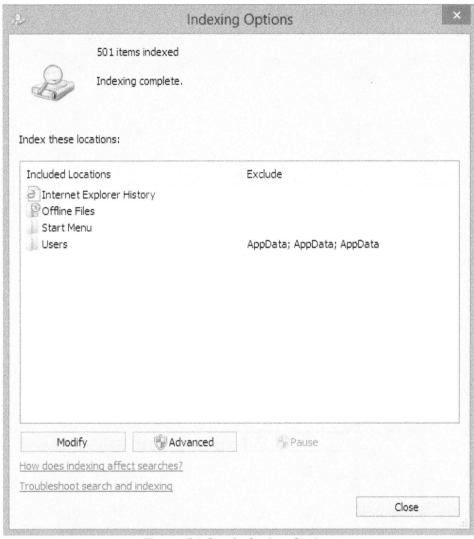

Figure 31.2 – Indexing Options

In figure 31.2 we can see the default indexing options. Under "Included Locations" you can see which places on your computer are added to the index. By clicking "Modify" it is possible to add other locations to the index, although we can only add locations on local drives, not network drives. Any folder you add to your libraries (as in lesson 24.2) will also automatically be added to the index.

Click on the "Advanced" button to change the advanced options. Figure 31.3

277

shows the advanced indexing options.

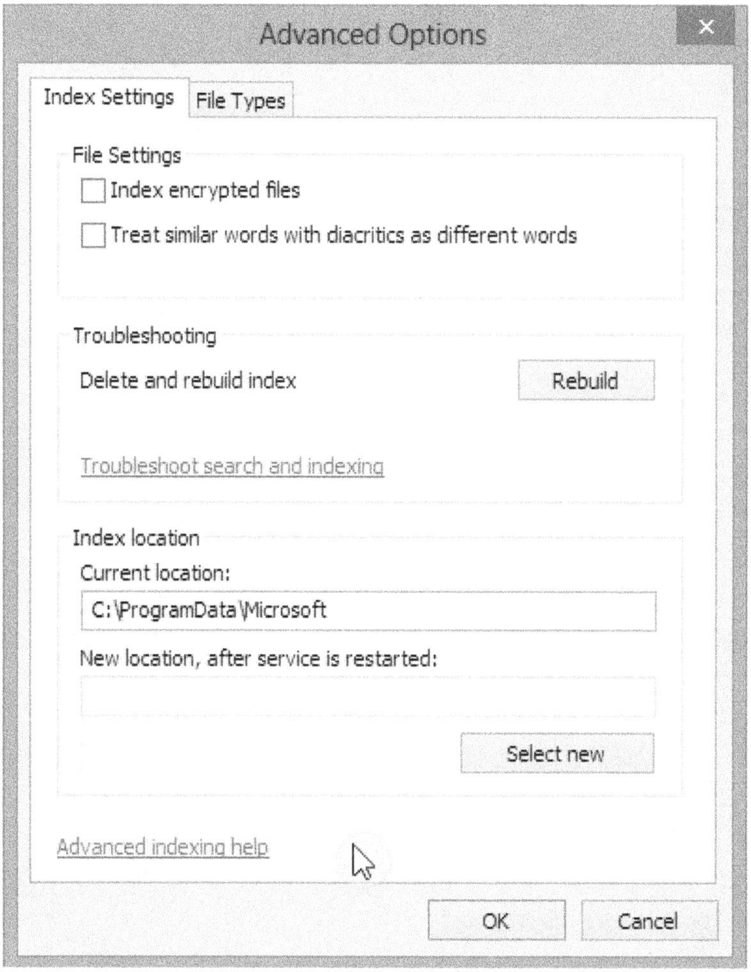

Figure 31.3 – Advanced indexing options

Under "File Settings" we can firstly choose to index encrypted files. This only applies to Windows encrypted files and not, for example, Truecrypt or PGP encrypted files. This option is off by default as it represents a security risk, since the contents of the encrypted file can be stored in the index in an unencrypted state. This option might not be present on all versions of Windows 8 and we do not cover encrypted files or Bitlocker in this course.

The second option under File Settings is "Treat similar words with diacritics as different words". What are diacritics? Diacritics are often called accents (though in actual fact an accent is only one of many different types of diacritic), and the English language doesn't generally use them. In other languages, such as French, they can be applied to letters to change the pronunciation. For example 'é' and 'e' are distinct because of the diacritic on the letter.

If you regularly work with other languages you may wish to turn this option on, but for those of us who work only in English, it can safely stay off.

Under "Troubleshooting" is the option to rebuild the index. If you find yourself searching for files and getting no results back, there is the possibility that the index is corrupt. Click on "Rebuild" to rebuild and repair it. Normally you will not need to do this as Windows is capable of maintaining the index on its own.

Finally, under "Index Location", it is possible to move the index to another drive. If you have a secondary hard drive it may be faster to store the search index separately from the Windows system drive, though for most users the default location is fine.

Clicking on the "File types" tab at the top of the window lists the current file types that are indexed. Figure 31.4 shows this window.

Figure 31.4 – Windows indexes hundreds of different file types

You can see from figure 31.4 that Windows knows about and indexes all kinds of files. For some types of file such as plain text or Microsoft Word documents, Windows will also index the contents of these documents.

At the bottom of the window you can add your own file types just by typing in the file extension (we covered file extensions in lesson 26.5). If the file does not contain text, you should choose "Index Properties Only" to avoid cluttering up the index with junk data, since Windows isn't clever enough to recognise file contents in picture or sound files just yet.

When you are done changing indexing options, click on "OK".

31.3 – Tips for searching in Windows 8

Not being able to find what you are looking for is frustrating and the nice thing about storing information digitally is that computers can look for things much quicker than we can in the physical world. Having said that, computers are pretty dumb, so be sure to tell yours exactly what you are looking for and where, to avoid frustration. Here are a couple of tips to help with the searching process.

Click the magnifying glass icon or press enter after typing a search on the Start screen to see more results:- Remember when searching on the Start screen, if you click the magnifying glass icon or press enter after your search, you will be taken to a page containing more search results. You may need to do this to find all of your tagged images, for instance.

When searching in File Explorer, the search starts from the current location:- If you use the built in search in File Explorer, keep in mind that it does not search your entire computer. For example, if you are in your video folder and you search for a photograph, it is unlikely that the search will find anything (unless you are in the habit of storing photographs in your video folder). The search will only search within the current folder and any sub-folders in that folder.

Searching in File Explorer does search through tags and meta data:- If you want to find a picture you tagged, you can search from the Start screen or from File Explorer. This is different to Windows 7 where searching in Windows Explorer would not search through tags.

Use the Search Tools tab on the ribbon:- If you are struggling to find a certain file, let Windows know that you are not interested in text files or other types of file by telling it exactly what type of file you want to find. Click on the search box in File Explorer and then use the Search Tools tab on the ribbon to filter files by type or size, figure 31.5 shows an example of this.

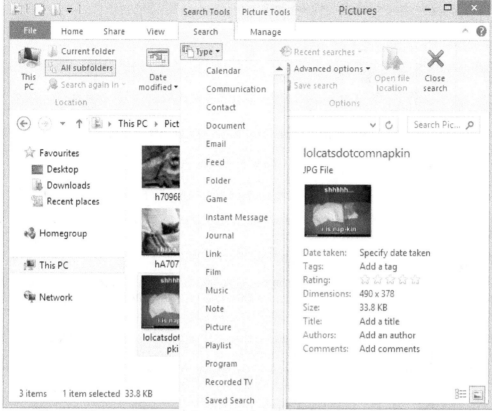

Figure 31.5 – Using the Search tab on the ribbon to filter searches

Be sure to try these techniques for yourself. The Windows 8 search facilities are the most powerful yet. Learn to use them and you will potentially save yourself a lot of time.

That is the end of this lesson and this chapter. The next chapter deals with computer and data security, starting with lesson 32 which deals with backing up your computer, a very important subject that many users still neglect.

Chapter 7 – Securing Your PC and Your Data

If you have been following this course so far, you are probably excited to dive head-first into your new Windows 8 PC and start changing, tweaking and trying all kinds of things. Indeed, we encourage you to do this, it is the best way to learn. Before you start getting too carried away however, it is time to consider security, the security of your computer and your important data.

This chapter firstly tackles the subject of backup. An alarming number of people still do not backup their data at all. Computer hard drives are mechanical devices and will eventually fail through wear and tear. Without a proper backup strategy, any information you have on a hard drive which fails may well be lost forever.

Once we are done backing our system up, we will look at the various security mechanisms in Windows itself. We will show you how to create additional accounts for other family members and how to secure your account against malicious software, using User Account Controls. If you plan to go online with your computer you should understand about security software including Antivirus software like Windows Defender, the Windows 8 firewall and about keeping your PC up to date.

Lesson 32 – Planning a backup strategy

It is important to remember that files and folders on your PC can vanish into oblivion at any time if you do not have a proper backup strategy. Hard drive failures are the most common hardware fault on modern PCs. While it is more usual for a hard drive to fail when it is old, it is not uncommon for hard drives to fail randomly at any time.

In this lesson we will discuss how to plan a backup strategy around the capabilities of the Windows 8 backup utility. If you are planning to use a third party backup solution this lesson might also be useful to you, but it is focused on the backup utility provided with Windows 8.

32.1 – Backup methodologies

Using the new Windows 8 backup software is not too complicated but understanding what to backup often is. Luckily Windows 8 backup supports two different kinds of backup, image backup and file history backup. What is the difference between these two options?

Image backup:- This option takes a snapshot of your entire computer, you can think of it like creating a time capsule and putting your current hard drive inside it. When you restore from an image backup, all information (programs and data) on your hard drive reverts to the state it was in when the backup was taken. You can only restore the entire snapshot, you cannot select individual files from an image backup (this is true in Windows 8 backup, though some third party backup solutions do not have this restriction). You can however, restore your computer in the event of a total failure of your computers hard drive or operating system.

File History backup:- This option backs up individual files and folders. It works in the background and monitors changes to your files, creating a new backup whenever a file is changed. If you need to recover a file that has been deleted or changed, you can then go into the file history vault and recover it. File history backup does not backup programs and system files, so cannot be used to restore your operating system in the event of a hard drive failure, for instance.

Consider the information on your computer, we can split it roughly into two categories.

Programs:- These are the things you install and run on your computer, including the actual operating system itself. It also includes word processors, web browsers, games, music players and anything and everything that runs on your computer. It changes infrequently compared with data.

Data:- This is information that programs work with. It includes word processor documents, spreadsheets, music and video files, digital photographs, saved game positions and anything and everything that the programs you run on your computer work with.

Data is personal to you and usually needs extra protection compared with programs which can usually be reinstalled from their original media or from the internet. Windows 8 File History backup makes it easy to protect your data.

Windows 8 does include image backup too. The feature is called "System Image Backup" in Windows 8.1. It is pretty well hidden, to find it you will need to go to the control panel and open the "File History" section under "System and Security". You should then find it in the bottom left hand corner. Windows 8 offers only the bare minimum image backup facilities, we recommend that if you want to create full system images on your PC, you should investigate one of the many third-party backup tools available.

32.2 – Do you have operating system recovery media?

There may come a time when you want to revert your computer back to the state it was in when you first bought it. Perhaps you have clogged your computer up with too much third party software and you just want a clean start, or maybe you are selling your PC and want to make sure that no unlicensed software or personal information remains on it. Windows 8 does give you the option to refresh and reset your PC from the settings menu and we look at these options in lesson 64. However, if your PC cannot start, you will need operating system recovery media. This can be a USB device or a DVD disc.

If you purchased your copy of Windows 8 from a store, your operating system recovery DVD is the same DVD you used to install Windows 8 in the first place, so you are covered. If you purchased your computer with Windows 8 pre installed, the manufacturer might not have provided operating system recovery media. Most manufacturers include a special recovery file/partition on the computers hard drive instead of a DVD. This is fine unless your hard drive fails (and your hard drive will eventually fail). If you do not have any recovery media, you should make some now. We will show you how in lesson 35.

32.3 – Where to backup

If you are still reeling from the cost of buying your new PC, you won't be happy to discover that you are going to need to spend a little more money on a backup solution. However, backing up to the same hard drive is just not an option. If your hard drive fails then so does your backup. The Windows 8 File History backup gives you two main options for backup media, namely secondary hard drives and network drives. Let's take a look at each option.

Secondary hard drives:- These can be either internal hard drives (typically in a desktop computer) or external. External drives usually connect by USB, though some connect via other kinds of interface such as eSATA and (increasingly rarely) Firewire. External drives provide easily expandable storage that is ideal for backup. Most, if not all modern Windows computers have USB connectors. Figure 32.1 shows two USB ports.

Figure 32.1 – Two USB ports on a computer, notice the white USB 'octopus' logo at the top left

When choosing a secondary drive, choose one that is bigger than the system drive in your PC. At least twice as much capacity is desirable, so there is plenty of room for your backups. Remember that we showed you how to determine the capacity of a hard drive attached to your computer in lesson 28.3. Figure 32.2 shows a typical external hard drive that connects to the computer via USB.

Figure 32.2 – A typical external hard drive. Like the vast majority of external drives, this drive connects via USB

Let's look at the advantages and disadvantages of secondary hard drives for backup now.

Advantages:- Fast, affordable high capacity storage. Hard drives continue to increase in capacity and decrease in price.

Disadvantages:- For external hard drives, the user must remember to connect the hard drive prior to the scheduled backup. Fitting an additional internal hard drive requires some technical know how.

Local network backup:- Once the exclusive realm of businesses, network backup around the home is gaining in popularity. Using network storage can be more convenient than attaching an external hard drive. As long as the network is available any and all computers in your home can access network attached storage. It is usually much easier to remember to leave your Wi-Fi network enabled while you work rather than having to lug in an external drive and attach it. Local network backup uses devices attached to your home network and should not be confused with online or cloud backup which works across the public internet. Figure 32.3 shows a network attached storage device (NAS).

Figure 32.3 – More expensive network storage solutions like this Netgear ReadyNAS can hold multiple hard drives which copy or mirror each other, providing some protection against random hard drive failure

Network backup solutions can be expensive however and they often require technical configuration to get the best out of them. If you are unable to start your operating system and you need to recover from an image backup, you may find that your computer cannot connect to the network and thus your backup is inaccessible.

Let's sum up the advantages and disadvantages of network backup.

Advantages:- Convenient, can be used by several computers in the house. Backups are fast and can be configured to work automatically with little or no user intervention.

Disadvantages:- Relatively expensive, may require expert configuration, restoring image backups from the network is often not possible.

In this guide, we will be showing you how to backup using an external USB hard drive, as that is the configuration that we recommend for home users. We will also show you how to create rescue media so that you can repair your operating system in the event of a hard drive or operating system failure.

32.4 – A note about storing your backups

Remember that hard drive failure and system crashes are not the only disaster you may encounter. Fire, theft, natural disaster and other unfortunate accidents could see both your computer and your backup copy wiped out in one go. To mitigate this danger, you might want to store backup copies at a friends house (you could store his or her backups in exchange) or perhaps in a locked drawer at the office. Another option is to use one of the many new online backup services which backup your data and save it in several data centres. While the Windows 8 file history backup does not directly support online backup, you can use the OneDrive service to backup your most important files to your OneDrive account, as shown in lesson 16. You may wish to investigate online backup further, particularly if you run your business from home.

That concludes this lesson on preparing your backup strategy. Once you have purchased your external hard drive or backup solution of choice, you can enable automatic backup in Windows 8 easily, we will show you how in the next lesson.

Lesson 33 – Configuring File History backup

File History   In Windows 8, backup has been overhauled again and is
now called "File History". File History replaces the
"Previous Versions" feature in Windows 7, that nobody
used, with a fantastic backup solution that protects your files from accidental
deletion and accidental changes too.

33.1 – Choosing a File History drive

Just like in previous versions of Windows, we need to set up this feature in
order to start using it. Go to the Start screen and search for "file history"
and click the first icon that appears. The window shown in figure 33.1 will
then appear.

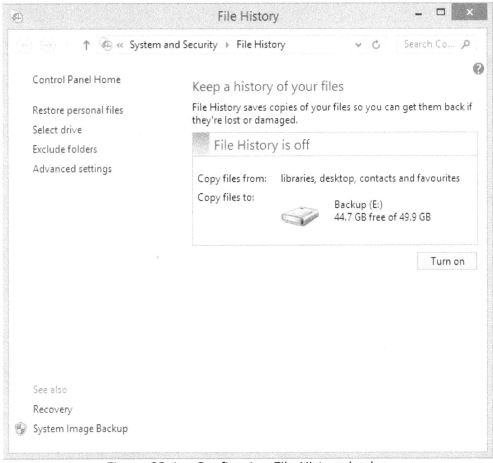

Figure 33.1 – Configuring File History backup

Figure 33.1 shows the initial setup window for File History. File History saves versions of your files, so that for instance if you accidentally delete or change a file, you can always recover it from the File History vault. To setup this feature, you will need a secondary hard drive, either internal or external, or a home network storage location. In the example shown in figure 33.1, we are using a secondary hard drive. By modern standards this drive is relatively small. In reality this device might not have enough storage space to backup a modern sized file collection and if you have a large media library on your PC you may need to invest in something with a bigger capacity.

To get started configuring File History, click on the "Select drive" option. It's the third option down from the top on the left of the window shown in figure 33.1. When you click this link, the window shown in figure 33.2 will appear.

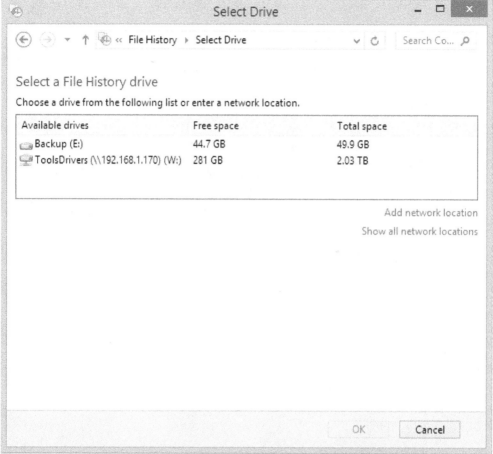

Figure 33.2 – Choosing a drive for File History

The window shown in figure 33.2 lists all the File History compatible drives in your system. Choose a drive, either internal or external, or click the "Add network location" to add a location on another computer or a network storage device such as a NAS or home server. To choose a drive, click on it from the list and then click "OK". You will then be returned to the window shown in figure 33.2, which will now show your target drive in the "Copy files to:" section.

33.2 – Starting the backup

Click on the "Turn on" button to start backing up. If you have configured a homegroup already (see lesson 56) you may see the following window appear.

Figure 33.3 – You can make your backup drive available to other users on the homegroup

If you choose "Yes" to the option shown in figure 33.3 then other users on your homegroup will be able to use this drive across the network for their File History backups. If you prefer to keep the space all to yourself, choose "No". Once you have made your decision (or if you're not connected to a homegroup) the window will change to the one shown in figure 33.4.

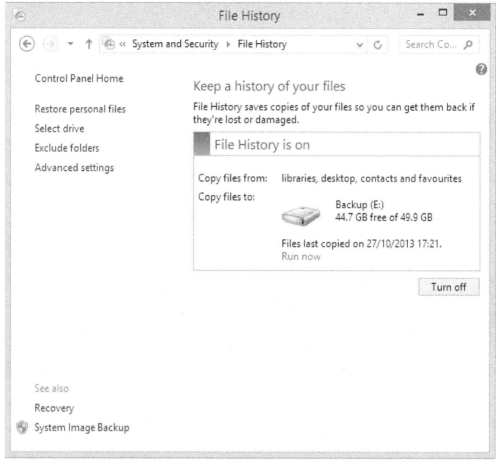

Figure 33.4 – File History is now enabled

Notice in figure 33.4 Windows tells us we are copying files from "libraries, desktop, contacts and favourites". These are the areas on your PC where you typically store information, so these are the areas that File History will protect. You can exclude certain folders from the backup by clicking "Exclude folders" from the options on the left of the window, then, just click "Add" and browse to the folder you want to exclude. If you want to include a folder that's not currently being backed up, you simply need to add it to your libraries, as shown in lesson 24.2, or place it in your personal folders.

File History is now configured and Windows will save copies of your files to the drive. By default, files will be backed up every hour. When you change any files or folders it will save a new version to the backup. That's all you need to do to set up File History. Before we wrap up this lesson, there are some advanced settings you may want to change.

33.3 – Advanced settings

To access the advanced settings for File History, click on "Advanced settings" from the options on the left. Figure 33.5 shows the Advanced settings window.

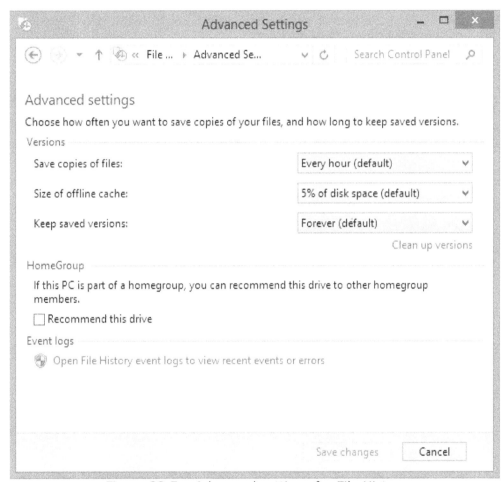

Figure 33.5 – Advanced settings for File History

There are a couple of settings you may want to consider changing here. Firstly, you can make backups more or less frequently than every hour by changing the top most option. The most frequent backup window is "Every 10 minutes". Increasing the frequency of the backups will put more workload on your computer but, of course, provides more security for files you are working with.

The "Size of offline cache" option relates to the cached File History information on your system drive. Generally this value can be left as the default.

Finally the "Keep saved versions" can be changed to automatically delete files that are older than several months or a year, or to automatically delete old versions when drive space is needed.

Remember to click on "Save changes" if you change any of the options available here.

That's all you need to know to use File History backup, in the next lesson we will look at how to restore files and also discuss some of the limitations of File History.

Lesson 34 – Restoring files from File History

 Backup copies of any kind are useless if you cannot easily restore data from them. In this lesson we will show you how to restore files from your File History backups.

34.1 – Restoring a file

To demonstrate the power of File History, consider the graphics file shown in figure 34.1.

Figure 34.1 – A photograph that's been 'creatively altered'

In figure 34.1 you can see that someone or some-thing has damaged the picture, by adding some scribbles over the top of it. These weren't in the original photograph. Using File History, we can restore a copy and repair the damage. Start File History from the Start screen as shown in the previous lesson (see figure 33.1). This time, choose "Restore personal files" from the options on the left. The window shown in figure 34.2 will then appear.

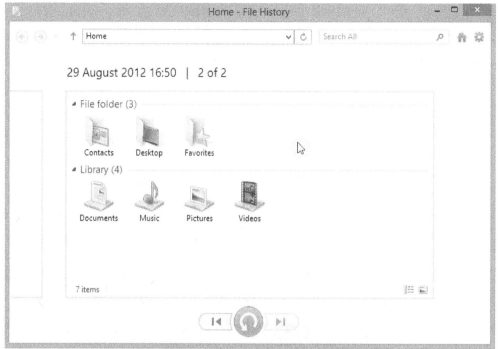

Figure 34.2 – Browsing File History backups

To restore a file or files from File History, simply browse to the files. For instance, the picture file shown in figure 34.1 was stored in the pictures library. Figure 34.3 shows the pictures library open in the File History explorer.

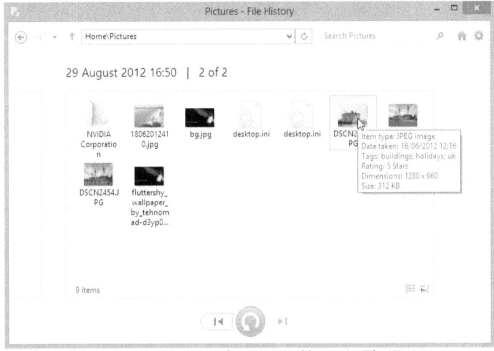

Figure 34.3 – Browsing the pictures library in File History

In figure 34.3 the user has identified the latest version of the picture we saw at the start of the lesson. Double clicking on this file will open it in the File History explorer. Figure 34.4 shows this.

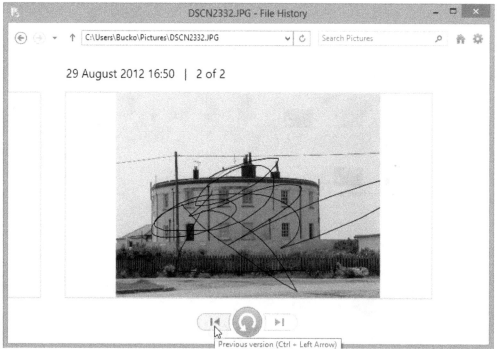

Figure 34.4 – The current version of the file in File History

Notice at the bottom of the windows shown in figures 34.3 and 34.4 that there is a button pointing to the left (next to the large round green button). Click on the button pointing left to go back in time to a previous backup. In the example shown in figure 34.4, when the user clicks on the button, the File History will move back in time to show the image displayed in figure 34.5.

Figure 34.5 – Going back in time to a different version of the file

Once the desired version of the file is located in the backup, it can be restored by clicking the big green button at the bottom of the window. Windows will warn you that there's already a file at that location. In our example, we know for sure that the current file is damaged so it would be perfectly fine to click on "Replace the file in the destination" and then the picture would be restored.

34.2 – Other ways of working with File History

As we can see in figure 34.3, you can work with several files while using the File History explorer, not just individual ones. Just like with File Explorer, you can use the forward, back and up controls near the top left of the File History window to navigate around. Note that you cannot drag and drop files between File History and File Explorer, however.

To restore several files from within the File History explorer, you can select them using any of the multiple file selection methods we discussed in lesson 23. For instance you could lasso the files using the mouse or your finger, or use the Control (Ctrl) key to select specific files. Once the files are selected, you can use the green button to restore them to their original directories. Of course, by doing this you may overwrite the current versions of the files. To restore the files to a different directory, right click and choose "Restore to". Figure 34.6 shows an example of this.

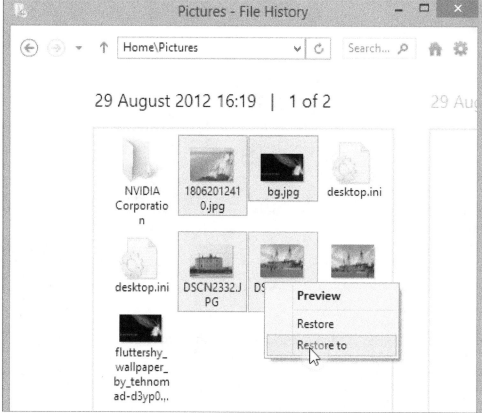

Figure 34.6 – Restoring several files at once to an alternative directory

Using this technique we can put the files anywhere on the PC, without having to overwrite the existing version.

That's all you need to know to use File History to protect your files. As you can see, backup in Windows 8 is now both extremely flexible and extremely easy. Before we round off this lesson, we'll take a quick look at some of the limitations of File History backup.

34.3 – Limitations of File History

To use any backup tool effectively you need to know about its limitations and File History is no exception. While File History might be an ideal solution for many users, it does have a number of shortcomings.

Does not back up program files:– File History backs up data stored in your libraries or personal folders only, it does not backup program files. When your computers hard drive eventually fails or if your operating system needs to be refreshed or reinstalled, any programs you use will need to be reinstalled as well. All tile-based software is linked to your Microsoft account and can be reinstalled automatically from the Windows store. Desktop software will need to be reinstalled from its original media or original download file.

Beware of older, legacy software designed for Windows XP and earlier. Some of this software stores data within its installation directory and not within your libraries or personal folders. Since File History doesn't back up the program files directory, this data will not be backed up either.

Cannot recover your operating system:– You should make sure you have some way of reinstalling your operating system. This could be your original Windows 8 installation DVD or other media or a system image backup. Hard drives will eventually fail and if you don't have means to reinstall your OS, you may be stuck with a drive full of File History backups you cannot access.

You can use tools such as System Restore (see lesson 63) and Refresh my PC (see lesson 64) to repair your operating system, but if you are a power user who installs dozens of applications and makes lots of modifications to the OS, you may wish to investigate system image backups. System image backups take a 'snapshot' of your entire computer, allowing you to restore it in full at any time. System image backup is not covered in this guide but it is still included in Windows 8.1 under "System Image Backup". There are also dozens of third-party backup tools for Windows that can manage system image backups in various ways.

Cannot backup using online/cloud services:– Windows File History does not directly support backup to an online service such as OneDrive. If, for instance, you store your backups at home and fire, theft or other disaster strikes your house, you will lose both your backups and your working copies in one go. Consider other backup strategies if you have particularly valuable data.

Backups are not encrypted:– If you require a greater level of security for your PC and your backups, you may need to consider third party backup tools that offer encryption, or use File History in conjunction with tools that add encryption to Windows drives such as Truecrypt.

Lesson 35 – Creating system repair media

 Create a recovery drive In this lesson, we are going to look at how to create bootable recovery media in Windows 8. A recovery drive can start your PC even if Windows is damaged, allowing you to start repair options such as System Restore (see lesson 63) or Refresh (see lesson 64). Since Windows 8 is designed to run on a wide range of PCs, Microsoft have changed the default rescue media from CD-ROM to USB device. As of Windows 8.1, you can no longer create system repair CDs, you can only use USB devices. To complete this process, you will need a USB drive that is at least 256mb in size, larger if you want to save your computers recovery partition.

35.1 – System repair USB device

To begin creating system repair media using a USB storage device, insert your USB device into the computer. Figure 35.1 shows "This PC" (see lesson 28) with a USB drive attached.

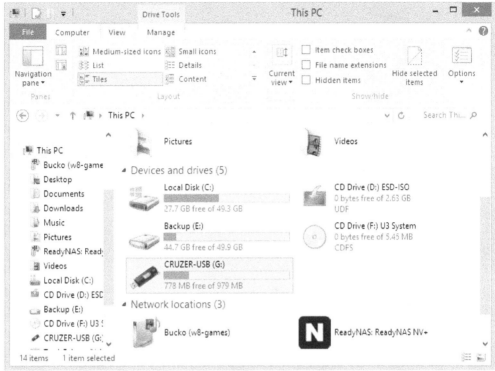

Figure 35.1 – A USB pen/thumb drive attached to the PC will show up under "This PC" like this.

To start the process of creating the recovery media, search for "Create a recovery drive" on the Start screen and click the icon that appears. Enter your password and/or click on "Yes" when the User Account Control prompt appears. The window in figure 35.2 will then be shown.

Figure 35.2 – Starting the recovery drive wizard

In figure 35.2 we can see one very useful new feature, the option to copy the systems recovery partition to the USB drive. What does this mean exactly? Many PCs have a hidden area on their hard drives which can reset the PC back to factory fresh settings. This is great if the operating system fails completely and you cannot start your PC. However, this is no help at all if the hard drive itself fails and needs to be replaced. With this option you can back up this important area of your hard drive, so you should choose this option if it is available. If this option is not available, you should make sure you have some way of reinstalling your OS completely, as you won't be able to do it from the recovery media in this case.

Click on "Next" to get started, the window shown in figure 35.3 will then be displayed.

Figure 35.3 – Choosing a drive to use as a recovery drive

In figure 35.3 the recovery drive wizard has found the E: drive, so we can use that. Note that all the information currently on the drive you select will be erased, so make sure you make a backup copy of anything you want to keep. Furthermore, make sure that you have definitely selected the correct drive to use. Cross check using This PC like we did at the start of the lesson if you are in any doubt.

With the correct drive checked and selected, click on "Next". The window shown in figure 35.4 will then appear.

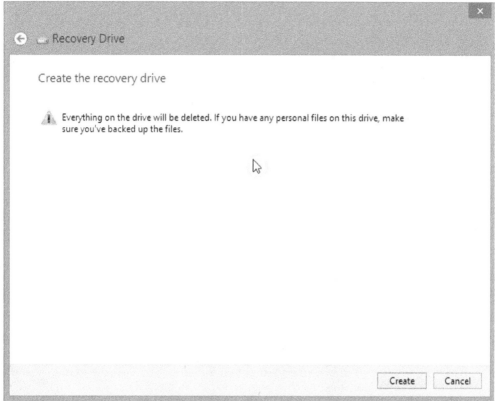

Figure 35.4 – Last chance before your USB drive is re-purposed as a recovery drive

Windows gives us one last chance to copy any information from the USB device. Click on "Create" to begin the process of creating the recovery drive. Windows will then copy and configure the necessary files, this will take a moment, especially if you are copying the recovery partition too. When the process is complete, the window shown in figure 35.5 will be displayed.

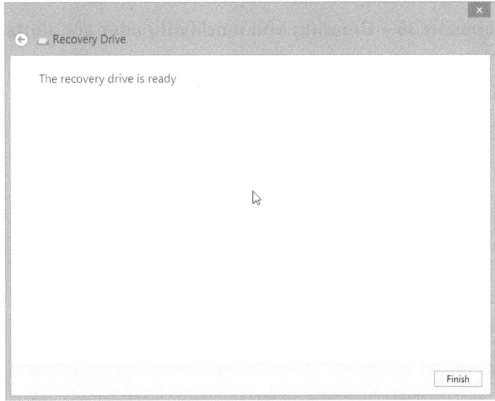

Figure 35.5 – The recovery media is now ready for use

The repair media has now been created. You should reboot your PC and test that it works immediately, then store the media away somewhere safe. If you have trouble starting from the repair media, you may need to change the BIOS or early startup settings on your PC, the details of this vary between PCs. Consult the instructions that came with your PC or motherboard for more information on how to do this.

Lesson 36 – Creating and modifying user accounts

Windows 8 lets several users share a computer by creating separate user accounts for them. Each user will have their own personal folders on the computer and their own settings and preferences. Creating separate user accounts for all your family members is highly recommended. By creating limited accounts for your children, for example, you can prevent them changing important settings on the computer while exploring.

Even if you are the only user of your computer, if you want to take advantage of the added security benefits of running as a standard user rather than an administrator then you should create two accounts for yourself. A standard, limited account for day to day use and an administrator account for those times when you do need to change system settings. We will explain more about this in lesson 37.

36.1 – Adding a user

In Windows 8, new user accounts are added through the "PC Settings" section on the Charms Bar. Simple customisations to existing accounts, such as changing an account picture, can be done from this section too. Go to the Start screen and open the Charms Bar. Click on the Settings Charm and then choose "Change PC settings" at the bottom right of the screen. The PC settings section will open, from the options on the left, choose "Accounts" and then "Other accounts". Figure 36.1 illustrates this.

Figure 36.1 – Adding a new user to your Windows 8 PC

Note:- If you don't see the "Other accounts" option, then you are not signed into your PC with a administrator account. In this instance, someone else has already added a new user account to your PC.

To add a new user, click on "Add a user". When you click this button, the screen shown in figure 36.2 will appear.

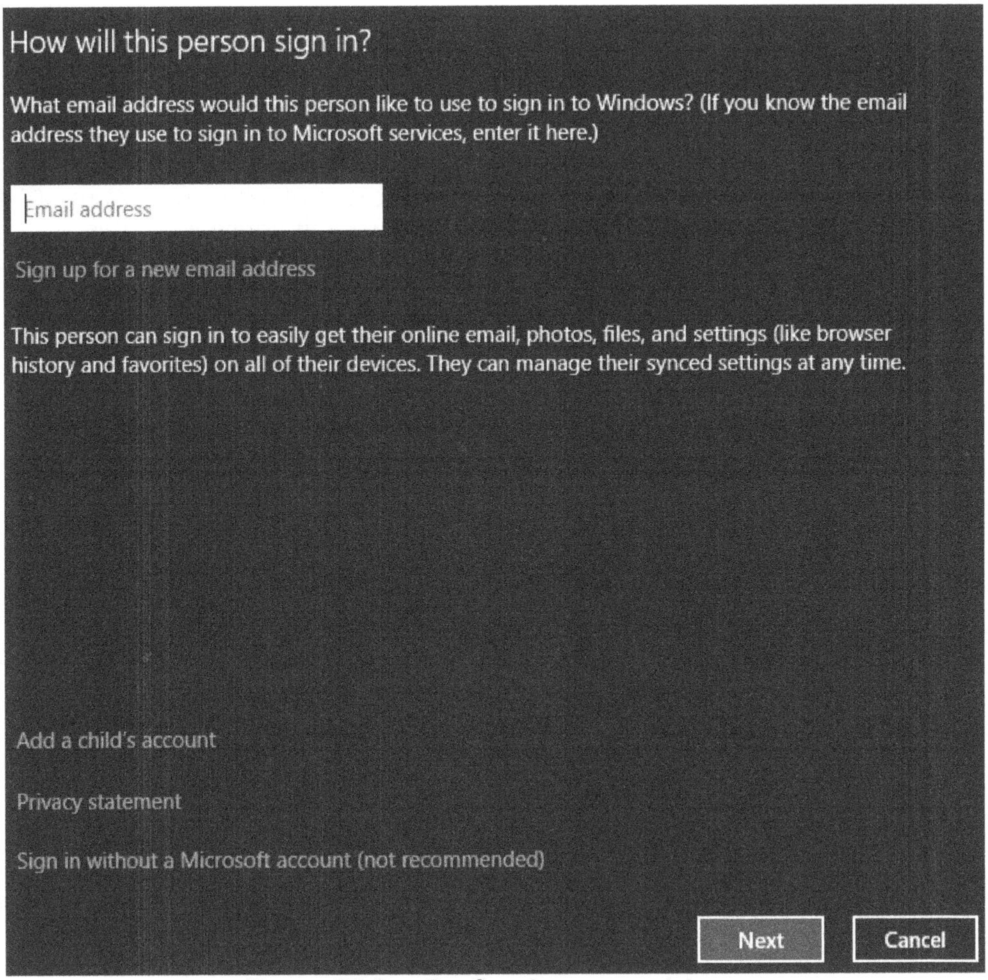

How will this person sign in?

What email address would this person like to use to sign in to Windows? (If you know the email address they use to sign in to Microsoft services, enter it here.)

| Email address |

Sign up for a new email address

This person can sign in to easily get their online email, photos, files, and settings (like browser history and favorites) on all of their devices. They can manage their synced settings at any time.

Add a child's account

Privacy statement

Sign in without a Microsoft account (not recommended)

Next   Cancel

Figure 36.2 – Configuring account types

36.2 – Microsoft accounts vs local accounts

As we discussed way back in lesson 1, accounts on a Windows 8 machine can be linked to your Microsoft account if desired. If you do this, your account is tied to Microsoft's other online services on the web, such as Hotmail, Xbox

Live and OneDrive. Using a Microsoft account will synchronise your settings between all the PCs you use, as well as sign you in automatically to services like the App Store and OneDrive.

There are also standard Windows accounts (or local accounts), which aren't linked to Microsoft accounts and act the same as they did in previous versions of Windows. If you are heavily into your home networking for instance, you may have set up your home network with user names and passwords on your shared devices, so you might want to carry on using the traditional Windows user account. With this setup you may need to manually sign into the App Store and other online features with your Microsoft account credentials.

For this example we will use a Microsoft account to add a new user to the PC. Fill in the users e-mail address on the screen shown in figure 36.2, this will usually be the users Hotmail or Outlook.com address. If the user is using any Microsoft services online already, be sure to enter the address associated with their Microsoft account. If your new user doesn't have a Microsoft account yet, he or she can get one by clicking "Sign up for a new email address" near the bottom of the screen.

Once you have entered the users e-mail address, click on "Next", the screen shown in figure 36.3 will then appear.

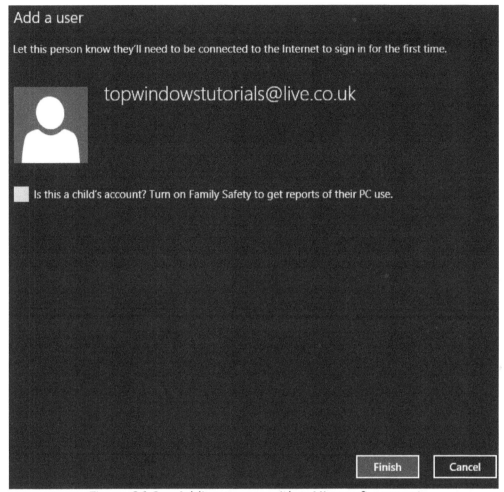

Figure 36.3 – Adding a user with a Microsoft account

Now our new user is set up. If this account belongs to a child, you can turn on Family Safety features by ticking or checking the box on this screen. The first time the new user signs into this PC, the computer will need to be connected to the internet. They will, of course, also need their Microsoft account password. Click on "Finish" to complete the account creation process. You will then be returned to the screen shown in figure 36.1. You can now add more users or simply continue to use your PC. When you are done using your PC, don't forget to log out (we showed you how in lesson 5.3) so that your new user can log in with his or her account.

36.3 – Standard users and Administrators

 The standard Windows 8 account settings do not give us the option of configuring the accounts security level. All new accounts added to the PC will default to standard user accounts. This is of course, usually the correct behaviour. Because Administrators can perform system wide changes, gain access to other users files and documents and completely reconfigure the PC, most users should not have administrator rights. To change account security levels, we will need to go to the Control Panel. Search for "user accounts" on the Start screen and then click the icon shown at the start of this paragraph. The window shown in figure 36.5 will then appear.

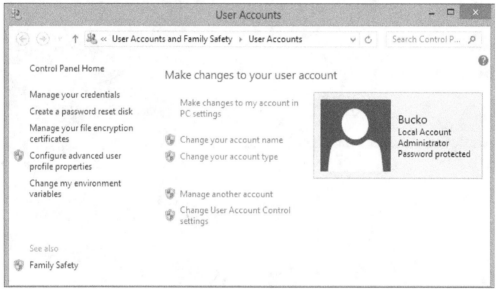

Figure 36.5 – Use the Control Panel to make advanced changes to user accounts

From the Control Panel window shown in figure 36.5, we can change account security settings. Notice how the account shown is an administrator. There has to be one administrator for a PC. This is the user responsible for installing new software and changing any system settings. The other account security setting is "Standard user". It is important to understand the difference between these two security levels that an account can have.

Administrators:- have full access to everything on the computer (including potentially the personal folders of other users) and can change any and all settings on the computer. This includes installing new software, changing networking and internet settings or storage configurations. Administrators can basically do whatever they choose.

Standard users:- can run and use programs but usually have to ask permission from an administrator before they can change global system settings or install new software. Note that in Windows 8, standard users are free to install new tile-based apps but not most desktop apps.

Normally, a family computer would only have one administrator, typically this would be the parent or head of the house, or the adult with the most computer experience. Everyone else, especially younger members of the family, should have standard accounts.

36.3.1 – Changing account security levels

To change a users account security level, click on the "Manage another account" link shown in figure 36.5. You will then be taken to a list of user accounts on the PC. Click once on the account you want to change. The window will then look like figure 36.6.

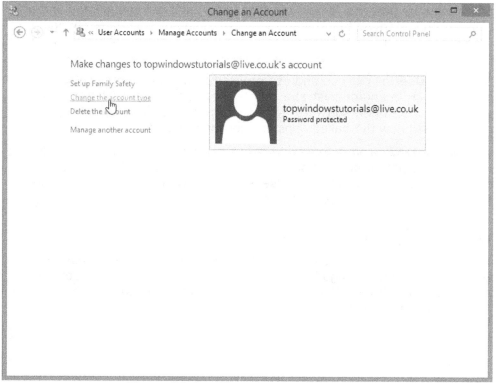

Figure 36.6 – Changing account types

Click on "Change the account type". You will then see the options shown in figure 36.7.

Choose a new account type for topwindowstutorials@live.co.uk

topwindowstutorials@live.co.uk
Password protected

⦿ Standard
Standard accounts can use most software and change system settings that don't affect other users or the security of this PC.

◯ Administrator
Administrators have complete control over the PC. They can change any settings and access all of the files and programs stored on the PC.

Why is a standard account recommended?

Figure 36.7 – Selecting security levels for a user

Note – Windows will use the term "Account type" to refer to standard user accounts and administrator accounts. Account type can also refer to Microsoft accounts and local accounts. Usually it's pretty easy to know which one is being referred to by context.

You can now choose between Standard and Administrator accounts for this user. As you might expect, only administrator accounts have the power to change other users account security levels. Repeat this process for any other accounts you want to change.

36.4 – Creating local accounts

The method of creating a local account is very similar to creating a Microsoft account. In this part of the lesson we will be creating a local account.

Here's a technique you can use to boost your PCs security. If you are the one responsible for maintaining the PC, create yourself two accounts, one with administrator privileges and one without. To do this, go back to the Start screen and use the Settings Charm to add another user account. This time we will create the account without using a Microsoft account by clicking the "Sign in without a Microsoft account" link shown at the bottom of figure 36.2. When you do this, the screen shown in figure 36.8 will appear.

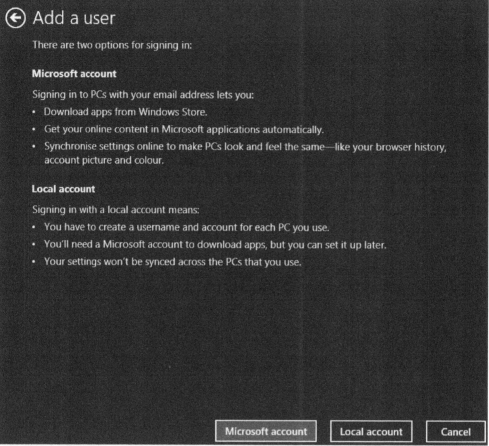

Figure 36.8 – Confirm you want a local account by clicking the "Local account" button

Windows gives us a little information on creating the two different account types, confirm that you want a local account and then the screen shown in figure 36.9 will be displayed.

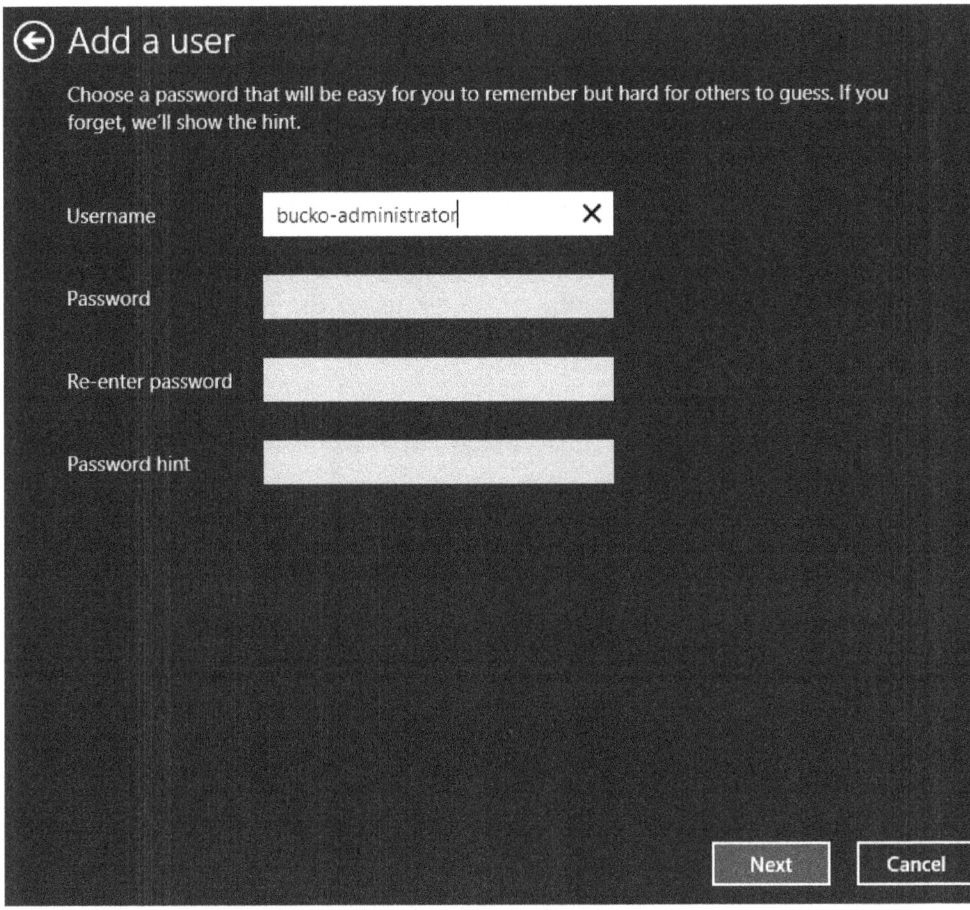

⊘ Add a user

Choose a password that will be easy for you to remember but hard for others to guess. If you
forget, we'll show the hint.

Username   bucko-administrator   ✕

Password

Re-enter password

Password hint

Next   Cancel

Figure 36.9 – Creating a local user account

Choose a user name for your account, when creating a separate
administrator account, you might want to use your regular user name with
the "-administrator" part tacked onto the end, like the user in figure 36.9 has
done.

Set up a password in the password entry box then confirm it in the box
below, then enter a password hint. Make sure not to choose anything too
obvious for your password hint as anyone who has access to this PC will be
able to see it. Click on "Next" when you have entered all the relevant
information. Windows will then show a screen similar to figure 36.3, giving
you the opportunity to turn on Family Safety. Click on "Finish" to finish
creating the account. You will then be returned to the PC settings screen as
shown in figure 36.1.

36.5 – Running as a standard user

As discussed previously, all accounts created using the PC settings screen are created as standard accounts. The next step would be to change this newly created account to be an administrator. Follow the steps outlined earlier in the lesson (36.3.1) to change the account type.

When you are finished making changes, you will need to log out of your regular account and log back in again with your newly created administrator account. Now, use this newly created account to change your day to day account to be a standard user account, again using the steps shown in lesson 36.3.1. Sign out and then sign back in again with your normal account when you are finished.

By using a standard account for your day to day computing tasks, you make your PC much more secure against viruses, malware and hackers.

So, now you know how to configure user accounts on your Windows 8 PC and you understand the distinction between administrators and standard users as well as local accounts and Microsoft accounts. The next lesson will look at User Account Controls and how this helpful feature can make using standard user accounts much easier than it was back in the Windows XP days.

Lesson 37 – The low down on User Account Controls

In the previous lesson we looked at how to create user accounts and discussed the security advantages of running a standard account rather than an administrator account. In this lesson we will show you how User Account Controls (UAC) work to make running as a standard user more convenient. Firstly, we will discuss in more detail why Microsoft implemented User Account Controls. In Vista, many users did not appreciate that UAC is attempting to fix a fundamental problem in the Windows security model. Instead, they berated the persistent annoying prompts that never appeared in Windows XP. In order to understand why UAC is not your enemy, we need to look at how Windows XP handled account security and why for the most part it was a failure for home users.

37.1 – Halt! Who goes there?

In the last lesson we learned that there are two different security settings for users on a Windows 8 machine, namely standard users and administrators. Generally, administrators can make changes to the computers configuration and install new software. Standard users, on the other hand, are forbidden from making system wide changes and are only cleared to run software already installed. In Windows 8, standard users are free to add new tiles to their accounts through the App Store, since each users tiles are unique to his or her account. This security model seems fine at first glance, but what about when a standard user wants to install some new desktop software? Certainly if you are running a family PC, it's likely that other users in the house will want to run their own software and not just software from the App Store tile. Children might want to install games, for example, which often run in desktop mode.

In Windows XP and Windows 2000, if you wanted to install some new software for a standard user account, you would need to switch to an administrator account, install the software (making sure to make it available to all users), log out of your administrator account and switch back to the standard account. This process was long winded and unfortunately it gets worse.

Lots of older, or simply badly written software just doesn't run under a standard account at all. Because of the fact that most Windows XP machines were pre-configured to run as administrator and because of the frustrations and headaches associated with running as a standard user, most Windows XP users ran administrator accounts all the time.

What is the big deal with running as an administrator? It's my computer, I can change it however I want, right? Unfortunately, running as an administrator also means that your system is wide open to attack from viruses and spyware. If you have full access to your computer, so does any program you run (or accidentally run) while using it, meaning that viruses can very easily propagate, hijack and sabotage key parts of your computer, often without you even knowing about it. With the new tile based applications in Windows 8, Microsoft have taken additional steps to safeguard users. By making every app pass a special vetting process before it is available in the store and restricting what tiles can do, Microsoft hope to mitigate the risk of malware even further. Nevertheless the vast majority of Windows users are still going to want to run desktop software. Even with antivirus and other security software running, running as an administrator is a security risk, but running as a standard user is too inconvenient for most people, or at least it was until User Account Control was introduced.

37.2 – User Account Controls to the rescue

User Account Controls work in two ways, when running an administrator account it prompts you to grant permission to make changes to the system. When running as a standard user, it allows you to temporarily elevate to administrator by entering your administrator password, thus saving you the hassle of switching accounts. Figure 37.1 shows a typical User Account Control prompt.

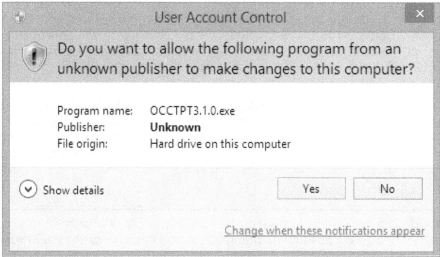

Figure 37.1 – User Account Control prompt on an administrator account

In figure 37.1, Windows has detected that a program we started wants to make changes to the computer. If this alert popped up out of the blue, you would certainly have cause for alarm. In this case it appeared because we started an installation file for a desktop application. Installation files are used to add new programs and features to Windows. Clicking on "Show details" will show where the program is located (the address or path of the file).

You might have noticed the shield icon, like the one on the left here, as you worked through this guide or experimented with your computer. Wherever you see this shield icon next to a task or program it indicates a task which makes changes to your computer and so may generate a UAC prompt. You may have also noticed (especially if you were a Windows Vista user) that clicking on most tasks on the Control Panel no longer results in a UAC prompt window appearing. Why is this? Microsoft scaled back the amount of alerts you typically see by default with Windows 7, and Windows 8 works the same way. If you are running an administrator account then UAC prompts will not appear by default when you change Windows settings. This decision upset some security experts[1] who rightly pointed out that by doing this you are actually making Windows less secure, seems like you can't please everyone.

37.3 – Changing User Account Control settings

To open the UAC settings window, open the System and Security section of the Control Panel and then choose "Change User Account Control settings" under "Action Center". Alternatively, search for "change user account control settings" on the Start screen and click the icon that appears. Figure 37.3 shows the User Account Control Settings window.

---

1   See http://www.osnews.com/story/21499/Why_Windows_7_s_Default_UAC_Is_Insecure

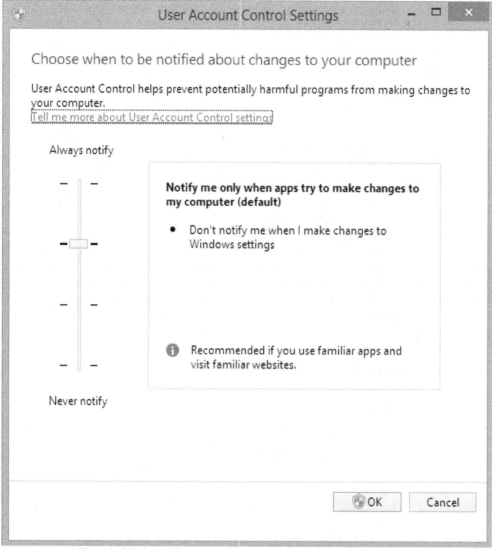

Figure 37.3 – Changing User Account Control settings

On the UAC settings window we can choose from four different settings. The settings are as follows.

Always notify me:- This is the highest security setting and the same behaviour as was seen in Windows Vista. With this setting, UAC asks for your permission every time a program or a Windows system setting is changed. **To get the very best security however, you must create and use a**

324

standard user account as discussed in lesson 36.4 to 36.5.

Notify me only when apps try to make changes to my computer:- This is the default setting. A UAC prompt will appear when you install a new program or run a program which requires administrator access (such as a backup utility). Changing Windows settings will not generate a UAC prompt. This setting aims to balance security with convenience but some more security conscious users have speculated that malware might find a way to impersonate a Windows setting and thus bypass the UAC notification process.

Notify me only when apps try to make changes to my computer (do not dim my desktop):- This is exactly the same as the setting above, except without the screen dimming effect seen when a UAC prompt is displayed. This effect is part of a mechanism which stops malware from hijacking the UAC notification and answering for you. If your PC struggles to display the screen dimming effect, choose this setting instead of the default setting.

Never notify me:- This setting disables UAC altogether. This is not recommended.

37.4 – User Account Controls and standard accounts

As discussed at the start of this lesson, UAC really comes into its own when used with standard accounts. Windows users can finally stop using administrator accounts for day to day computing tasks and enjoy the improved security of a standard account.

Figure 37.4 shows a UAC prompt window on a standard user account.

Figure 37.4 – User Account Control prompt on a standard user account

Notice in the picture above, we are asked for the administrator's password, why is this? This user account is only a standard account and therefore does not have the necessary rights to make system changes. With UAC we can temporarily activate another account which DOES have these rights. Under Windows XP or Windows 2000, we would have to switch user accounts to make the changes and switch back again. As you can imagine, being able to immediately switch to an administrator account thanks to UAC is much more convenient.

Running as a standard user rather than an administrator is one of the best ways to improve security on your PC. Thanks to UAC, this is now possible and convenient.

That concludes this lesson on User Account Controls. This was a long lesson with a lot of theory and so give yourself a pat on the back for getting through it. We hope that you understand the advantages of limited accounts now and that you won't curse at UAC prompts quite so much in the future. The next lesson covers updating your Windows 8 machine and is not as long winded, we promise.

Lesson 38 – Updating your PC

Keeping your Windows 8 PC up to date is essential if you want to stay ahead of hackers and security threats. New updates improve the security and stability of your operating system and should be applied as soon as they are available. Fortunately, in Windows 8 the update process is highly streamlined and is designed to update your PC without you even knowing about it.

38.1 – Manually checking for updates

Windows updates (and updates for all other operating systems) happen frequently in this highly connected digital age. When possible security vulnerabilities or other faults are found in the operating system, Microsoft issue updates to remedy the problems. To ensure that your operating system receives these updates as quickly as possible, we recommend that you enable automatic updates. This is the default setting, but you can still check for updates at any time. To do so, open the Charms Bar and click on the Settings Charm. Now select "Change PC settings". From the options that are then displayed, choose "Update & Recovery" right at the bottom. Finally, make sure the "Windows Update" option is selected. Figure 38.1 shows the screen that will then be displayed.

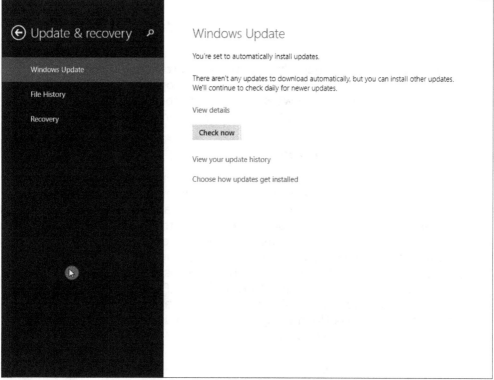

Figure 38.1 – Basic Windows Update settings

You will now see this simple update screen. If there are updates pending, you can install them now, otherwise, click the "Check now" button to check for updates. If an update is found it will then be displayed. Click on the View details text to see details of available updates, figure 38.2 shows an example.

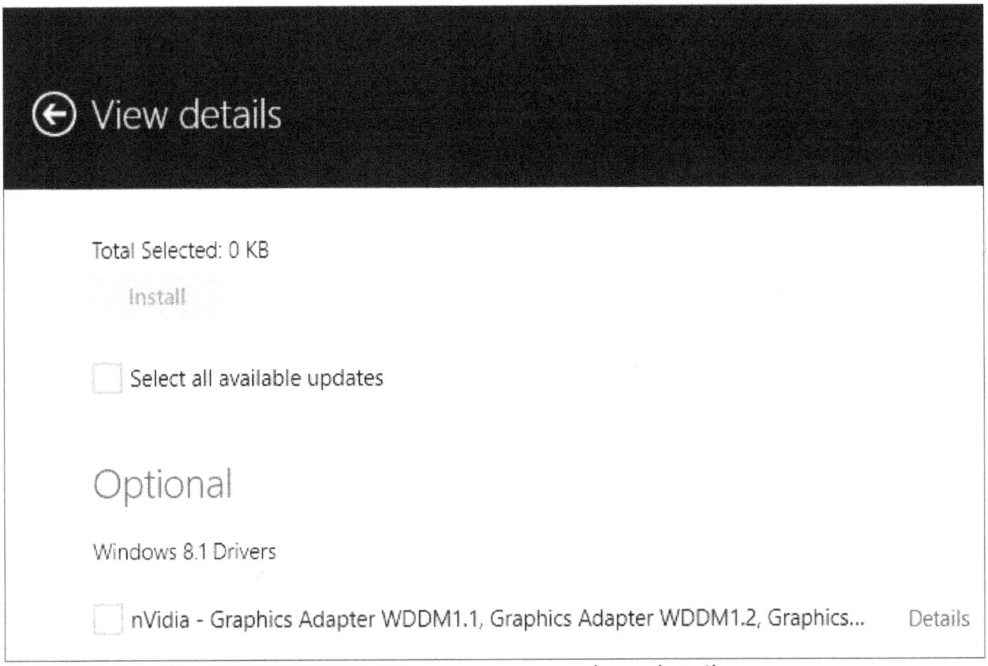

Figure 38.2 – Viewing update details

You can now either select individual updates or simply click on "Select all available updates" to install everything. Once you have selected the updates to install, click or tap on the "Install" button to install the update or, for important updates, simply navigate away from the Windows Update section to have the update install in your PCs scheduled maintenance window. We'll discuss what this means later in the lesson.

38.2 – Advanced update options

If you want more control over your Windows updates, you can use the Control Panel. From the Start screen, search for "control panel" and click the icon that appears. Then, on the Control Panel window, search for "windows update" and click on the top result. Figure 38.3 shows the window that will then open.

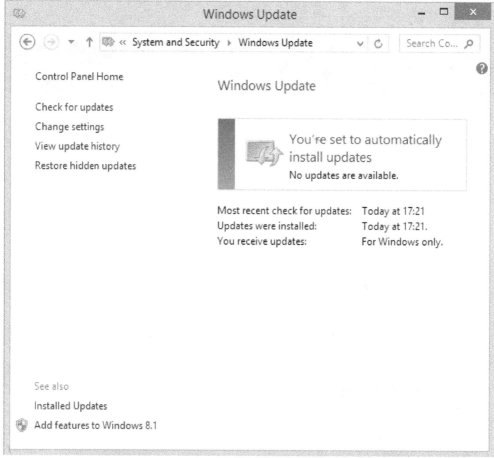

Figure 38.3 – Accessing advanced update options

The Windows Update window shown in figure 38.3 is a lot like the one that existed in Windows 7. Using the options on the left, you can check for updates from here, view the history of installed updates or restore a hidden update, that is, an update that you have specifically told Windows Update to ignore.

Clicking on "Change settings" will open the window shown in figure 38.4.

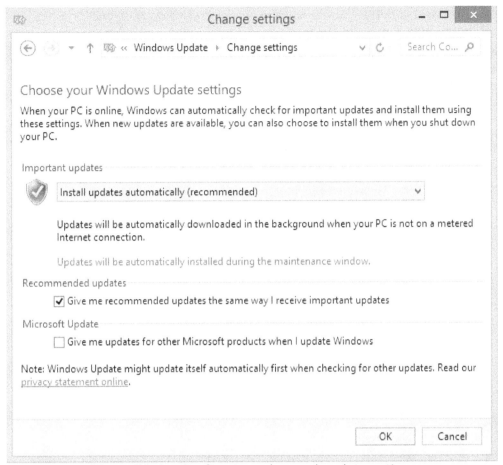

Figure 38.4 – Configuring advanced update options

In the update settings window shown in figure 38.4, we can choose between four different update options.

Install updates automatically (recommended):- With this option the updating process is entirely automatic. Updates are downloaded and installed in the background. This is the option we recommend you choose. Some users disable automatic updates because they are worried about an update causing a problem with their system or some software or hardware component they have installed. While this does happen, it is uncommon. It is far more risky to leave your system without a security update.

Download updates but let me choose whether to install them:- If you prefer to check which updates are being installed before installing them, you can choose this option. Some power users prefer to do this, but for most ordinary users this is not necessary.

Check for updates but let me choose whether to download and install them:- With this option, Windows simply notifies you that there are updates available. Some users on slower internet connections prefer this option since they can postpone the downloading of updates until they are finished on the internet. Windows update is designed to download in the background and not interfere with your internet or computing session, so this option is not usually needed.

Never check for updates (not recommended):- If you choose this option, you need to manually check for updates on a regular basis. We do not recommend choosing this option.

At the bottom of the window there are two other significant options. Enabling "Give me recommended updates the same way I receive important updates" will allow Windows update to install recommend updates as well as critical updates. Recommended updates do not help protect you against hackers or malware but they do improve features of the operating system. We recommend you select this option.

Enabling "Give me updates for other Microsoft products when I update Windows" will allow Windows update to download and install updates for other Microsoft software, such as Microsoft Office.

38.3 – The maintenance window

New in Windows 8 is the "maintenance window". The idea of the maintenance window is so that updates can install at a time that suits you, so that your work-flow is not interrupted by your PC running more slowly as it updates itself. If you click on the blue text that reads "Updates will be automatically installed during the maintenance window" (as seen in figure 38.4), you can change the update window. Figure 38.5 demonstrates this.

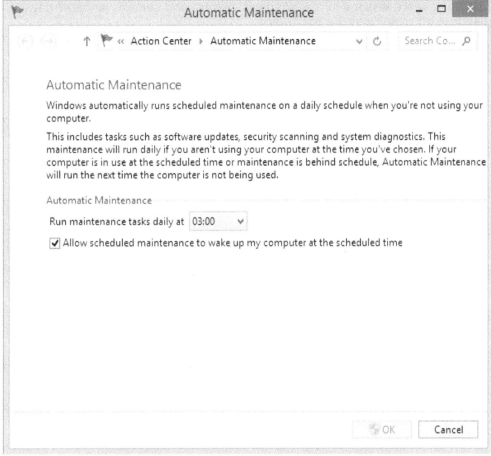

Figure 38.5 – Changing the maintenance window

In figure 38.5 we can see that computer maintenance is scheduled for 3:00 or 3 am. At this time Windows will install any pending updates. If your computer is turned off at this time, Windows will install the updates the next time it is turned on, which could result in updates being installed first thing in the morning if, for instance, your PC is normally off at the time shown. Change the maintenance time to a time that suits you. Perhaps you take a lunch break at mid-day, for instance, this would then be an ideal time to let Windows carry out any maintenance tasks.

When you are done changing update options, be sure to click on "OK" to save your changes.

That is all you need to know about keeping your Windows 8 PC up to date.

Just three more lessons in our Windows system and security chapter now, then it is on to some more fun topics.

Lesson 39 – Privacy options

Windows 8 has been designed to work with Microsoft's various online and cloud based services. This means that now, more than ever, you should carefully consider exactly what information you and your family put into your PCs. You should also keep in mind where you let that information end up and who you trust to safeguard it. In this lesson, we are going to take a brief look at the Windows 8 privacy options. Privacy options have been beefed up in Windows 8.1, with lots more options to help you keep your private information secure.

39.1 – Configuring privacy options

To access the privacy options, go to the Start screen and open up the Charms Bar. Click on the Settings Charm and then choose "Change PC settings". Now, from the options that appear on the left, click on "Privacy". The options shown in figure 39.1 should now be displayed.

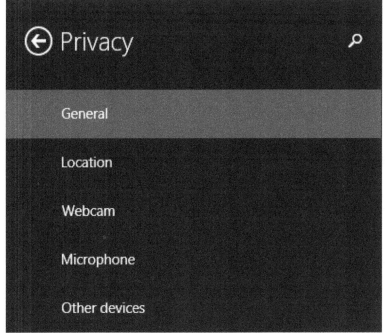

Figure 39.1 – The five categories of Privacy options

39.2 – General privacy settings

Click on the "General" option to access the general privacy options for a Windows 8 machine. Figure 39.2 shows the resulting options.

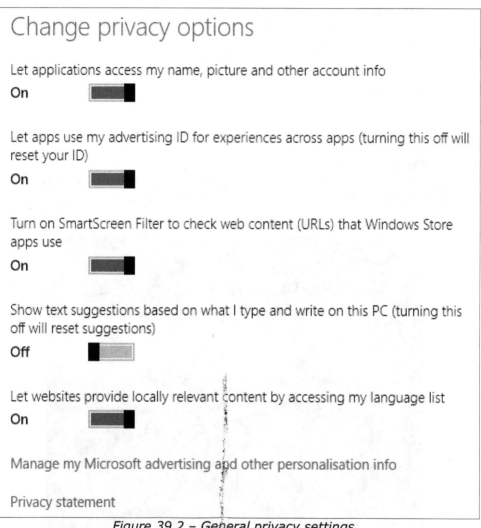

Figure 39.2 – General privacy settings

There are five options available under general privacy settings.

Let applications access my name, picture and other account info:-
Fairly self explanatory, this allows apps to use your name, account picture

and any information you have made public on your account, as you work with them. For instance, you could be using an app to post content to the internet. With this setting turned on, the app could then post your user name and account picture along with the content you post. If you use your own photograph for your account picture and don't want your mugshot appearing online, you can turn this option off, but usually it is pretty harmless.

Let apps use my advertising ID for experiences across apps:- Many app tiles on Windows 8 are supported by ads. By leaving this setting on, you let advertisers tailor the adverts more specifically to you, based on what you do with your Microsoft account. If you play Xbox games often, for instance, you may see more adverts for other games. If you consider this to be an invasion of your privacy, turn this setting off. You will still see ads in apps with this setting off, but they won't use this extra data to tailor them to you.

Turn on SmartScreen Filter to check web content (URL's) that Windows Store apps use:- This option extends Internet Explorer 11's smart screen filter to also inspect any download content that might appear in a Windows Store app. Usually this is a good idea, since it can stop an app from downloading data from some malicious internet sites. This does mean anonymously submitting which pages the app is visiting to Microsoft for analysis however.

Show text suggestions based on what I type and write on this PC:- With this option on, Windows will store some information based on what you type into the PC and use it to tailor web-search results. If you find the automatic web searches that take place and appear when you search your PC for apps or files intrusive, turn this option off.

Let websites provide locally relevant content by accessing my language list:- This is, in basic terms, a long winded way of saying "can a website look at my language list to see what country I am in?". Even with this option off, websites you visit have other ways of determining a rough geographic location for their visitors.

Finally, you can view your Microsoft advertising preferences (these affect all the Microsoft services you use with your account) and view Microsoft's privacy policy in full by using the links at the bottom of the screen.

39.3 – Location privacy settings

Select "Location" from the menu shown in figure 39.1 to view the location privacy settings. Figure 39.3 shows these options.

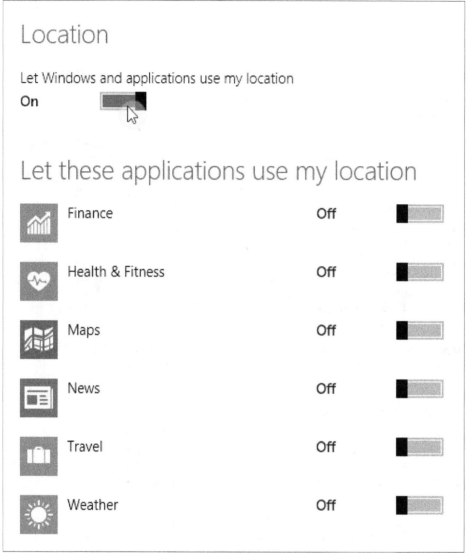

Figure 39.3 – Location privacy options

There are a number of options here, the most important one is the first one.

Let apps use my location:- This is mainly for portable PCs with GPS devices, but it can apply to other computers too. Even without a GPS, you can establish a rough geographical location by checking the computer's internet connection. With this option turned on, apps will be able to query and use your location. Perhaps you are on the road and have an app which recommends nearby restaurants, with this setting enabled the app could know where you are and point out somewhere nearby to eat. Of course, having the apps on your PC know exactly where you are can also be a privacy concern, perhaps an app might leak out your location onto the public internet somehow. Turn this option off if you prefer to keep where you're travelling secret.

In Windows 8.1, you can enable or disable location information on a per-app basis. So for instance if you had downloaded an app that requested to know your location for no good reason, you could deny the app while still allowing the apps you trust to use your location.

Under "Let these applications use my location", you can see which apps are allowed to use your location. When a new app is installed, this setting will be set to "Off" automatically. The first time an app wants to use your location, Windows will ask you for permission. If you deny an application permission and change your mind, you will need to access these settings to change the permissions.

39.4 – Webcam, Microphone and Other devices

The Webcam, Microphone and Other Devices options work in the same way as the Location settings. Just like with your location, apps must ask permission to use your Webcam and your Microphone and you can restrict individual apps from using these devices as you see fit. The "Other devices" section can control access to special hardware and will be empty on most PCs.

39.5 – Desktop software and privacy

Remember that these settings apply to tile applications only. Desktop software can ignore these settings and spyware that runs in desktop mode will not pay any attention to how you configure your privacy settings here. To help combat against spyware, we will be looking at the new improved Windows Defender in lesson 41. We also discuss other PC privacy related issues on Top-Windows-Tutorials.com, see http://www.top-windows-tutorials.com/PC-Privacy.html

Lesson 40 – Windows Firewall

 The job of a firewall is to monitor and restrict the internet traffic flowing in and out of your computer. There are two types of firewall that home users typically use. Software firewalls, like the Windows 8 firewall, are programs that run on your computer. Hardware firewalls are physical items that plug between your internet connection and your PC. Typically home users will buy a router with an inbuilt firewall. We discuss this in lesson 52.

40.1 – About the Windows 8 firewall

The Windows 8 firewall provides a basic level of protection against hackers and malware. To access the firewall settings, search for "windows firewall" on the Start screen and click on the "Windows Firewall" icon that then appears. Figure 40.1 shows the window that will then appear.

Figure 40.1 – The basic configuration window for the Windows Firewall

In Windows 8, there are two types of network configuration you might typically connect to. Private networks and Guest or public networks. Private networks are networks like your network at home, where you can reasonably trust most people and devices using the network, as long as you have secured your internet connection of course.

Guest networks are networks where you cannot be certain of security, for instance a public Wi-Fi access point. Using Guest networks is more risky, since they are open to attack or interception from other users in range or could be controlled by hackers or malicious users themselves.

In figure 40.1 we can see that for "Private networks", Windows Firewall is on (Windows Firewall state: On). We can also see that incoming connections will be blocked unless the program is on the list of allowed programs.

Our wired network, called "Network" is listed next to "Active private networks". Looking below to "Notification state" we can see that if Windows Firewall blocks a program it will notify us.

To view settings for Guest or public networks, click on the downward pointing arrow button next to "Guest or public networks". Figure 40.2 shows the resulting window.

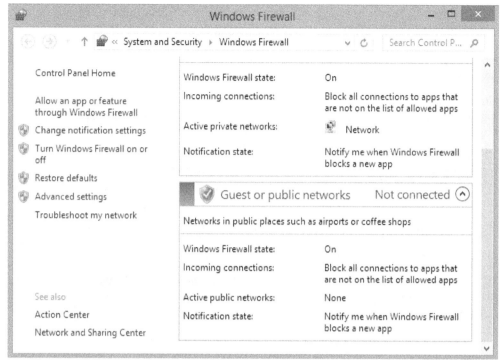

Figure 40.2 – Viewing the public network settings for Windows Firewall

By default, the basic settings for public networks are exactly the same as for private networks. One of the advantages of the Windows 8 firewall for power users is the fact that the firewall can be configured for different network connections. So, if you connect to your office via a virtual private network, but you have a network at home, you are not restricted to one firewall configuration for them both.

40.2 – Changing firewall settings

To change firewall settings, click on "Change notification settings" from the options on the left. Figure 40.3 shows the window which now appears.

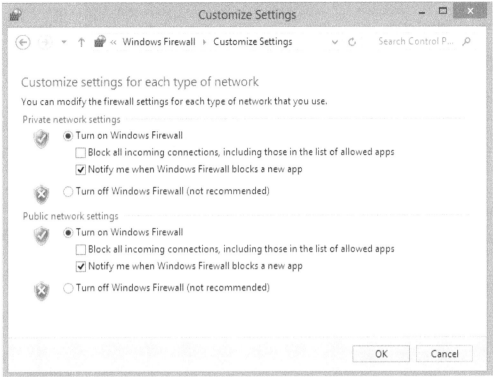

Figure 40.3 – Customising basic firewall settings for each type of network

From this window we can tweak the firewall settings for each connection type. We might decide to block all incoming connections when we are on a public network and doing so does not affect our settings for our private network.

It is also possible to turn the Windows Firewall off entirely, by selecting the option next to the red shield icon. We do not recommend turning the firewall off unless you have a third party firewall to use instead, but it might occasionally be necessary for troubleshooting purposes.

When you are done changing settings, click on "OK". You will then be returned to the previous window.

40.3 – Windows Firewall with Advanced Security

You may notice another icon while working with your PC or following this tutorial for something called **"Windows Firewall with Advanced Security"**. Clicking on this item will open up some advanced settings for the

Windows Firewall. We can also access these same advanced firewall settings simply by clicking "Advanced settings" from the options on the left in figure 40.1. The advanced settings are really only for IT experts and so we won't be covering them in this Superguide.

40.4 – Third party firewalls

The Windows 8 firewall lacks many of the features of the more advanced third party firewalls. Firewalls such as ESET Personal Firewall, Zone Alarm and Outpost firewall include individual program control and easy to configure outgoing connection protection amongst other features. Is this extra protection necessary? It is debatable, but many users prefer a third party firewall over the Windows Firewall, even in Windows 8. Figure 40.4 shows a typical third party firewall alert.

Figure 40.4 – A typical third party firewall alert message

In the picture, we can see that individual programs need to ask for access to the internet. This is true in many third party firewalls. In this system, a malicious program should be intercepted before it could send out any information from your computer. You will see similar alerts from Windows Firewall under certain circumstances too. If you are considering a third party firewall, be sure to visit Top-Windows-Tutorials.com for information on our recommended firewall software packages.

That concludes our lesson on the Windows Firewall. You are becoming quite the security expert now. Next lesson we will finish our chapter on system security by discussing the new Windows Defender software.

Lesson 41 – Windows Defender

 Windows 8 is the first version of Windows to come with an antivirus solution pre-installed. While Windows Defender was present in previous versions of Windows, in Windows 8, Windows Defender includes anti-virus capabilities too, while the older versions simply focused on anti-spyware. In this lesson we will take a brief tour of Windows Defender.

41.1 – What is antivirus software?

Computer viruses are computer programs, (just like everything else that runs on your PC). What makes computer viruses different however is the fact that they are designed to copy themselves throughout your computer's memory or hard drive, or even across the internet. Many computer viruses have malicious components too and may try to cause all sorts of mischief from slowing down your computer to allowing hackers to gain entry and steal confidential data.

Antivirus software is designed to watch for these particular rogue programs and stop them from running and causing whatever brand of mischief they were written for. Historically, Windows has not had the best track record when it comes to security, though this reputation is slowly changing thanks to Microsoft's hard work in this area. Windows is also the most commonly used operating system around the world and this has established it as the favourite target of computer virus designers.

41.2 – Starting Windows Defender

Windows Defender is automatically enabled and doesn't generally need any reconfiguration. It will start with your PC and work in the background. If you need to access the programs interface for any reason, simply search for "windows defender" from the Start screen and then click the icon that appears. Figure 41.1 shows the main Windows Defender window.

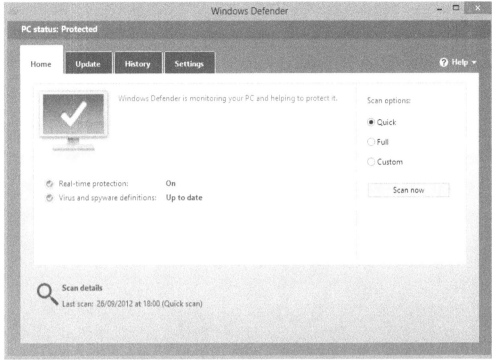

Figure 41.1 – Windows Defender

Figure 41.1 shows Windows Defender running normally. We can see that real time protection is enabled and virus and spyware definitions are up to date. New virus definition updates, which contain updated information about new malware, will download with Windows Update (see lesson 38). To change settings for the program, click on the "Settings" tab. Figure 41.2 shows the available options under the settings tab.

Figure 41.2 – Windows Defender options

41.3 – Windows Defender Options

There are only a few settings you need to be aware of in Windows Defender. Occasionally anti-virus programs will falsely identify a program as malicious when it is not. In this case, you can add an exception by going to the "Excluded files and locations" option (second from top). Figure 41.3 illustrates this option.

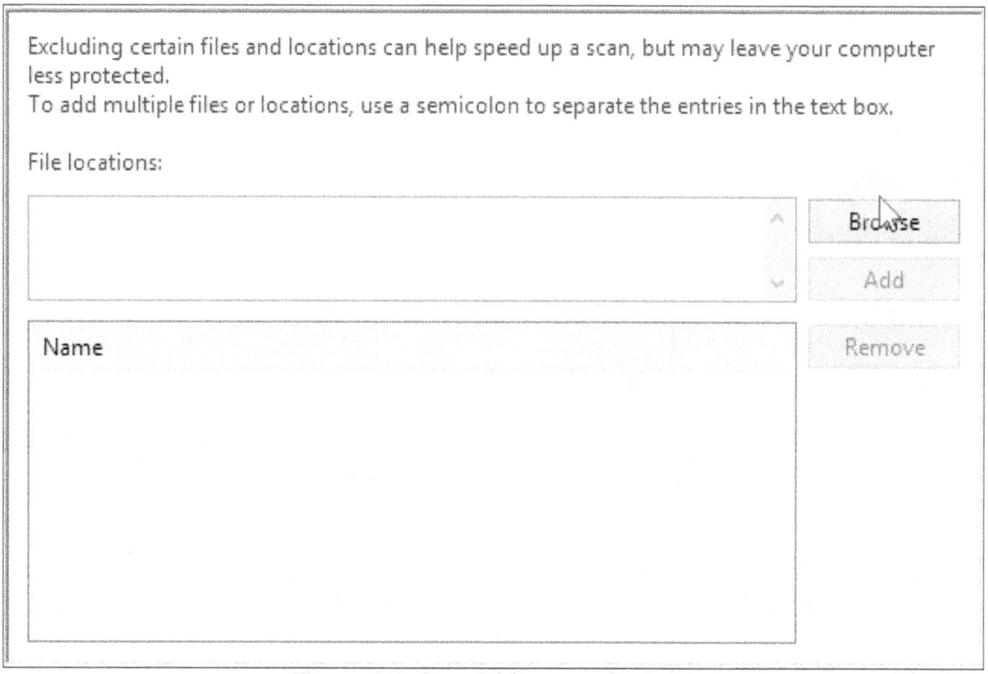

Excluding certain files and locations can help speed up a scan, but may leave your computer less protected.
To add multiple files or locations, use a semicolon to separate the entries in the text box.

File locations:

	Browse
	Add

Name | Remove

Figure 41.3 – Adding exclusions

Click on "Browse" and then simply browse to the directory where your file is stored. You can add individual files or folders to the exclusions. Be careful doing this, any files you exclude will not be checked for any kind of malware. Do not assume a detected file is a false positive unless you're absolutely certain.

The second option that you may want to reconfigure is the "MAPS" option. This option can be seen second from bottom in Figure 41.2. MAPS stands for "The Microsoft Active Protection Service". This service sends information about detected malware on your machine to Microsoft. This data is then used to help improve Windows Defender for everyone. You can choose between "I don't want to join MAPS", "Basic membership" and "Advanced membership".

Advanced membership sends more information to Microsoft, although no personally identifying information should be sent. There's always a slim chance that some information may be leaked along with the virus samples submitted, so keep this in mind when choosing the options.

41.4 – Manually scanning your computer

Windows Defender can run a manual scan of your system at any time, just as with most other antivirus packages. Scans are started from the Home tab. In figure 41.1 you may be able to make out the scanning options on the right, they are "Quick", "Full", and "Custom". Quick scan scans the areas on your PC most likely to be targeted by malware, "Full" scans all areas on your PC, except removable devices and "Custom" allows you to choose exactly where to scan. Custom scan can be useful if you want to scan some media that a friend or colleague gave to you, for instance.

Choose a scan type and then click on "Scan now". If you choose Custom scan you will then be required to choose the drives or locations you want to scan. Otherwise, you will be sent straight to the window shown in figure 41.4.

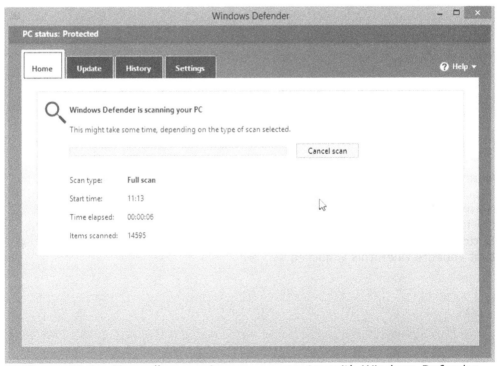

Figure 41.4 – Manually scanning your computer with Windows Defender

The scanning process may take some time, particularly for a full scan. When the scan is complete, you will see the window shown in figure 41.5 if any malware was found.

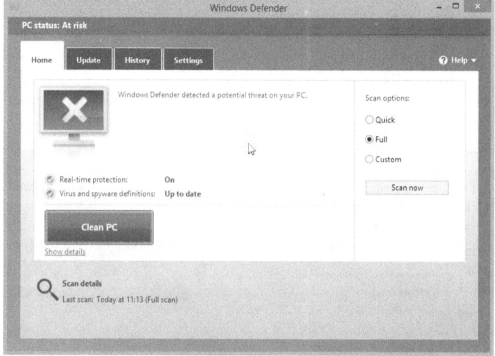

Figure 41.5 – A threat was detected on the PC

Notice how the Windows Defender window in figure 41.5 has turned red, to indicate an active threat on your PC. Actually the program has found the harmless 'trojan simulator' that we placed on the PC as an example. To clean the infection automatically, click on the large "Clean PC" button. Below the button there is a link labelled "Show details". Figure 41.6 shows the window that appears when this is clicked.

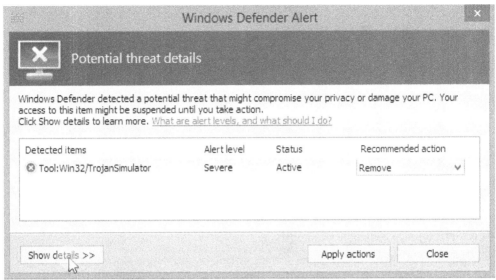

Figure 41.6 – Viewing detected threats

From the window shown in figure 41.6 we can see each individual threat and the recommended action to take to remove it. By clicking one of the detected threats in the list and then clicking on "Show details >>" you can see exactly where the threat was found on your PC. By changing the option under the "Recommended action" column, you can choose either "Remove" or "Quarantine". If you quarantine an infection, it is removed from your PC and stored in a special virus vault where it cannot do any more harm to your system, but you can inspect it. Quarantine is useful for any files you suspect might be false positives, or if you are an expert user and you want to preserve the file for further investigation without risking the security of your PC. You can view any quarantined items by going to the History tab on the main Windows Defender window.

Click on "Apply actions" to remove or quarantine the detected threats from the Window shown in figure 41.6, or simply close the window and use the "Clean PC" button shown in figure 41.5.

41.5 – Automatic scanning

Of course, you don't need to run a scan to detect malware, Windows Defender can detect it in real time. When Windows Defender detects an intrusion, it will notify you immediately. Figure 41.7 shows the notification that will appear.

Malware Detected
Windows Defender is taking action to clean
detected malware

Figure 41.7 – A Windows Defender notification

If you see this notification, don't panic, you don't have a virus, Windows Defender has protected you against one. You can open the programs interface and go to the History tab to get more details about what was detected and removed.

41.6 – Third party antivirus packages

It is great that Windows 8 comes with antivirus software right out of the box, but many users still prefer to use a third-party solution. Third party solutions may integrate other security features too, such as advanced firewalls, web content filtering or e-mail protection. There are dozens of third party antivirus packages available on the market. Some are free, others require a yearly subscription. Traditionally the free antivirus packages have provided a reasonable level of protection, whereas the better paid-for solutions have had better detection rates and less of an impact on system performance. Of course, results vary widely. You can find tutorials for several recommended antivirus packages on our website at http://www.top-windows-tutorials.com/Computer-Viruses-Tutorials.html. AV Comparatives regularly test several anti virus packages, you can find their website at http://www.av-comparatives.org/

Here are a couple of pointers to keep in mind when choosing an antivirus solution.

Avoid little known antivirus packages that use flashy advertising:- There are dozens of fake antivirus packages available through the internet. These packages claim to clear viruses from your computer but actually are a huge security risk in themselves and are often exceptionally difficult to remove. Do not install antivirus software unless you are sure it is legitimate.

Expensive and popular does not always mean the best:- Two of the most popular antivirus solutions, Norton Antivirus and Mcafee have in the past been outperformed by free alternatives such as Avast.

Free is not necessarily bad:- Free antivirus packages like Avast can provide good protection and additional features above and beyond what Windows Defender offers.

That concludes this lesson and also this chapter on computer security. Now that your bits and bytes are secure, we can move on to more exciting topics like customizing your PC and installing new software.

Chapter 8 – Your PC your Way

It will not be long before you want to add your own personal touch to your computer, be it adding some new software or changing the look of the desktop or the Start screen. This chapter is all about making your computer uniquely yours. Yes, it is finally time to leave boring old security behind and have some fun with your new Windows 8 machine!

Lesson 42 – Customising the mouse

 If you have been experiencing difficulty using a mouse (or touch-pad) with your Windows 8 PC, this lesson shows you some ways that you can change the behaviour of the electronic rodent in order to make it easier to use.

In Windows 8.1, there are actually two places you can tweak mouse settings. If you search for "Mouse" on the Start screen and click the first option that appears, you will be taken to the Mouse & Touchpad configuration settings on the tile interface. However, there is a more in-depth mouse configuration tool we can access. To get to it, open the Control Panel and search for "mouse", then click on "Change mouse settings". The window shown in figure 42.1 will then appear.

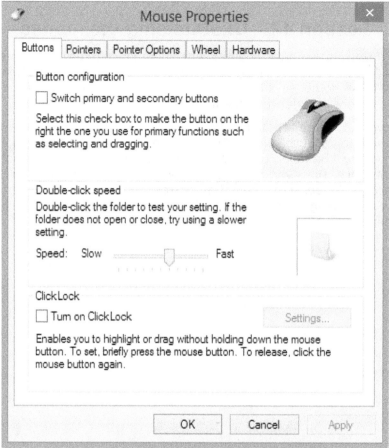

Figure 42.1 – The Mouse Properties window

42.1 – Left handed use and other button options

If you are left handed and place the mouse at the left of the keyboard, you may find it easier to switch the primary and secondary mouse buttons. This makes the mouse much easier and more natural to use if you are a left handed user. Just remember that when this guide talks about 'right clicking', it is referring to the mouse in the default configuration.

To switch primary and secondary (left and right) mouse buttons, select the box labelled "Switch primary and secondary buttons".

If you have issues with double clicking, you can change the double click speed using the sliding control in the middle of the window. If you make the double click speed too slow you may end up double clicking by accident, so be sure to try out your new setting on the practice folder on the right.

If you find dragging icons difficult, you can use "ClickLock". With this setting, you only need to hold down your mouse button for a second to "lock" it down, then hold it for a second again to release it.

Don't forget to click "Apply" when you are done changing the options.

42.2 – Pointers and pointer options

If you have difficulty seeing the mouse pointer, it is possible to choose a larger pointer scheme. Firstly, click on the "Pointers" tab at the top of the Mouse Properties window. Figure 42.2 shows the window which will then open.

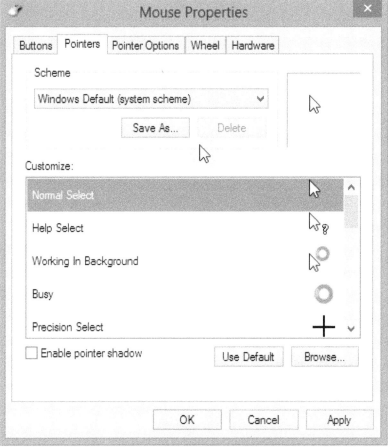

Figure 42.2 – Changing mouse pointers

Using the drop down box at the top of the window, you can choose from a range of Windows pointer schemes. Some, such as the extra large ones, are useful for people who have difficulty seeing smaller pointers.

If you like, you can customise each individual pointer by using the "Customise" box in the middle of the window. Click on a pointer type you want to change and then click "Browse..." to choose a new pointer or "Use Default" to reset the selection back to default.

Once you have chosen a pointer scheme, don't forget to click "Apply" to start using it. There are more pointer options you can configure on the "Pointer Options" tab. Figure 42.3 shows this tab.

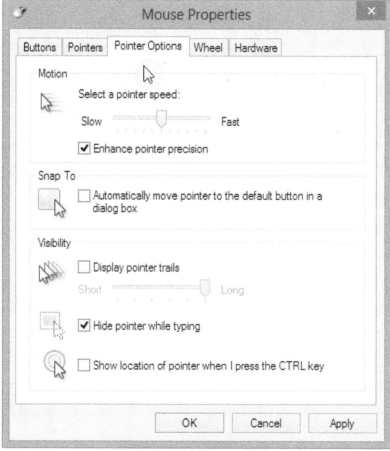

Figure 42.3 – Pointer options

If you find the mouse pointer moves across the screen too quickly, you can adjust its speed using the sliding control under "Motion" at the top of the window. Changes you make on this control take effect immediately, so you can see for yourself if the new speed is more suitable.

The "Snap To" option below the Motion control makes the mouse pointer automatically jump to buttons in windows. This can save some time but beginners usually find this confusing, so we do not recommend this.

Under "Visibility", there are three options. Choosing "Display pointer trails" makes a trail follow your mouse pointer as you move it around the screen. The trail looks like a gang of other mouse pointers relentlessly pursuing the pointer as it cruises around the screen. This makes it easier for some users to spot the mouse pointer as it moves. You can also change the length of the trail by using the sliding control underneath the tick/check box.

Below the pointer trails option is the "Hide pointer while typing" option, this is fairly self explanatory, if you do not want the pointer distracting you while typing, make sure this option is enabled.

If you still have trouble spotting the mouse pointer, select the option "Show location of pointer when I press the CTRL key." The CTRL or Control key is the key in the bottom left and bottom right of the keyboard. It does not matter which one you use. When this option is enabled, a circle will appear around your mouse pointer when you press Control, helping you locate it on the screen.

42.3 – Mouse wheel options

Some mice have a wheel between their two buttons. If you are using a laptop with a touch pad or a mouse without a wheel this will not be relevant to you. If your mouse has a wheel, you can alter the behaviour of the mouse wheel on the Wheel tab. Figure 42.4 shows the Wheel tab.

Figure 42.4 – Setting options for the mouse wheel

If your mouse has a wheel, you can use the wheel to scroll up and down text in a document or web page. By default, one click of the wheel will scroll down three lines of text.

Some mouse wheels move left to right too, though these are rare and most only go up and down. If your wheel moves left and right, you can set the amount of characters to scroll with each click by changing the value in the bottom half of the window.

That concludes our lesson on mouse properties. Hopefully, if you have been struggling to master the mouse, this lesson will have made things a little easier for you. In the next lesson, we will discuss customisation options for tiles on the Start screen.

Lesson 43 – Customising Start screen tiles

In this lesson we will be looking at how to change and personalise the tiles on the Start screen.

43.1 – Rearranging tiles and groups

You will probably have noticed that when using your Windows 8 PC the tiles on the Start screen are arranged into groups. To move a tile between groups, just click and hold with your mouse, or hold with your finger on a touch screen and drag it wherever you like. To create a new group, you simply drag a tile to an empty space.

While you can't create sub-folders on the new Start screen, you can create and name groups. This is done slightly differently in Windows 8.1 Update 1. If you are running a touch screen PC, swipe up from the bottom of the touch-screen with your finger. A customise button will appear in the bottom right hand side of the screen. Tap on this button to enter customise mode. Figure 43.1 shows a typical Start screen in customise mode.

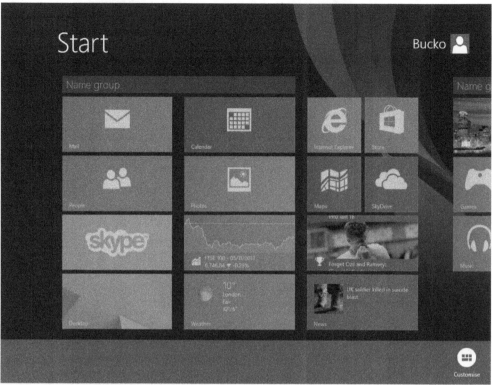

Figure 43.1 – Customising the Start screen

In customise mode you can move tiles around freely just by dragging them. To name a group of tiles, simply tap on "Name Group" above any group of tiles and then type any name you like. The group will now be named, you will see the name when you browse the Start screen. To remove a name from a group, repeat the process then simply tap and delete the old name.

To leave customise mode, simply click or tap on a blank area of the Start screen.

If you're using a keyboard and mouse, Microsoft have added a handy shortcut in Windows 8.1 Update 1. You can now rename groups simply by right clicking on a blank space on the Start screen and selecting "Rename groups".

Naming groups of tiles may make it easier to find them visually, but unfortunately you cannot search the Start screen for group names. For instance if you create a group called "My favourite desktop programs" then try to search for "My favourite desktop programs", Windows won't direct you to the group.

43.2 – Options for individual tiles

If you tap on a tile while you are in Customise mode, an extra menu will open from the bottom of the screen. Figure 43.2 shows this menu.

Figure 43.2 – Options for individual tiles

Using the "Unpin from Start" button, you can remove a tile from the Start screen. If you unpin an app from the Start screen, it will still show up in a search. For instance if you were to unpin the Finance tile, then later decide you wanted it back, it is just a matter of searching for "finance" then selecting it (with a right click or finger swipe) from the search results and then choosing "Pin to Start".

The "Pin to taskbar" button can be used to make an app appear permanently on the taskbar, even when it is not running. Since Windows 8.1 Update 1, this works for both desktop and tile apps, and can provide a convenient shortcut to your most used programs.

The Uninstall button will only appear here for tile apps. Clicking on this button will remove an app entirely from your PC. To reinstall it you will need to re-download it from the App Store. We cover uninstalling both desktop and tile apps in lesson 60.

The "Resize" button can change the size of the selected tile. Have you noticed how some tiles on the Start screen are bigger than others? Tiles on the Start screen can have their sizes changed. There are four sizes, Large, Wide, Medium and Small. The Store tile we can see in figure 43.1, for instance, is set to large size. If you use a program often, you can set it to large or wide size so that you can find it quickly. Only live tiles (the tiles that cycle through different information on the Start screen) can be set to large or wide size, while tiles representing desktop apps can only be set to medium or small size.

The "Turn live tile off" (or on) button will only appear for apps that have a live tile. Turning the live tile off will change the tile to display a static icon type image.

Keyboard and mouse users can access these options from a handy context menu by simply right-clicking on any tile on the Start screen.

43.3 – Other Start screen options

There are several other options we can set for the Start screen. To access these options, open the Charms Bar and select the Settings Charm, then click on "Tiles". You will then see either two or three extra options, depending on your computers configuration. Figure 43.3 shows these options.

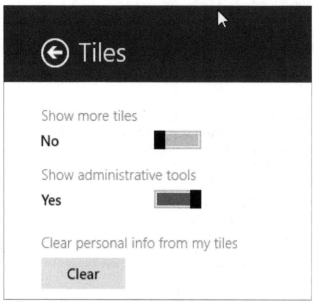

Figure 43.3 – Additional Start Screen options

Selecting "Show more tiles" will increase the number of tiles shown on the Start screen, making better use of available screen space, but potentially making your Start screen more cluttered. It is entirely up to you if you want to use this option. If you have a screen resolution of 1280x1024 or less you will not see this option.

Choosing "Show administrative tools" will add a whole set of new tiles to your Start screen which give you shortcuts to places on the Control Panel. Without this option on, you can of course still search for these tools when you need them.

Finally, clicking on "Clear personal info from my tiles" will reset any personal content on the live tiles. This is useful if you want to clear out snippets of a messenger conversation you'd rather someone else not see over your shoulder, for instance.

43.4 – Adding tiles from the desktop

If you have a program, shortcut or folder on your desktop or anywhere in File Explorer or Apps view and you want it to appear on the Start screen, you can easily pin it to the Start screen using the context menu. Simply browse to the item you want to use and then right click on it and choose "Pin to start".

That concludes this lesson. You now know all about adding, removing and customising tiles on your Start screen. In the next lesson we will look at some more personalisations that affect the look and feel of the Start screen.

Lesson 44 – Customising Start and Lock screens

In this lesson we are going to take a look at how you can add your own personal touch to the Start screen and a few other areas on your Windows 8 PC. To get started, go to the Start screen and open up the Charms Bar, then click on the Settings Charm. Now, click on "Personalise". Figure 44.1 shows the options that will then be displayed.

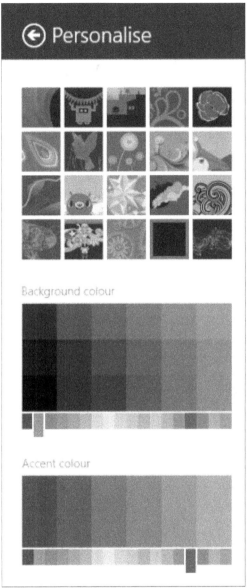

Figure 44.1 – Start screen personalisation options

44.1 – Start screen personalisations

Windows now shows you a selection of patterns, background colours and accent colours. To see what a background picture looks like, just click on it, the Start screen background will then instantly change.

For each picture, it is possible to choose a background colour and an accent colour. The accent colour affects the colour of the picture elements on the background picture. You can experiment with any colour combination you like. If you create something that looks ghastly, simply click again on the background picture you chose originally and the colours will reset.

If you don't like any of the default pictures that come with Windows, see Lesson 48.5. In this lesson you will learn a trick to put any picture you choose on your Start screen.

44.2 – Customising the Lock screen

There are several customisations you can do to the lock screen. The lock screen is the screen you see before you log into your PC. By default it will show a static image and a digital clock. To get started customising the lock screen, go to the Start screen and open up the Charms Bar, then click on the Settings Charm. Now, click on "Change PC settings". The PC settings menu will then open, choose the "PC and devices" option and then make sure "Lock screen" is selected. Figure 44.2 shows the screen you will now see.

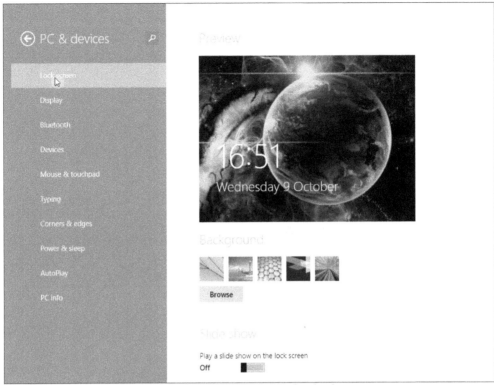

Figure 44.2 – Customising the lock screen

We saw how we could customise the lock screen image from within the Photos app in lesson 10.3. This customisation can also be done here too. Click on a picture thumbnail on this screen to set it as your lock screen picture. If you don't see the picture you want to use, use the browse button to browse anywhere on your PC for an image.

New for Windows 8.1 is the option to use a slide show for the lock screen. By scrolling the screen down and turning this option from Off to On, several new options are revealed. Figure 44.3 illustrates them.

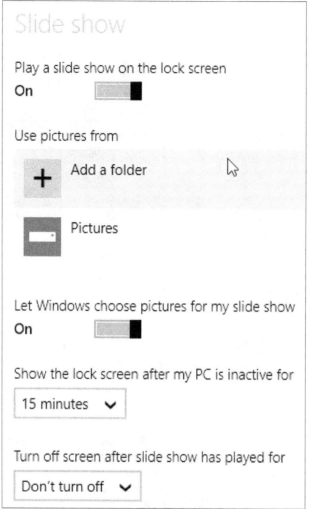

Figure 44.3 – Lock screen slide show options

For your lock screen slide show, you can either use your pictures folder or add a folder from anywhere on your PC. Using what you learned about File Explorer earlier in the guide, you could create a folder on your PC just for pictures you wanted to appear on your lock screen. Or, you can simply use the pictures folder.

By turning on "Let Windows choose pictures for my slide show" Windows will choose the pictures that fit best for the lock screen. If you'd rather just show all your pictures, turn this off.

Next, there is the option to automatically show the lock screen after a time interval. This can be good for security as it automatically locks your PC. It can also replace the legacy Screen Saver function we discuss in lesson 49. Strangely, this option is only available if we are using the slide show feature.

Finally, by using the last option we can opt to stop the slide show and turn the screen off after 30 minutes, an hour or three hours. This helps preserve battery life if your Windows machine is left dormant.

44.3 – Lock screen apps

By scrolling the screen down below the slide show options you can find the Lock screen apps options. Figure 44.4 shows these options.

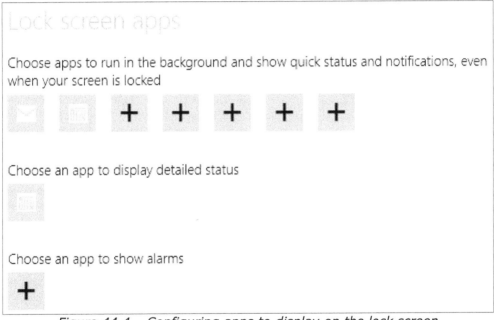

Figure 44.4 – Configuring apps to display on the lock screen

Certain apps can show notifications on your lock screen. This could be useful if, for instance, you wanted to see if you have received an e-mail while you were away from your PC. Click on one of the plus shaped icons shown in figure 44.4 to see a list of apps that can display information on the lock screen. You can also choose one app to show a "detailed status". Only certain apps are compatible with this setting.

New in Windows 8.1 is the option to use an app to "show alarms". Alarms typically play a sound and take over the entire lock screen for a moment. If you want to use your Windows 8 device as an alarm clock for instance, make sure to click the plus button in this section and choose the "Alarms" app so that your wake up call can appear on the lock screen. We will look at how to set the alarm at the end of the lesson.

44.4 – Lock screen camera

If you have ever used an iOS device such as an iPhone or iPad, you may be familiar with the way you can quickly snap a picture without having to unlock your device. This option is now available in Window 8 too. If you want to be able to access your devices camera from the lock screen, make sure the "Use camera from the lock screen" option, available at the very bottom of the lock screen options, is turned on.

44.5 – Setting an alarm

As we saw earlier in the lesson, Windows 8.1 allows alarms to sound on your lock screen. To set an alarm, search for "Alarms" on the Start screen and click on the tile that appears. Figure 44.5 shows an example of setting an alarm in the Alarms app.

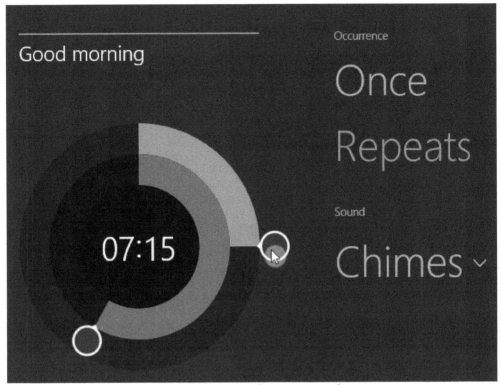

Figure 44.5 – Configuring an alarm

To turn an alarm on, click the bell button at the bottom (not seen in figure 44.5). You will now be able to configure the alarm by clicking on it. To set the alarm time, drag the two curved controls around, as seen in figure 44.5. The outer control changes minutes and the inner one changes hours. Change the Occurrence settings to set which days the alarm sounds and click the Sound option to hear different chimes. Click on the save button when you are done (the floppy disk icon in the very top right of the screen). You can add another alarm by clicking on the plus button in the top right hand corner of the Alarm app's window.

That's all there is to personalising the Start screen on Windows 8, in later tutorials, we'll look at personalising the desktop too. Remember if you use your Microsoft account to login then many of these settings will be synchronised across any Windows 8 machines you use.

Lesson 45 – Notification options

Windows 8 is the first version of Windows to introduce a standard notification system. Now all programs, desktop and tile, can send you notifications (those small pop-up messages) in a unified manner. In this lesson we will investigate the notification options.

45.1 – Accessing notification options

To view or change the notification options, open up the Charms Bar and then select the Settings Charm. Next, choose "Change PC Settings". The PC Settings menu will then appear. From the menu, click on "Search & apps". Now, make sure that the "Notifications" option is selected. Figure 45.1 shows the notification options open on a Windows 8 PC.

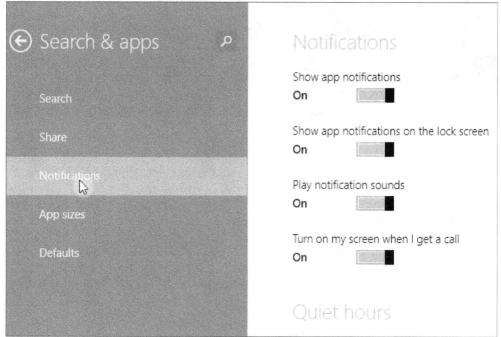

Figure 45.1 – Notification options

Using the topmost option we can toggle notifications on or off entirely. If you turn this option off you may miss notifications from your applications. Remember that if you want to temporarily disable notifications you can do so from the Settings Charm, we showed you how in lesson 5.2.

The second option determines if notifications are shown on the lock screen. Notifications may contain snippets of IM conversations, for instance, so you might want to avoid having them appear on the lock screen if other people might see your PC when it is locked, but it's entirely up to you.

Using the third option you can enable or disable sounds for your notifications. You cannot change the sound the notification makes, however.

The fourth option enables Windows to turn your PCs screen back on if you get a call. If you use a service like Skype for instance, you can have the PCs screen light up to let you know there's an incoming call. This option doesn't work if your PC is powered down completely.

45.2 – Quiet Hours

New for Windows 8.1 is the "Quiet Hours" option. The idea of the Quiet Hours option is so that you can stop notifications appearing and disturbing you when you're asleep, for instance. By default, this quiet spell is between midnight and 6am, though using the controls on this screen you can change it to any time you like. You can also opt to ignore any incoming calls in the quiet hours too.

45.3 – Notification settings for individual applications

By scrolling the screen shown in figure 45.1 downwards, you can see the notification settings for individual applications. Figure 45.2 illustrates this.

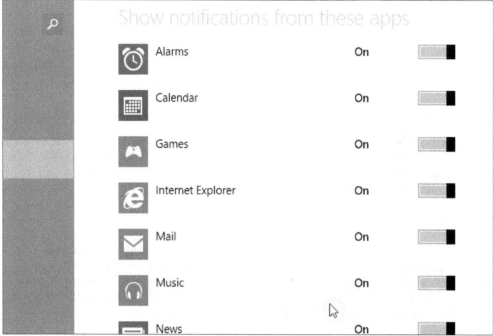

Figure 45.2 – Notification settings for individual apps

Every application that is registered to send notifications will appear here. As time goes by more applications will start to use the Windows 8 notification system. If you are not interested in notifications from certain apps, you can turn them off here. On my desktop PC, for instance, I normally turn off notifications from the mail application. This is because I use an e-mail program designed for desktop PCs rather than the e-mail tile, so I'm not interested in notifications from that application.

That is really all there is to managing notification settings in Windows 8. In the next lesson we will be looking at adding new desktop applications to the computer. While the tile software can be useful, it is desktop software that really shows off the power of your PC. This is especially true if, like most users, you are using a traditional PC with a mouse or pointing device and a keyboard.

Lesson 46 – Installing new desktop software

Windows 8 is compatible with a huge amount of software. Whatever you want to do on your computer, chances are there is an application out there to do it. Typically there are three ways you might purchase or acquire new software. You can use the store tile to purchase (or download for free) Microsoft approved software directly to your PC. We cover the store tile in lesson 11. You can also purchase desktop software on a CD or DVD disc from a retail store, or as a download from an internet website. All the methods have advantages and disadvantages. The Microsoft store offers a good selection of pre-approved software for your Windows 8 PC, but software you can buy there is limited to what Microsoft approves. Many developers are unwilling to work directly with Microsoft to have their applications officially certified, preferring the more open nature of the traditional Windows desktop. Digital downloads from the internet can be very convenient, but owning a physical disc gives you a backup copy of your software and license. Many industry analysts expect digital distribution to grow and physical distribution to decline, but it may be several years before we see the end of physical software sales entirely.

This lesson will concentrate on choosing and installing desktop software. While the tile software can be useful, it is desktop software that has the greatest power and flexibility. Desktop software is also usually optimised for traditional PCs with a keyboard and pointing device such as a mouse or trackpad.

46.1 – Choosing software

When choosing software for your Windows 8 PC, look carefully at the packaging or the website you are buying/downloading from. Look especially for the compatibility information on the packaging/website.

Software labelled as compatible with Windows 8 is guaranteed to work on your Windows 8 PC as long as your system meets the minimum hardware requirements as specified. Check the packaging or the website for details of this.

Almost all software that is labelled as compatible with Windows 7 will work with Windows 8. There are very few exceptions to this.

Almost all software that is labelled as compatible with Windows Vista will work with Windows 8 though there are a few exceptions. It's worth checking on the website or asking in store before purchasing.

Software which is labelled as compatible with Windows XP may work with Windows 8, but a significant number of titles will not work correctly or will need a compatibility update from the publisher. You may also need to use the compatibility options which we discuss in the next lesson.

Windows 8 is even compatible with *some* software designed for versions of Windows that pre-date Windows XP, though to take full advantage of Windows 8's features you should always look for a more recent version of the software if you are able to do so.

46.2 – Free software versus paid

There are a lot of fantastic free programs available on the internet, from Office applications to instant messengers and games. Many new computer users eye these freebies with suspicion. "There's no such thing as free!" or "There must be a catch!" they think. Well, a good deal of free software is both free and high quality. There are bad apples of course, software which installs spyware or other less welcome components is common. With a little research on the web you can eliminate these rogue applications and enjoy some really high quality free software. Don't forget to check Top-Windows-Tutorials.com for some great free software recommendations too.

46.3 – Starting installation from optical media

Installing most desktop software you buy pre-packaged from a store is just a matter of inserting the disc into a compatible drive. When you insert a CD or DVD with a Windows program on it, a notification like the one shown in figure 46.5 will usually appear.

DVD RW Drive (H:) DIRT3
Tap to choose what happens with this disc.

Figure 46.5 – Click or tap this notification to install software from a CD or DVD disc

By clicking on the notification, the window shown in figure 46.6 will appear.

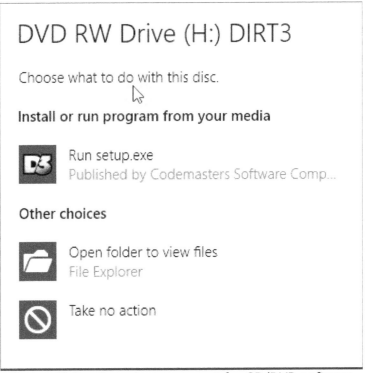

Figure 46.6 – An autorun prompt for CD/DVD software

Choose the option under "Install or run program from your media". In most cases the programs installation routine will then start. Some titles will run directly from the CD or DVD, but most will require installation to your computers hard drive. See your products accompanying documentation for more details.

If you miss the notification shown in figure 46.5, you can either eject and then re-insert your media or open Computer and locate the CD/DVD drive, right click on it and choose "Install or run program from your media".

46.4 – Installation examples

Software you download from the internet can usually be installed simply by opening your download folder in File Explorer and then double clicking on the downloaded program file. You need to be running an administrators account or have your administrator password available in order to install new desktop software. Care must be taken when installing new software from the internet, as less reputable sites often lace their downloads with spyware or viruses. Files you download from the internet are stored in your downloads folder, inside your personal folder. If you are not familiar with downloading files from the internet, we cover that in the next chapter.

Every program you download or install from a disc will have a slightly different installation process, though there are a couple of elements that are common throughout most software. Firstly, the end user license agreement (EULA). This is a wordy, legal document which explains your legal rights when running the software. For CD/DVD software this may be in the packaging, though usually it is displayed during the installation process.

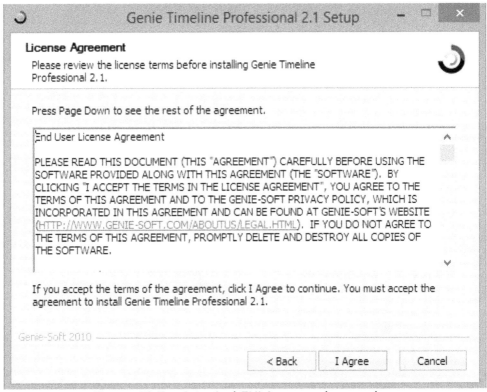

Figure 46.7 – A typical EULA, several pages long

An EULA is like the small print on a contract, we all know that we should read it but few of us do. However, you will not be able to proceed and install the software without indicating that you accept the terms and conditions in the EULA.

Most installers will also give you the option of changing the default installation directory. By default, programs will install to the program files folder on the C drive. However you can change this to be any folder on your computer if you wish. If you have used up all the space on your primary hard drive, you could install to a secondary drive for example. Usually, however, the default location is fine.

Many programs will ask you if you want to make desktop or Start menu shortcuts too. Windows 8 will put Start menu shortcuts on the Start screen, while desktop shortcuts will, of course, appear on the desktop. Finally, some software will offer to run as soon as your computer starts up. Remember that this will increase the amount of time it takes for your PC to start, so think carefully before allowing a program to do this.

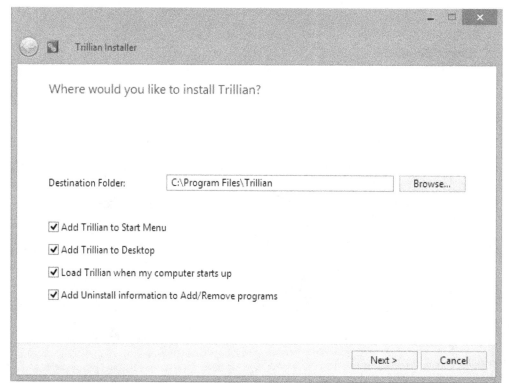

Figure 46.8 – Most software will allow you to change the default installation directory

Often, software will ask you if you want to install for all users. If you have multiple user accounts on your system and you want to make sure that all users have access to the software, select this option.

Increasingly, software you download from the internet may bundle additional components such as toolbars. In figure 46.9, the installer for the program "Trillian" is offering to install an additional browser toolbar.

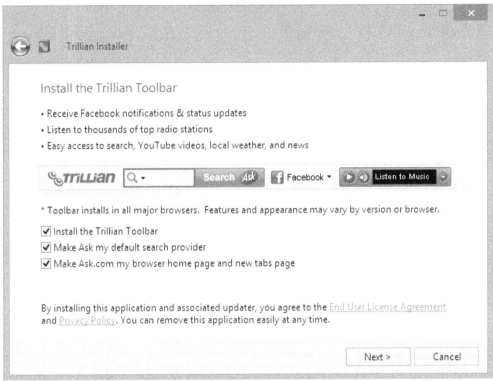

Figure 46.9 – Think carefully before installing additional components like this

While new browser toolbars like this can be useful in some instances, usually they are unnecessary. You do not need to install the toolbar offered in figure 46.9 in order to use the program, you can simply deselect the options and click on "Next >" to continue installing the software.

When the installation process is finished, the installer will let you know. Beginners are often caught out by the progress bars or meters in installers. Frequently they indicate that the installation is 100% complete before the installation is actually finished. Do not be tempted to close the installer if it stops on 100%, wait for it to complete and close on its own. You can then start to use your new software.

You now know how to add new desktop software to your Windows 8 machine! There are thousands, maybe even millions of useful programs for Windows machines for you to discover that go far beyond what's offered in the Windows store.

In the next lesson we will take a look at the Windows 8 compatibility options that can help run some older software.

Lesson 47 – Legacy software and compatibility

Operating systems, like everything else in the world of technology, keep evolving and improving. The unfortunate consequence of this is that certain older software will no longer work on more modern systems. To help with compatibility, Windows 8 has several compatibility mode options you can set for applications. This can often help older software to run on your new operating system.

Note – If you aren't having any compatibility problems with older software, you can skip this lesson.

47.1 – Windows 8 64-bit edition

Are you running a 64-bit version of your operating system? When you bought your computer or installed Windows 8, if you bought a system with a large amount of memory (RAM) you may have the 64-bit version pre-installed. The 64-bit version of the OS has better performance and can use more memory than is possible in the 32-bit version.

64-bit versions bring about a whole new range of compatibility problems however. Early versions of Windows ran software for 16-bit processors. This refers to the largest value the processor can work with in one go. On a 16-bit machine, that number is 65535. Clearly this was not going to be adequate for long, so way back in Windows 3.11, Microsoft began to move to 32-bit. In order to maintain compatibility with the programs designed for older processors, a special compatibility layer was added.

However, when running a 64-bit version of Windows, a new compatibility layer works to ensure that 32-bit applications can run and 16-bit applications are no longer supported. Although few users need to run 16-bit Windows applications from the pre-Windows 95 days any more, unfortunately lots of installers for older games and applications were actually 16-bit executables. This means that installing legacy software on 64-bit systems can be somewhat hit and miss.

Figure 47.1 – 16-bit applications will not run on 64-bit versions of Windows

If you ever see the window shown in figure 47.1, you have tried to run a 16-bit application on a 64-bit operating system. No amount of setting compatibility options will help you this time.

47.2 – Using compatibility options

If you are installing software from a CD or DVD and the installation process itself is failing, you might need to configure the programs installer to run in compatibility mode. To do this, insert the CD or DVD into your computer, but don't click on the notification. Now, open "Computer" from the Start screen and locate your CD/DVD drives icon. Right click on this icon and choose "Open". Figure 47.2 shows an example.

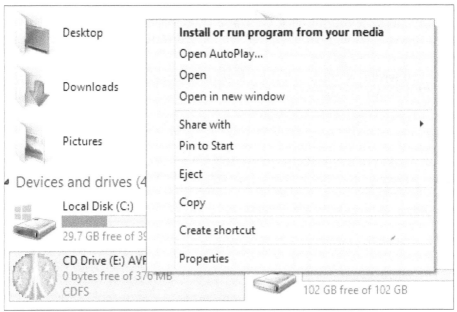

Figure 47.2 - Opening a CD/DVD to investigate the contents

File Explorer will now show the contents of the CD or DVD. In order to determine which file loads when the CD is started, we need to open a file called autorun.inf (which may appear as autorun). Locate this file in the File Explorer window and then right click on it. Choose "Open With..." from the context menu which then appears and then choose "Notepad" from the list of recommended programs. A Notepad window will then open showing the contents of the file. Figure 47.3 shows an example.

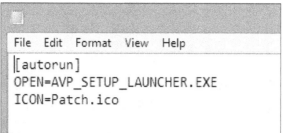

Figure 47.3 – The Autorun file shows us which file the computer opens when the CD or DVD is installed

In the example shown in figure 47.3, we can see that the file we need to work with is called "AVP_SETUP_LAUNCHER.EXE". Find this file in the File Explorer window and right click on it and choose "Properties" from the context menu (just like we did when we looked at folder properties in lesson 25).

The file properties window will then appear, choose the "Compatibility" tab, figure 47.4 shows an example.

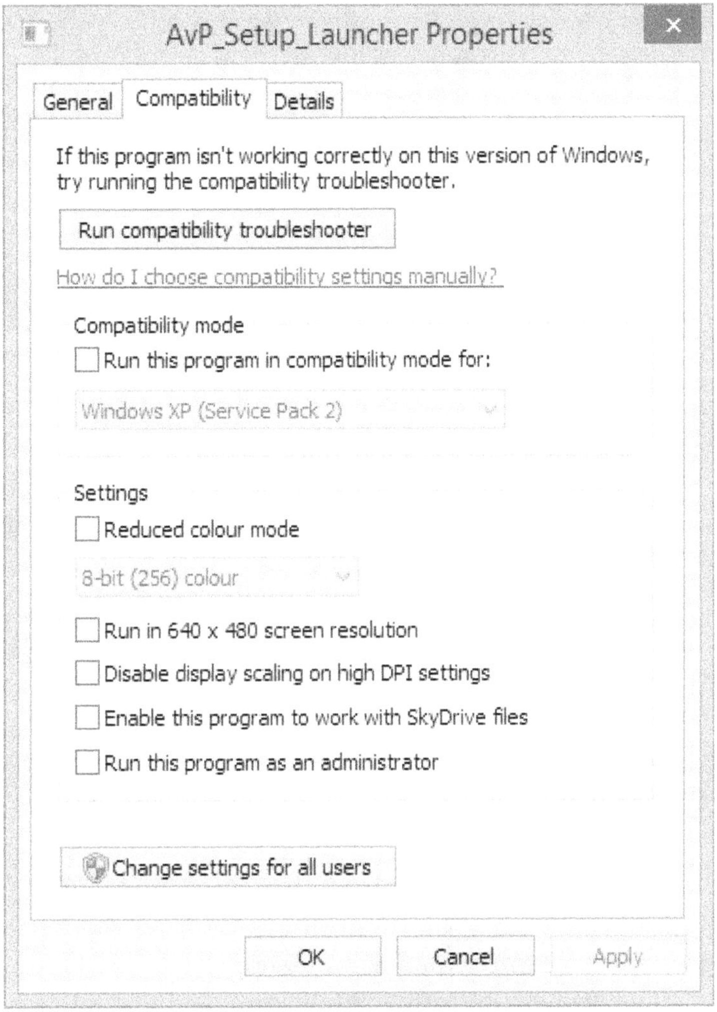

Figure 47.4 – Setting compatibility options

There are several options on this window. New for Windows 8 is the "Run compatibility troubleshooter" option. Using this option, Windows will try to determine the best compatibility settings for this program. You may want to try this first, before moving onto setting the compatibility options manually.

The most important compatibility settings are the "Run this program in compatibility mode for:" options and the "Run this program as an administrator".

When you select the box labelled "Run this program in compatibility mode for:" you can then choose the operating system the software was designed for. Check the programs packaging or instructions on the web for details of which option to choose.

Many older or badly programmed Windows programs also require that they be run as administrator. There are two ways to do this, the first way is to select the "Run this program as an administrator" option on this window. The other is to right click on the program icon and choose "Run as administrator" from the context menu. If you're launching the program from the Start screen, you can run as administrator by selecting the program with a right click or a finger swipe and then using the menu at the bottom of the screen. Keep in mind that when you run a program as administrator, it gives the software full control over your PC. Never run a program as administrator unless you fully trust it. If you are running a program like this from a standard user account, you will need your administrator password every time you start it.

There are several other compatibility settings that you can try in the middle of the window, although in our experience they rarely make any difference. The "Reduced colour mode" and the "Run in 640x480 screen resolution" options can be helpful for some very old (Windows 95/98 or even earlier) games software. If your old application appears wrong or distorted or has incorrect colours when it is running then choosing some of these options may help, but experimentation is required on a case by case basis.

There's one new option in Windows 8.1, that is the "Enable this program to work with OneDrive files" option. You can try this setting if the program can't see or open files in your OneDrive.

You can set compatibility options for any desktop program you run or install on your PC. Sometimes software will install correctly but fail to run. To set compatibility options for software you have already installed, simply search for the program on the Start screen and then right click on the icon and choose "Open file location". You will then be taken to a File Explorer window. Figure 47.5 shows an example.

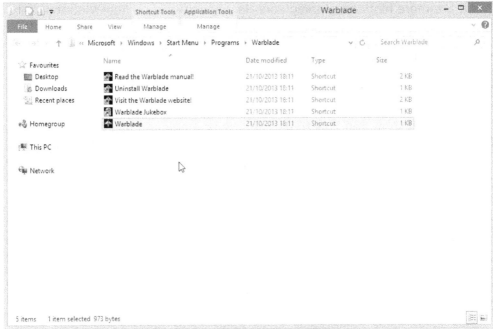

Figure 47.5 – Open file location has taken us to this folder, where we can work with the programs shortcut

Rather than take us directly to the programs folder, Windows has actually taken us to the location of the shortcut instead, but we can work just fine with the programs shortcut in this case. Select compatibility options by right clicking on the programs icon and choosing Properties, then selecting the Compatibility tab just like in 47.2 previously.

47.3 – My software still won't run

Setting compatibility mode options will not help in every case. Some programs simply won't run on Windows 8. There are several other things you can try when faced with a program like this. Firstly, check the publisher or developers web site, if you can find it. They may have issued an update or they may sell a new, improved and fully compatible version.

If that is not an option, you may be able to use virtualization software to install an older version of Windows, such as Windows XP. When you use this kind of software, a window appears on your desktop with an entire copy of Windows XP inside it, running just as it would do on a normal XP PC. However, virtualization is usually not suitable for multimedia or games software. We don't cover virtualization software in this guide.

There are more hints on running your legacy software on Top-Windows-Tutorials.com, visit http://www.top-windows-tutorials.com/windows-vista-compatibility.html to learn more. If you have an older game title you are struggling to get running, check out our new site http://www.play-old-pc-games.com , where you can find step-by-step instructions for running several popular old PC games, with more games added all the time.

That concludes this lesson on application compatibility options. In the next lesson we will show you how to personalise the look and feel of your desktop by changing your desktop backgrounds.

Lesson 48 – Changing the desktop background

If you are bored with the default background on your desktop then it's time to change your desktop background (also called desktop wallpaper). This fun little modification has always been popular and in Windows 8 it's really easy to do.

48.1 – Getting started with desktop backgrounds

To get started, open the desktop and then right click on a blank space on the desktop and choose "Personalise".

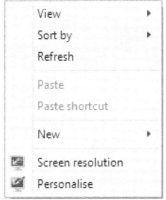

Figure 48.1 – The Personalise option is at the bottom of the context menu

The Windows 8 desktop theme manager will then open. See figure 48.2.

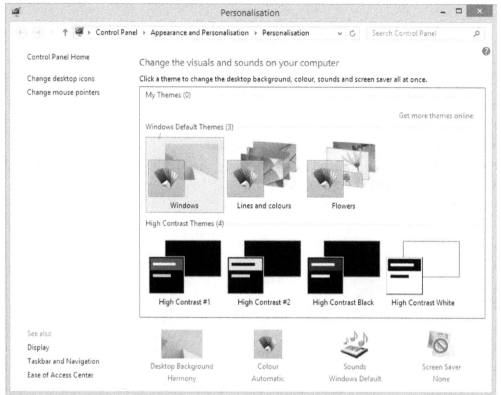

Figure 48.2 – The theme manager is under "Appearance and Personalisation" in the Control Panel and can also be accessed by right clicking on the desktop and choosing "Personalise"

To change desktop backgrounds, click on "Desktop Background" near the bottom left of the window. You will then be taken to the desktop background picture gallery. Figure 48.3 shows this.

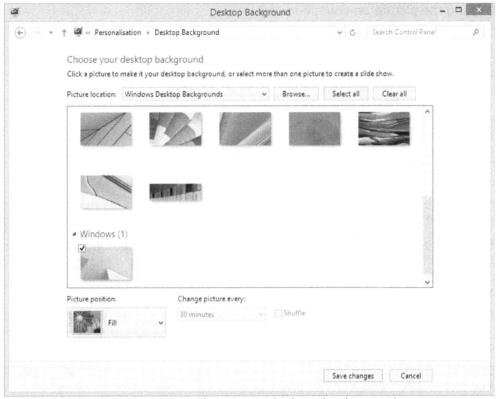

Figure 48.3 – Choosing a desktop background

Using the scroll control you can browse through a selection of pictures that come with Windows 8. To see what a picture looks like on the desktop, click on it once, then minimise this window if necessary. The picture should now be displayed on the desktop. Notice how in Windows 8, the colour of your windows changes to match the colours in the desktop background. We show you how to override this behaviour in lesson 50.2.

It is possible to use any picture stored on your computer as the desktop background. Near the top of the window is a drop-down box labelled "Picture location:". If a picture is in your personal pictures folder or your pictures library, simply select "Pictures Library". The gallery will now change to show pictures in your library (remember, we covered libraries way back in lesson 24). Now, choose a picture by clicking on it and it will appear on your desktop.

If for any reason you want to use a picture that is not in your pictures library or pictures folder, you can do so by clicking the "Browse..." button and locating the picture on your computer.

48.2 – Picture positioning options

Since both pictures and desktops come in a variety of sizes, most pictures will not fit exactly into the dimensions of a desktop. To compensate for this, we can choose how the picture is displayed. There are now five different ways to adjust desktop pictures. These adjustments only affect the desktop background as it is displayed, they do not change the actual image file on your computer. You can change the picture positioning options by using the "Picture position:" drop down box, which is near the bottom left of the window. The picture positioning options are as follows.

Fill:- Expands the image and crops the edges if necessary, so that it fits to the current screen resolution (desktop size).

Fit:- Keeps the pictures aspect ratio (the aspect ratio of an image is its width divided by its height, if this value is ignored when resizing a picture it can become stretched or distorted). Blank space or bars are placed at the top and bottom of the image, if necessary.

Span:- If you have two or more monitors connected, you will see this option. This will cause the current image to span across all of your monitors. This can look very impressive with panoramic pictures, for instance.

Stretch:- Expands the image to cover all of your desktop. Does not always maintain aspect ratio and can make photographs look distorted or out of proportion.

Tile:- Repeats the image across your desktop in a tile pattern, this only works with images smaller than your current desktop.

Centre:- Places the image in the middle of your desktop with blank space around it.

48.3 – Slideshow backgrounds

Just like in Windows 7, Windows 8 has a desktop background slideshow feature. When selecting a desktop background, in the top left hand corner of the picture thumbnail, there is a small box with a tick or check mark. Selecting this box includes the picture in your slideshow. If we do that for several other pictures a custom slideshow will then be created.

By using the drop-down box under "Change picture every:" we can specify how long it takes before one image transitions to another, while selecting "Shuffle" will make the pictures appear in a random order.

48.4 – Desktop backgrounds from the internet

We cover connecting to the internet in the next chapter, but if you are already connected then you may want to try this next technique. Lots of sites on the internet offer desktop wallpaper or desktop backgrounds for you to use. For this example we visited the BBC's Planet Earth website at http://www.bbc.co.uk/nature/animals/planetearth/wallpaper/ where a range of free animal themed wallpapers are available. Most websites that offer wallpaper downloads offer them in a choice of screen resolutions. You should choose the wallpaper that is closest to your screen resolution. You can find this by right clicking on the desktop and choosing "Screen resolution".

When you find a picture on the web that you want to use as your desktop background, simply right click on it and choose "Set as Background". Figure 48.4 shows this in Internet Explorer.

Figure 48.4 – Getting a desktop background/wallpaper from the internet

Alternatively, choose "Save picture as..." and place the picture in your pictures folder. You can then download several other pictures in the same way and create a slideshow with them.

48.5 – Desktop backgrounds on the Start screen

Here is a neat new trick that Windows 8.1 introduced, if you don't like any of the default backgrounds for your Start screen, you can set your desktop background to appear on your Start screen too. To do this, firstly right click on the taskbar and choose "Properties" from the context menu. Now, in the window that appears, click on the Navigation tab. Figure 48.5 shows the resulting Window.

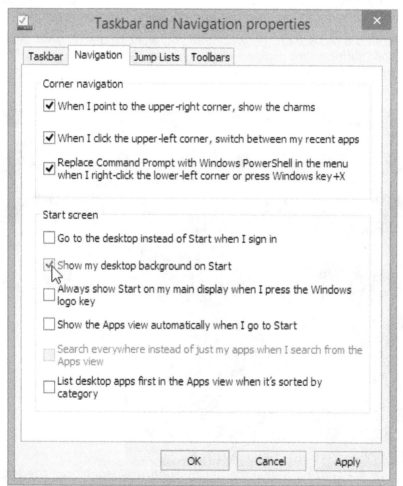

Figure 48.5 – Showing desktop backgrounds on the Start screen

Now choose the "Show my desktop background on Start" option and click

"OK". When you go back to the Start screen you will now see your desktop background has been applied to the Start screen background too.

That's all there is to changing desktop backgrounds or wallpapers in Windows 8. Give it a go yourself and have fun.

In the next lesson we look at another popular customisation, screen savers.

Lesson 49 – Changing screen savers

A screen saver is a pattern or animation that appears on your computer screen, over the top of your windows, after a period of inactivity. Screen savers were designed to change the image on the screen to protect monitors from "burn in". This can occur when static images are left on a screen for long periods of time. On modern monitors this problem has virtually been eliminated and in these days of increased environmental awareness, monitors that are left idle for long periods of time should really be turned off. Nevertheless, many users still find the screen saver an amusing distraction, something to make a coffee break more interesting perhaps!

49.1 – Windows 8 and screen savers

Windows 8 still supports screen savers, though there aren't any enabled by default. To get started, go to the desktop from the Start screen and then right click on the desktop and choose "Personalize", just like we did in the previous lesson. The theme manager will then open (see figure 48.2).

From the options displayed in the theme manager, choose "Screen Saver" in the bottom right corner. The following window will then appear.

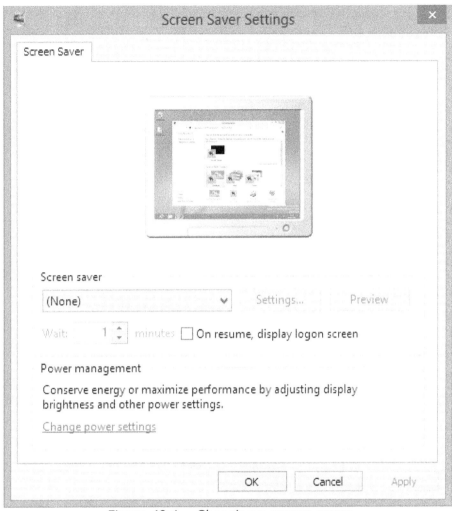

Figure 49.1 – Choosing a screen saver

Here you can choose from a range of screen savers that come with Windows. Choose one by using the drop down box near the middle of the window.

You can then see a preview of the screen saver you selected in the picture of a monitor on the top half of the window.

49.2 – Configuring screen savers

Some screen savers have extra options. For example the 3D text screen saver, which displays a message in 3D letters on your screen, can be configured to show a message of your choice. When a screen saver has extra settings like this, the "Settings..." button will become available. The settings will be different for each screen saver. Figure 49.2 shows the options for the 3D text screen saver.

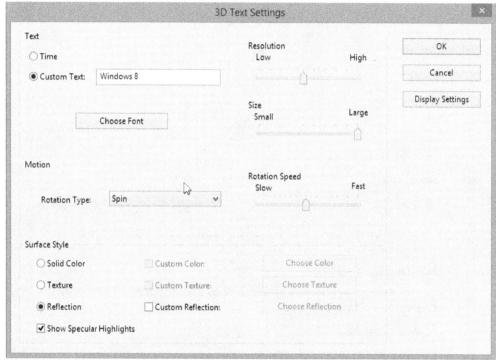

Figure 49.2 – Configuring the 3D Text screen saver

To configure the message shown when the screen saver is enabled, simply edit the text in the "Custom Text:" box. Click "OK" when you are done changing settings.

To see what a screen saver looks like at full screen size, click on the "Preview" button. You can see this button around the middle right of the window shown in figure 49.1. To exit from a screen saver, you normally just move the mouse, but on a small number of screen savers you need to press the Escape (Esc) key instead.

You can also adjust the amount of time before the screen saver starts by changing the value in the "Wait:" box. By selecting "On resume, display logon screen" you can make it so that you are required to login again when the screen saver exits. This can be useful for stopping other people using your PC while you are temporarily away from your desk.

49.3 – Downloading new screen savers

If you get bored with the screen savers that come with Windows 8, you can find new screen savers on the internet. We cover connecting to the internet in the next chapter, but if you are already connected, you may want to try out some new screen savers from the web. Be careful to download them only from reputable sites and always have an antivirus package running to avoid accidentally installing any malware.

WinCustomize.com is a great and safe site for obtaining new screen savers. For this example we downloaded a fiery screen saver from WinCustomize.com. The file was downloaded as a zip file. To use a screen saver it must first be copied outside of the zip file into a suitable location (e.g. your personal documents folder). Figure 49.3 shows a typical screen saver file ready for use.

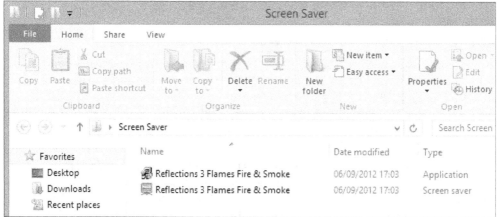

Figure 49.3 – Most screen savers are downloaded as zip files, double click a zip file to open it, then copy the contents to a suitable location

Once you copy the screen saver out of the zip folder, double clicking on it will either start an automatic installation utility or, in the case of this screen saver, it will preview it. Windows 8's new SmartScreen features will prevent you from automatically previewing most screen savers (and many other types of file that would have run automatically in Windows 7). See figure 49.4 for an example.

Figure 49.4 – SmartScreen filter will initially block most screen savers you download

This warning appears because screen savers have, in the past, been used to install malware. Enter your administrator password (if you are not running an administrators account) and click on "Run anyway" if you trust the download.

If you like the preview, you only have to right click the screen saver and choose "install" from the context menu. Make sure the screen saver settings window (figure 49.1) is closed before you try this. The screen saver will then be installed and selectable from your list of screen savers. To uninstall a screen saver, simply delete it from your computer.

Other screen savers you find on Wincustomize.com may install slightly differently, so check the download notes for more information. Remember that with some screen savers, you need to press the Escape key (Esc) to exit them.

You now know all you need to know to use screen savers on your Windows 8 PC. In the next lesson we will finish off our tour of Windows 8 desktop customizations by looking at themes.

Lesson 50 – Windows 8 desktop themes

Windows 8 themes let you quickly and easily customise several parts of the desktop with one quick click. Themes have been popular throughout the history of Windows. Windows 7 drastically improved theme support and Windows 8 improves on these features further still. In this lesson we will show you how easy it is to use desktop themes.

50.1 – The desktop theme manager

You have already seen the theme manager in the previous two lessons. To access it, simply right click on the desktop and choose "Personalise". The theme manager will then appear, just like you saw in figure 48.2. In figure 50.1 we can see the theme manager again, after setting the desktop background we demonstrated in the last lesson.

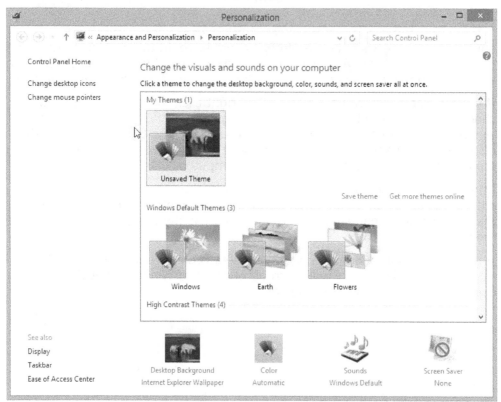

Figure 50.1 – The theme manager

In figure 50.1 we can see that the "Unsaved Theme" is selected. By choosing a new desktop background in the previous lesson, we have started to create our own theme. To choose another theme, simply click on it. There are three themes to choose from under "Windows Default Themes" and four under "High Contrast Themes".

When you change themes, you will see that the desktop background is instantly changed. Furthermore, the window colours are changed based on the theme and also the sound scheme is changed, though not all themes have associated sound schemes. Some themes have screen savers associated with them too, in which case they will be automatically applied, although the default Windows 8 themes do not include screen savers.

You can individually personalise all the components of the theme. This is done by clicking the icons at the bottom of the window, in exactly the same way as we showed you in the previous two lessons.

50.2 – Automatic colours

You might have noticed that when changing the desktop background, the colours of the windows changed too. This is a new feature in Windows 8 called Automatic Colour. When Colour is set to automatic, Windows will try to pick the window colours based on the current desktop background. If you want to change this behaviour, click on "Colour" near the bottom of the theme selector window. The window shown in figure 50.2 will then appear.

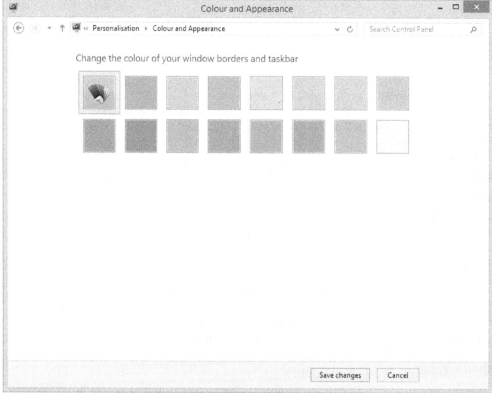

Figure 50.2 – Choosing theme colours

Use the window in figure 50.2 to choose the colour of your windows, simply click the colour of your choice or select the icon on the top left to use automatic colours. When you have picked your colour scheme, click the "Save changes" button at the bottom of the window.

50.3 – Saving themes

When you change theme elements, such as backgrounds or colours, Windows will name the theme "Unsaved Theme" and place it into the "My Themes" category at the top of the list. In figure 50.1, you can already see the "Unsaved Theme" at the top of the window. This is because we changed the desktop background in lesson 48. Click on the "Save theme" link next to the theme to save it on your computer. You can also right click on any theme you create and choose "Save theme for sharing", this will create a theme file package that you can then send to your friends or family.

50.4 – Downloading themes

What if you want to download more themes for Windows 8? As long as you are connected to the internet, you can click on the "Get more themes online" link near the top of the Personalisation window. This will open a web browser and take you directly to Microsoft's own theme gallery. Figure 50.3 shows this theme gallery open in Internet Explorer.

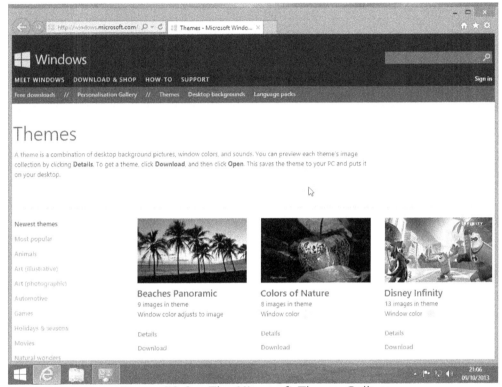

Figure 50.3 – The Microsoft Theme Gallery

Select a theme category from the left to view themes in that category. Below the themes title, the gallery tells you how many images it has in it. Themes with two images or more will change backgrounds automatically like a picture slide show. To download any theme just click on the "Download" link. Internet Explorer will ask you if you want to open or save the theme. Choose "Open" and the theme will be downloaded and applied automatically.

Certain third-party websites offer their own theme galleries and themepack files. If you download themes from other sites, remember to download them only from reputable sites and always have an antivirus package running to avoid accidentally installing any malware.

That concludes this lesson and our lessons on the theme manager. If you are still hungry for more customisation tips, visit http://www.top-windows-tutorials.com/Windows-skins.html where you can find out even more ways to customise your PC.

Lesson 51 – Devices and Printers

 As well as great support for a huge range of software, Windows also supports a massive range of hardware too. When choosing new hardware to use with your Windows 8 PC, look for the "Certified for Windows 8" logo to ensure compatibility.

51.1 – Delving into Devices and Printers

In this lesson, we are going to take a look at the "Devices and Printers" Control Panel section. This is a feature first introduced in Windows 7 that aims to make it easier for users to manage hardware devices on their computers, such as printers, game controllers and monitors. To get started, open the Start screen and search for "devices and printers", then click on the icon that appears. Figure 51.1 shows the resulting window.

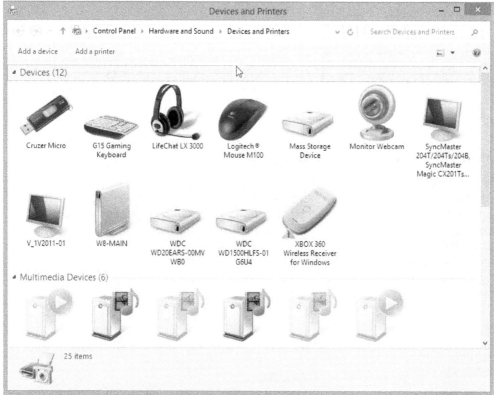

Figure 51.1 – Devices and Printers makes it easier to work with hardware

Devices and Printers gives us a very user friendly way of viewing our hardware. Your window will look different to this unless you have exactly the same hardware in your computer.

For hardware that Windows knows all about, you even get a custom icon that looks like the actual hardware device, such as the icon for the Cruzer Micro USB drive in the top left. In figure 51.1 we can also see a keyboard, USB audio headset, mouse, external hard drive, webcam, two monitors and various other hardware too. The second icon from the left on the second row down represents the actual computer.

By scrolling the window down, we can see even more hardware, see figure 51.2 for an example.

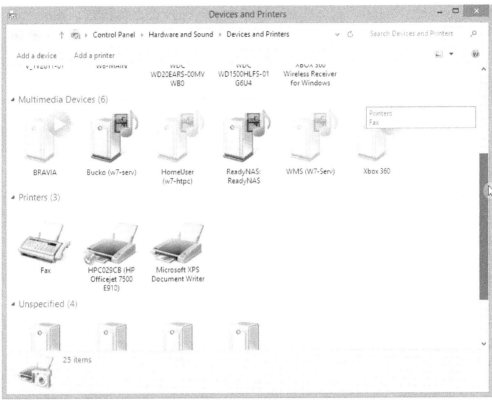

Figure 51.2 – More hardware in Devices and Printers

In figure 51.2 we can see "Multimedia Devices" and "Printers and faxes". The Multimedia Devices section lists various devices on our home network. These could be smart TV's or network attached storage devices like the ReadyNAS, or even other PCs with media or file sharing services enabled.

Printers are listed on the next row. In figure 51.2 we can see the generic Windows fax machine, which requires an old fashioned telephone modem to work. The next icon represents an HP Officejet printer and the final icon on this row is an XPS Document Writer. By default, Windows comes with a printer called the "Microsoft XPS Document Writer". This is not a real printer but it can act like one. Any program which can print documents can use this pseudo printer and the document will be saved to XPS format rather than being physically printed. The green tick or check mark next to a printer means that this is the default printer. If you want to change the default printer, right click on any printer in Devices and Printers and choose "Set as default printer".

411

Devices that Windows recognises but does not have detailed information on are shown at the bottom of the list under "Unspecified", with a generic white box icon.

51.2 – Using Devices and Printers

The Devices and Printers window is great for performing common tasks with your hardware and troubleshooting hardware problems. If we right click on a device, there is a list of actions we can take. For the Cruzer Micro for example, we can browse files or eject the device. For a monitor, we can change screen resolution.

Devices with a warning icon over them, like the Xbox 360 wireless receiver (last item on the middle row in figure 51.1), potentially have a problem. This isn't always accurate as the Xbox 360 device was working fine, it simply didn't have a controller connected to it, so Windows suspected that there might be a problem with this device.

If a hardware device has a problem you can attempt to troubleshoot it from this window. Right click on a device and choose "troubleshoot". The Windows hardware troubleshooter will then attempt to fix the problem, usually by reinstalling the drivers (drivers are software components that allow Windows to 'talk' to hardware devices). If the troubleshooter fails, you might want to check with the manufacturers for an updated driver.

That concludes our tour of the Devices and Printers section of the Control Panel and concludes this chapter. You now know how to add hardware, software and how to personalise the look of the operating system. In the next chapter we will take you into the world of the internet and home networking.

Chapter 9 – Networking and the Internet

When the first version of Windows launched way back in the mid eighties, there were relatively few computers connected to the internet, or networks of any kind. Home computers usually sat in isolation, never talking to the outside world.

Flash forward to the modern day and millions of homes now have internet connections. Computers now talk to one another across small home networks and the web is part of many peoples daily routine. Windows 8 is well equipped to traverse the information superhighway. You already know about its beefed up security software and its new cloud computing capabilities. In this chapter we will show you how to get your PC online, how to surf the internet and also how to share files and resources in your home with some basic networking tutorials.

Lesson 52 – Choosing an ISP and networking hardware

Before you can take your Windows 8 PC online, you will need an internet service provider (ISP) and some hardware. Choosing an ISP depends a great deal on where you are located geographically. Deals vary widely and shopping around can often save you money. We will discuss some of the things to look for in an ISP in this lesson to help you make your decision.

52.1 – Types of internet connection

There are lots of technologies used to deliver internet connections, each with their own particular advantages and disadvantages. For domestic internet, there are four technologies that are most common. We will look at each of these technologies now and discuss the advantages and disadvantages of each.

Cable broadband:- Cable internet connections are usually considered the best way to get online. A dedicated wire which provides internet access is connected to your home and a cable modem connects between the incoming wire and your PC or your router (we discuss routers later in this lesson). Fast and reliable, cable connections are highly recommended if they are available where you live.

ADSL:- ADSL is a technology which lets phone companies provide fast internet access through regular telephone lines. ADSL connections can be as fast as dedicated cable connections in some areas. The technology is not as robust as cable but for most users it is more than adequate.

Satellite:- Satellite internet connections are available in regions where no cable or ADSL connection is available. Satellite connections can have good download speeds but have very high latency. Latency is the measure of time between sending information (such as a page request) across the internet and the request arriving at the destination. Because of their high latencies, satellite connections are not suitable for online gaming for example.

Cellular or mobile broadband:- Cellular connections use the now ubiquitous cellular telephone network to connect you to the internet. If you're frequently out on the road, why trust potentially expensive or even dangerous public Wi-Fi access points when you can purchase internet access from your mobile phone service provider? Modern cellular data connections can be almost as fast as cable and ADSL connections, though they are often subject to more stringent download limits and may be charged per amount used rather than simply as a flat fee each month.

Windows 8 has full support for cellular data connections, when you insert a supported mobile broadband adaptor, you can connect instantly to your provider by opening the Charms Bar, choosing the Settings Charm and then clicking on "Network". Figure 52.1 shows an example of this.

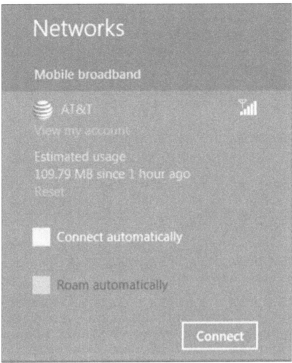

Figure 52.1 – Connecting to a cellular or mobile broadband connection

Windows is smart enough to know that mobile broadband can be expensive. To combat this, you will always be automatically connected to your Wi-Fi or wired internet connection in preference to the mobile broadband connection. Windows will also defer the downloading of any updates except critical security updates while you are connected using your mobile broadband.

Dial up:- Dial up connections use the existing phone lines to transmit data. They are typically used where no alternative is available or the user is only a light internet user. Dial up connections are very slow and have high latency but are relatively easy to set up. Because of the affordability of faster internet connections, the number of companies offering dial-up access is diminishing quickly.

52.2 – Choosing an ISP

To get the most out of the internet, we recommend choosing an ISP that provides either a cable or ADSL internet connection where possible. When choosing an ISP, do not just look for a provider who gives you the fastest speeds. Many ISP's now limit the amount of information you can access on the internet in a month or even in a day. Before signing a contract be sure to ask about download limits. On a broadband connection, it is not hard to use several gigabytes of bandwidth a month just surfing the web and watching online videos.

It is also worth checking what hardware the ISP provides with the package. If you have more than one PC in the house then you will need a router to share the internet connection between the computers (or other connected devices like games consoles). Read on to find out more about networking hardware.

52.3 – Types of internet hardware

There are lots of devices that can attach to a domestic broadband connection. Your ISP should be able to advise you on what hardware you need. We will give you a few pointers here so that you don't get confused with the techno-babble when dealing with your ISP. Some terms you will need to know about are now listed.

Modem:- A modem is actually a technical anachronism for the old style telephone modems that dialled up to the internet through a phone line. However, the term has been adopted to mean any device which connects to the incoming cable (or satellite). The modem then connects either to your computer, or to a router.

Router:- A router is a device that plugs into your modem (or sometimes is built into your modem). Routers share access to the internet amongst all the computers and connected devices in your home. Routers also help to keep hackers out by providing a hardware firewall, so they are recommended even for users with just one computer in the house. Generally, routers come in two types, wired and wireless.

Wired:- When we talk about networking equipment being wired, it refers to the connection used between the equipment. Wired routers connect to computers or other devices by a standard cable called an ethernet cable. Wired networks are faster, more robust, easier to configure and more secure than wireless networks. However, it is not always convenient to use wires to connect.

Wireless:- Wireless networking equipment (also known as Wi-Fi networking equipment) works without the need for cables. This makes it very convenient to use with laptop, tablet or other portable computers or devices, or simply where running a wire is inconvenient. Care must be taken however to ensure that proper security measures are put into place to avoid unauthorised users stealing your internet connection or even snooping around on your computer. Wireless routers usually offer the option of connecting both wired and wireless equipment, meaning you can use the more robust wired connection where it is possible to do so and then connect other devices through Wi-Fi.

52.4 – Connecting it all up

Actually connecting all your chosen networking equipment should be straightforward, but there are so many variations and variables that it is simply not possible to go into details here. Your chosen ISP should provide you with the instructions and technical support required to get connected. Remember that when you connect Wi-Fi equipment, you should set the security mode to WPA or WPA2 wherever possible. Do not be tempted to run your wireless connection without any security as this can leave you vulnerable to hackers and free loaders who may abuse your internet connection and even land you in legal troubles.

Windows 8 will connect to wired networks automatically as soon as you insert an ethernet cable. For wireless networks, Windows 8 will scan for networks in range and connect you to any network that you have previously authenticated. To see a list of Wi-Fi networks in range, to connect to a new network or disconnect, open the Charms Bar and click on the Settings Charm, then click on "Network". Figure 52.2 shows an example of a typical wireless network list.

Figure 52.2 – A list of wireless networks in range. Beware of connecting to an unsecured wireless network

To connect to a network, simply select it from the list and then enter your network key. You only need to enter the key the first time you connect, Windows will remember it for future sessions. Remember that connecting to an unsecured network (your own or someone else's, even at a coffee shop or internet café) represents a significant security risk as all your web traffic can easily be intercepted by a third party.

Lesson 53 – Internet Explorer 11 on the desktop

Windows 8.1 comes with not one but two different web browsers. Internet Explorer 11 comes in both touch friendly tile and power user ready desktop versions. In this lesson, we will show you the basics of starting to use the desktop version of IE11 to surf the web. Once you have an internet connection, the first thing most users do is try out the World Wide Web. IE11 is one way to access the web on a Windows 8 machine.

53.1 – Starting Internet Explorer 11

You can start the desktop version of IE11 in two ways. Firstly, you can go to the desktop and click on its icon on the taskbar. If you don't have an IE icon on your taskbar and want to create one, we showed you how to pin icons to the taskbar in lesson 19.2.

Secondly, if you have the tile version if IE11 open, either right click with your mouse or swipe your finger up from the bottom of the screen. A menu bar will then open, click on the spanner/wrench shaped icon and choose "View on the desktop". Figure 53.1 shows an example of this.

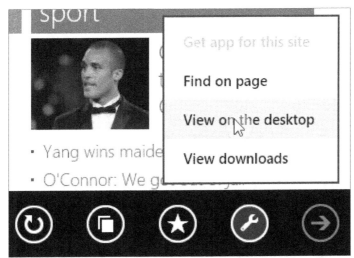

Figure 53.1 – Launching desktop IE from within the tile version

53.2 – Your first Internet Explorer 11 session

Figure 53.2 shows the main Internet Explorer 11 window.

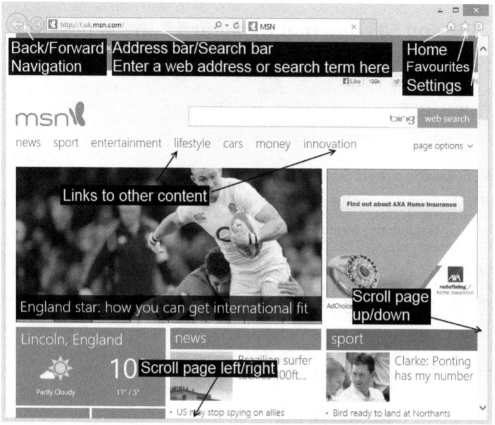

Figure 53.2 – Internet Explorer 11's main window

When navigating around a web page, use the scroll control on the right of the window to move up and down the page and the scroll control at the bottom of the window to move the page left and right. If you don't see these controls, move your mouse to the right or bottom edge of the browser window. If the page is small enough to fit in the browser window entirely, these controls will not be available.

Links on a web page take you to another page, links are coloured blue on some web pages but not all. If you suspect that some text may be a link, hover your mouse over it. Your mouse pointer will become finger shaped if the text is indeed a link. Clicking on a link will take you to another page.

When you click a link, the back/forward navigation controls will become active. To go back to the previous page, use the back button (the arrow pointing to the left). Clicking on the forward button will return you to the page you just went back from.

Unless you have a specific web address that you want to visit, you will probably want to search the internet to find what you are looking for. Fortunately, searching is really easy. In the box at the top right of the window, click once with the mouse and press the Delete key to clear the existing text. With the box empty, enter your search query. You can enter one word (e.g. "Pizza") or multiple words (e.g. "Pizza recipes with ham"). Once you have typed your search, either click the magnifying glass icon at the far right of the box or simply press the Enter key on your keyboard. You will then be taken to a results page, search results are ranked by the search engines own special criteria and do not necessarily reflect the pages accuracy or relevancy.

Finally, if you get a web address, perhaps from the TV or from a magazine article, you can enter it into the address bar. Click on the address bar once with your mouse and then use the Delete or Backspace key to delete the current address. Now, type the new address (also known as a URL) and press Enter. You need to enter the address exactly as given (although it doesn't usually matter if you use upper or lower case, www.MSN.com is exactly the same web address as www.msn.com).

If you entered the address accurately, you will be taken directly to that page on the internet.

53.3 – Home page

By clicking on the Home icon near the top right of the IE11 window, you will be taken to your home page. By default this will be the MSN search and information portal for your geographic location. From this page you can read news and perform a Bing search directly. We'll show you how you can change your home page in the next lesson.

We will cover more of the elements shown in figure 53.2 in the next lesson.

That concludes this lesson. You now know enough to start using Internet Explorer 11 and exploring the internet. In the next lesson we will look at a few other features to help make your web browsing more productive.

Lesson 54 – More on Internet Explorer 11

In this lesson we will finish our introductory tour of Internet Explorer 11 on the desktop by looking at some other useful things you can do in the browser as you explore the web.

Figure 54.1 shows an Internet Explorer window and the features we will be looking at in this lesson.

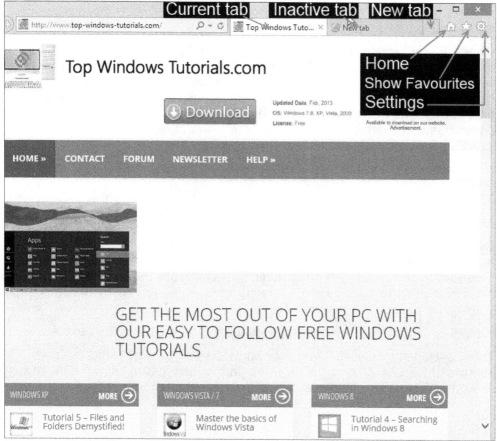

Figure 54.1 – More Internet Explorer features

54.1 – Tabs

Tabbed browsing is one of the most useful features to be added to modern web browsers. Tabs are useful when you want to work with two or more webpages at once, to compare prices for example. In figure 54.1 you can see two tabs currently open. To open a new tab, click on the area marked "New tab" in figure 54.1. To switch between tabs, simply click on them.

In any open tab it is possible to enter a web address into the address bar. You can also click on the home icon to go to the "home page" (our default starting page), or start a search. Navigating or searching for pages in one tab will not change the web content displayed in another, which means you can refer back to the content in another tab at any time just by clicking on the desired tab.

You can have as many tabs open as you like, just click to the right of your last tab to open a new one. Of course, having too many open tabs at once can become confusing!

54.2 – Favourites

When you find a website you want to revisit, you do not need to remember the address, you can add it to your Favourites (Favorites in the USA) list instead. This is often called "bookmarking" in other browsers. To add a site to your Favourites, open the page in the active tab and then click on the small star shaped icon labelled "Show Favourites" in figure 54.1. The window shown in figure 54.2 will then open.

Figure 54.2 – Using Favourites

The window shown in figure 54.2 lists all your favourite sites. To add the current site, click on the "Add to favourites" button at the top right of the window. Sites that are added as Favourites will appear under "Favourites Bar" by default. In figure 54.2 we can see two sites in our list of Favourites (Bing and Classic Shell) and two folders (Favourites bar and Computer Help Sites).

To visit a site, just click on it once from the list and it will instantly open. If you want to remove a site from your Favourites, right click on the site in the list and choose "Delete" from the context menu. Favourites that you delete like this are sent to the Recycle Bin and can be recovered from there if accidentally deleted.

You can also make your Favourites appear as a sidebar on the left of the Internet Explorer 11 window. To do this, click on the icon labelled "Open in Sidebar" in figure 54.2. Having your favourite sites show up as a sidebar can be convenient, if you are using a smaller screen however it may take up too much room on your monitor while you browse the web.

54.3 – Advanced IE11 options

There are some advanced settings we can change in the desktop version of IE11. To access these settings, click on the gear shaped icon in the top right of the browser window. The icon is marked as "Settings" in figure 54.1. When you click on the icon, the menu shown in figure 54.3 will open.

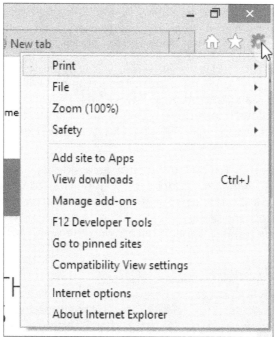

Figure 54.3 – Internet Explorer tools menu

From this menu you can access various tools such as zoom controls for the webpage and developer tools. For this lesson, we're interested in the Internet options menu item. Clicking this item brings up the window shown in figure 54.4.

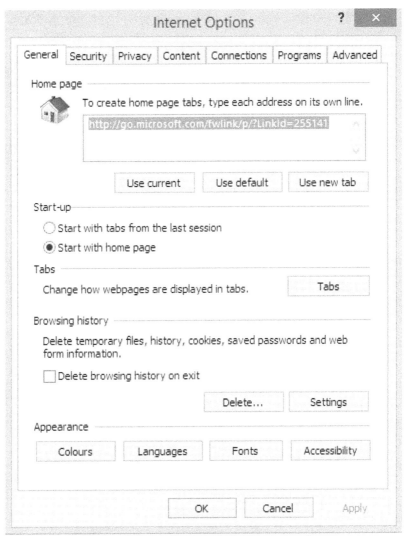

Figure 54.4 – Internet Options window

We won't be covering the Internet Options window in great detail in this guide, but there are a couple of items here that you may want to change.

On the General tab you can change the default home page. To do so, simply browse to the page you want to use as your new home page, then open the Internet Options window and click the "Use current" button. Note that if you have several tabs open when you do this, all the tabs will be set as your home page and they will open again whenever you click the home button. If

427

you only want one home page, make sure you only have one tab open when you click the "Use current" button.

Below the home page option is the option to start with the home page, or with the tabs you had open on your last browsing session. The tile version of IE11 will always start with the tabs from the last session, but it is entirely up to you how you set this option here.

In the bottom part of the window is the option to delete your current browsing history. Content from pages you visit on the internet is cached to your computer, along with search history and other potentially private information. If anyone else uses your PC and has access to your account, they can see which sites you have been visiting. If you don't want anyone to know about the sites you recently visited, click on the "Delete..." button to remove traces of them.

54.4 – Download manager

At some point during your internet use, you will probably want to download a file to your computer. Internet Explorer has an in-built download manager to make this easy. To access it, click on the gear icon and then, from the menu that appears (figure 54.3), choose "View downloads". The download manager window will then appear. Figure 54.5 shows a typical download manager window with several completed downloads.

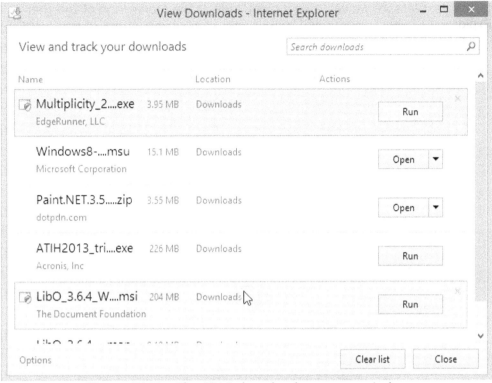

Figure 54.5 – The IE11 download manager window

Any files that download will appear in the download manager window. When a download is complete, click on the blue text link under "Location" to open the download folder and access your file. Alternatively, use the button on the right of the download to either "Run" or "Open" the file. Remember that files you download from the internet can contain malware. To minimise the risks, always make sure that your antivirus program or Windows Defender is running and is up to date and only download from reputable sites.

That concludes our tour of Internet Explorer 11 on the desktop. We have barely scratched the surface of what you can do with the web and with IE11, in fact we could probably make a whole new Superguide about IE11 alone! Don't forget that IE11 isn't the only way to browse, alternative browsers such as Firefox, Opera and Google Chrome have been increasing in popularity over recent years. Check them out when you become more confident, you may find you prefer them.

In the next lesson, we will take a quick look at the tile version of Internet Explorer 11, which is designed to be more accessible to those of you using touch screens.

Lesson 55 – Internet Explorer 11 – Tile version

We've seen IE11 on the desktop and in this tutorial we will take a look at using it on the tiled interface too. This version is optimised for touch screens and tablets, so use whichever version suits your hardware best.

To start the tile version of IE11, click the tile shown at the start of this lesson, the tile version of Internet Explorer will then open instantly.

55.1 – Navigating with IE11 on the tiles

Many things work exactly the same in the tile version of Internet Explorer as they do on the desktop version. Click or tap on a link on a page to navigate to another page. As before links are often coloured blue, or highlighted in a different colour on a page so that you know you can click them.

The forward and back buttons are located at the bottom edges of the screen. If you cannot see them, right click with your mouse or swipe upwards with your finger from the bottom of the screen. Figure 55.1 shows the menu bar that will appear.

Figure 55.1 – The navigation bar for the tile version of IE11

When you click on a link, the back button in the bottom left of the browser screen becomes active, click on that button to go back to the previous page. Clicking on the arrow pointing to the right will, not surprisingly, take you back again to the page you just clicked back from.

55.2 – Searching with Tile IE

Searching in this version of Internet Explorer works in exactly the same way. Simply type the search query into the address bar shown in figure 55.1. You can type one word or multiple words. Windows will search using the Bing search engine by default. Press enter or click/tap the right pointing arrow icon to see the results. Windows will also show you any results from your web surfing history above the search query as you type it. Figure 55.2 shows an example.

Figure 55.2 – An example search in the IE11 tile

If you have a specific web address, such as www.top-windows-tutorials.com, that you got from a magazine or business card for instance, you type it into the same box that you use for searching. Click or tap on the X icon at the far right of the search box to clear any existing text if necessary. When you enter a web address or 'URL', you will be taken directly to the page rather than a page of search results.

The tile version of Internet Explorer 11 doesn't have as many features as the desktop one, but there are still a few neat little things you can do. You can set Favourites and you can also pin sites to the Start screen, so if there's a site you visit regularly, you can get to it easily. To save a favourite or pin a site, first click on the Star icon on the navigation bar (shown in figure 55.1). The icons shown in figure 55.3 will then appear.

Figure 55.3 – Three buttons for saving websites you find

To save a site as a Favourite, click the star icon, shown on the left in Figure 55.3. Adding a site to your Favourites will make it appear when you click the star icon on the navigation bar. Favourites are also synchronised between the tile version of IE11 and its desktop counterpart. To pin a site, click on the pin-shaped icon, shown in the middle in Figure 55.3. Pinning a site to the Start screen will make it appear with all your other tiles. To remove a pinned site from the Start screen, simply right click and choose "Unpin from start".

The final button shown on the right of figure 55.3 is the share button. This works just like clicking on the Share charm (see lesson 6) and allows you to share the web page you are viewing with other apps.

55.3 – Tabs in the IE11 tile

Like its big brother, the tile version of IE11 supports tabs too. To open a new tab, open the top toolbar, either by right clicking (several times if necessary) or by swiping your finger up from the bottom of the screen. Figure 55.4 shows the menu bar that will open.

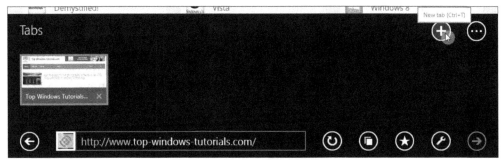

Figure 55.4 – Tab toolbar

Click the plus icon shown in figure 55.4 to open a blank tab. From the blank tab you can start a new search or access one of your frequently used sites or a site in your Favourites. To switch tabs, simply bring the tab toolbar back and then click or tap on the tab you want to use.

That concludes this tutorial on the tile version of Internet Explorer 11. Remember that if you need to view any page in the more powerful desktop version of IE, you can click on the spanner/wrench icon on the bottom toolbar and choose "View on the desktop". The page will then open directly in IE11 for the desktop.

Lesson 56 – Homegroups

 These days it is not uncommon to find two or more computers in one household. Many homes have one computer per family member. Even though the price of powerful hardware has tumbled in recent years, a computer, printer or storage device is still a significant investment for most people. Luckily, Windows now includes software that makes it really easy to share files and printers on your home network. Don't have a home network, are you sure? If you have a router that shares your internet connection between PCs in your home, either wired or wireless, then you already have a home network and you can begin this lesson. You can skip this lesson if you only have one PC in your home.

56.1 – Creating a homegroup

To get started making a homegroup, make sure all the family computers you want to share resources with are turned on and connected to the network (if they can access a web page then everything is good to go). Now, open the Start screen and search for "homegroup". Click on the "Choose HomeGroup and sharing options" item that appears, the item shown in figure 56.1 will then appear.

HomeGroup

With a homegroup you can share libraries and devices with other people on this network. You can also stream media to devices like TVs and game consoles.

Your homegroup is protected with a password, and you'll always be able to choose what you share.

Create

Figure 56.1 – Creating a homegroup

If you have never configured a homegroup on your network, Windows will now give you the option of creating one. This only needs to be done once, on one PC in your home. Click on "Create" to begin the process. There will be a short pause and then the options shown in figure 56.2 will appear.

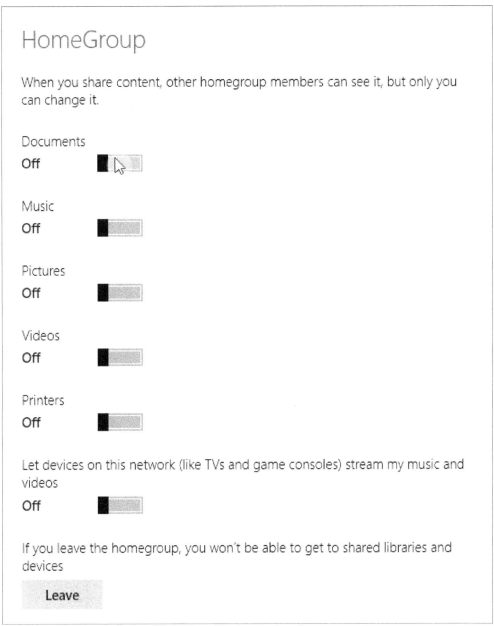

Figure 56.2 – Choosing file types to share on a homegroup

Choose the file types you want to share on your homegroup. You can share documents, music, pictures, videos and printers. Each of these options relates to the library or personal folder on your PC, so if you turn on music and picture sharing for instance, the content of these two libraries or folders will be available on the home network.

Sharing a folder on the homegroup like this opens up your files to other people on your home network. Keep this in mind when selecting what to share. You may have video content that isn't suitable for younger members of the family, for instance. By default, other users on the homegroup will be able to view and open your files but will not be able to change them. We will show you how you can limit which files and folders you share, later in this lesson.

Turning on the last option in the list, "Let devices on this network stream my music and videos" will let compatible media extenders, such as smart TV's or games consoles, play the media content on your homegroup.

If for any reason you want to leave the homegroup, simply click on the "Leave" button at the very bottom of the list of options.

By scrolling the screen down to the very bottom, you can see the homegroup password. Write this down exactly as it is shown on the screen. The password is 'case sensitive' which means that upper case and lower case letters are different ('A' is not the same as 'a'). Any computer joining your homegroup will require this password.

56.2 – Restricting access to files or folders

When you share files on the homegroup, all the files in your libraries or personal folders are shared. What if, for example, you had some video content that was not suitable for children? You could simply opt not to share videos at all, but then the children would miss out on everything. You could take the unsuitable content out of your video library and store it elsewhere, but then it won't show up when you use your video library. Fortunately there is a better solution.

Firstly, open up File Explorer and browse to the content you want to restrict. When you have located the file or folder you want to keep private, right click on it and choose "Share with → Specific people". Figure 56.3 shows the correct context menu option.

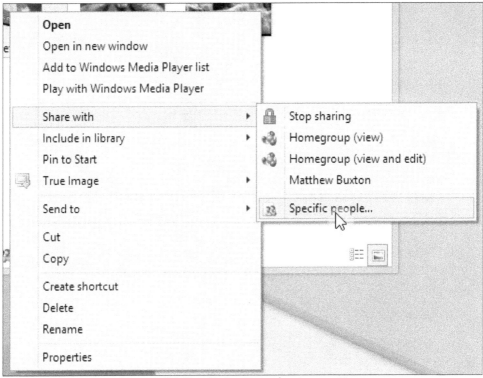

Figure 56.3 – Selecting sharing options

When you select this option, the window shown in figure 56.4 will appear.

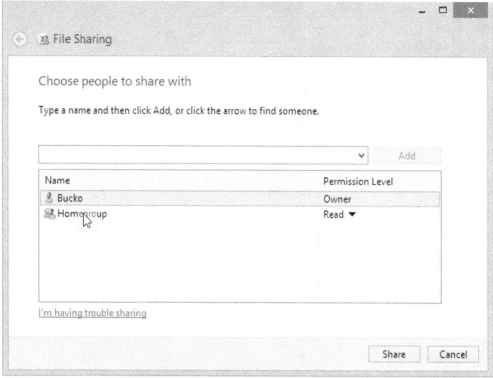

Figure 56.4 – Setting sharing options

In figure 56.4 we can see that the permissions for "Homegroup" are set to "Read". We can exclude a file from sharing completely by clicking the little arrow next to "Read" and then choosing "Remove", or we can give read (only) or read/write access to other users on the homegroup from the same menu. By default, other users on the homegroup can see your files but not change them. If you need to change files from another computer choose "Read/Write", but make sure you have a backup in case someone else in the house accidentally deletes your files. When you're done making changes, click on "Share" to close the window and activate the new permissions.

56.3 – Joining an existing homegroup

Connecting another computer to an existing homegroup is done in exactly the same way as setting up a homegroup in the first place. On the computer you wish to include in the homegroup, open the HomeGroup settings from the Start screen, exactly like we did at the start of the lesson. Instead of seeing the "Create" button, this time you should see the password prompt shown in figure 56.5.

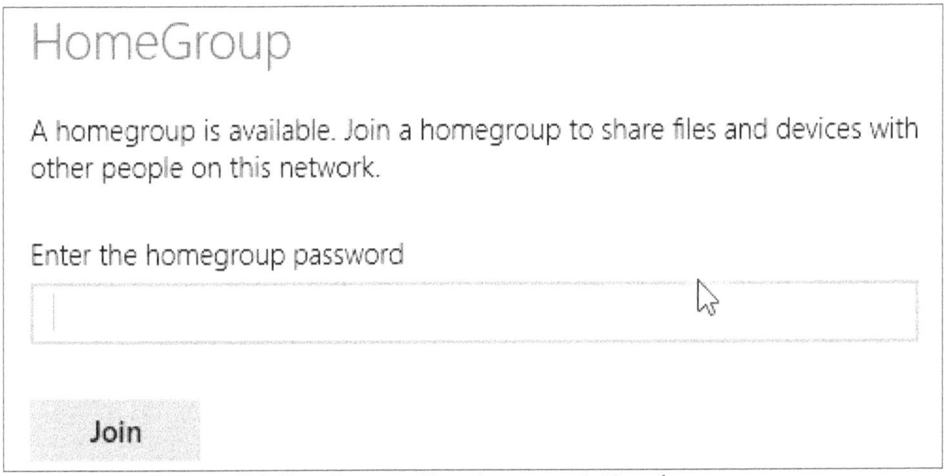

Figure 56.5 – Connecting to an existing homegroup

This time, Windows has detected an existing homegroup on the network. To join in and share files and printers, enter the homegroup password you wrote down earlier in the lesson and then click on "Join". You will then see the options shown in figure 56.2. Choose which of the libraries or folders you want to share from this computers hard drive, just like before.

Note - If you are running a third party security package that includes a firewall, you may have trouble connecting to a homegroup. Temporarily disable your firewall and try to connect again. If you can connect with your firewall turned off, contact the vendor of your firewall product for technical support and advice or to obtain an upgrade.

56.4 – Browsing a homegroup

You can browse a homegroup through File Explorer. Simply open up a File Explorer window and you will see the homegroup icon in the Navigation pane on the left of the window. Click on it and you will then see the other users PCs in your homegroup. Figure 56.6 shows an example of this.

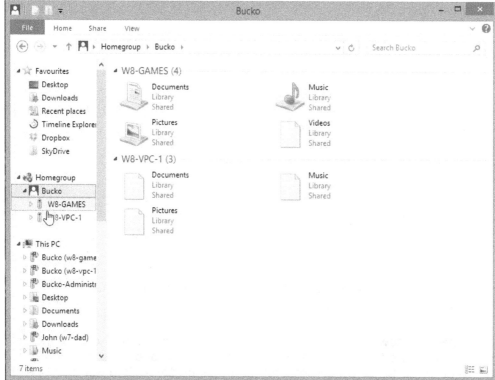

Figure 56.6 – Browsing a user's files on the homegroup

If a computer has more than one user, each user will have to log on, join the homegroup and authorise their files to be shared before they will show up under "Homegroup" in File Explorer.

You have now completed this lesson on homegroups and also this chapter on networking and the internet! In the next chapter we take a look at Windows Media Player. This program is, for many users, the preferred way to play and organise music on the Windows desktop.

Chapter 10 – Windows Media Player

In this chapter, we are going to focus on Windows Media Player. Windows Media Player is pretty much unchanged from Windows 7, but that's not necessarily a bad thing, since it was a very competent piece of software when launched. If you prefer to work on the desktop and not with the tiles, Windows Media Player is the best way to both organise and play your media files.

Lesson 57 – Introducing Windows Media Player 12

 In this lesson we will look at running Windows Media Player 12 for the first time. We will also show you how to play back both music and video. To get started, load Windows Media Player by going to the Start screen and searching for "windows media player", then click on the icon that appears.

57.1 – Running Media Player for the first time

The very first time you run the program, you will see the window shown in figure 57.1.

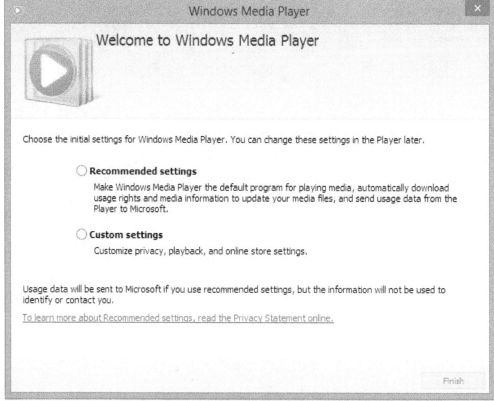

Figure 57.1 – First time setup of Windows Media Player

Windows Media Player uses your internet connection, if available, to download information about the media you are playing. Choose "Recommended settings" to get started right away or "Custom settings" if you want to analyse the settings and privacy policy in detail. For this example, we will choose the "Recommended settings" button, then click "Finish". You will then be taken to the main Windows Media Player window as shown in figure 57.2.

Figure 57.2 – The main Windows Media Player window

Unlike Windows 7, Windows 8 doesn't come with any sample music to get you started. Before continuing with this lesson you may wish to copy some media files into your libraries or music folder. If you purchased the Windows 8 Superguide DVD, you can use the Sample Media installer to install a simple music file called "A Hundred Pipers". Alternatively, go to lesson 58 where we add music from an audio CD.

Playing music and video with Windows Media Player is really easy. There are two ways to start playing a file that we will demonstrate in this lesson.

Firstly, we can drag and drop media files from File Explorer onto the Windows Media Player window. To do this, make sure the "Play" tab is selected, then open File Explorer and navigate to the folder where the media file you want to play is stored. To play a file, drag it, as if you were moving it, over from the File Explorer window onto the right hand side of the Windows Media Player window. The file will then play right away. Figure 57.3 illustrates this.

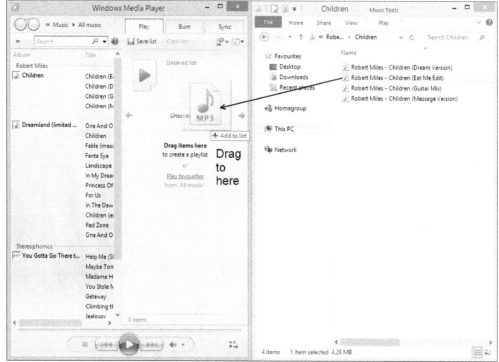

Figure 57.3 – Dragging a file to Windows Media Player

The first file you drag to Windows Media Player will start playing instantly. You can keep dragging files onto the window to create a playlist. Files on a playlist will play one after the other.

You can add video files to your playlist too, in exactly the same way. If you want to jump directly to an item on your playlist (to play it immediately), just double click on it.

57.2 – Playing video

Figure 57.4 shows Windows Media Player playing a video file.

Figure 57.4 – Playing a video in Windows Media Player 12

The picture shows the buttons available in video playback. The controls are the same when playing music (apart from the full screen control). We will take a look at each button now.

Shuffle:- This changes the order in which files are played from your playlist. When shuffle is on, files are played in a random order.

Repeat:- Repeats the current playlist (rather than just the file you are currently playing). When this option is disabled, playback will stop when the end of the playlist is reached. Otherwise it will resume from the beginning again (or a random point if shuffle is enabled).

Stop:- Stops playback of the current media file. You are then given the option of returning to the media library or resuming playback.

Previous:- Go to the previous file on your playlist.

Play:- When a file is playing, this button will pause playback. When a file is paused, pressing this button will resume playback.

Next:- Go to the next item on your playlist.

Mute:- Turns off all sound.

Volume:- Adjusts the level of the volume by moving the slide control.

Fullscreen:- Make the video play back in full screen mode, taking up all the space on your monitor. Not applicable for audio files.

Back to library:- Takes you back from the media file and returns you to your media library.

57.3 – The media library

Earlier in the lesson we showed you how to drag and drop media on to Windows Media Player in order to start playing it. This is handy for playing music on removable media, for example. Normally however, you would use the music library to play files from your computer. Any media files you add into your libraries or personal folders will automatically be available in Windows Media Player. The media library navigation pane is shown on the left of the Media Player window (see figure 57.2).

You can browse the library by file type, using the Navigation pane or search for media either by name or tags by typing into the search box near the top right of the window. Enter a search query then press Enter or click the magnifying glass icon at the right of the search box to start the search.

To play an item from your media library just double click it. To add it to your playlist, drag it across to the right and drop it in the same area we dropped the files from File Explorer.

To save a playlist, click on "Save list" then enter a name for your list. Saved playlists appear in the library under "Playlists". You could create playlists ready for a house party for example, or just to match your mood. To start playing a playlist, just double click it.

That concludes this lesson on Windows Media Player. Now you know how to play audio and video media files. In the next lesson we will look at how to copy your CD collection to your computer and create a digital jukebox of all your favourite tunes.

Lesson 58 – Ripping CDs

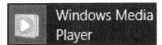 Have you ever wanted to create your own jukebox? By ripping your CDs to your computers hard drive you can do just that. Ripping a CD means taking a copy of the music on the CD and storing it in your computer. The copyright law in most countries allows you to do this, as long as you own a copy of the original CD. This means that you can access all your music without having to have the original CD in the CD drive or player!

To rip a CD, you will of course need an optical drive in your PC. If your PC didn't come with one, most computer stores sell external DVD drives that will do the job just fine. DVD and even Blu-ray drives are backwards compatible with CD, so any such drive will work with the techniques shown in this video.

58.1 – Setting ripping options

Before we get started ripping CDs, let us take a look at some options. On the main Windows Media Player window, click on the "Organize" menu and then choose "Options". Now, choose the "Rip music" tab. Figure 58.1 shows you how to do this.

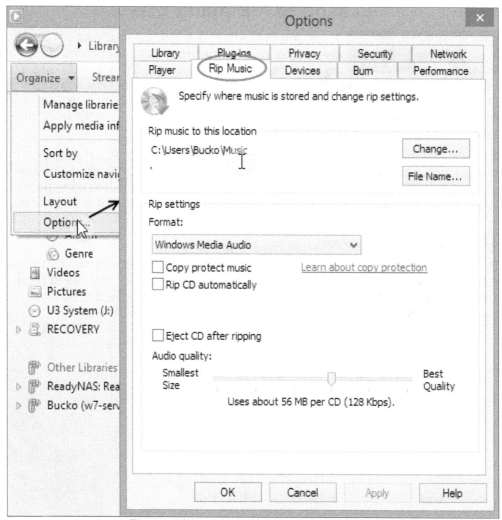

Figure 58.1 – Accessing ripping options

By default, music that you rip will be stored in Windows Media Audio format. If you are planning to use the music on a generic MP3 player, it might not be compatible with Windows Media Audio format. Choose "Mp3" in that case. You can change formats by using the drop down box under "Format:". If you are playing the music files back on high quality audio equipment, you may also want to up the quality of the copy, though doing so increases the file size. You can change quality settings by using the slide control at the bottom of the window. There is no right or wrong setting, experiment and find out what sounds best to you.

When you are done setting ripping options, click on "Apply" then on "OK". You will then be taken back to the main Media Player window.

58.2 – Ripping a CD

To rip a CD using Windows Media Player 12, firstly insert your audio CD. It should then show up in the Navigation pane, under "Music". Click on it once. Figure 58.2 shows a Media Player Window with an Audio CD ready to play.

Figure 58.2 – An audio CD in Windows Media Player

Just like regular media, you can double click on audio tracks to play them. You can also drag them over to the right (as long as the Play tab is selected) and make a playlist.

We could start ripping the CD right away, but first, check that the track names are set correctly. To save the hassle of renaming them later, you can look up the track names in the online CD database. Windows Media Player

449

will usually do this automatically. If you need to override this behaviour or look up a CD manually, right click on the CDs icon in the media library then choose "Find album info" on the context menu that appears. Media Player will then connect to the internet and look up the track names and information about the album. This saves you entering them manually later. Of course, you will need an internet connection for this to work. Figure 58.3 shows the "find album information" window.

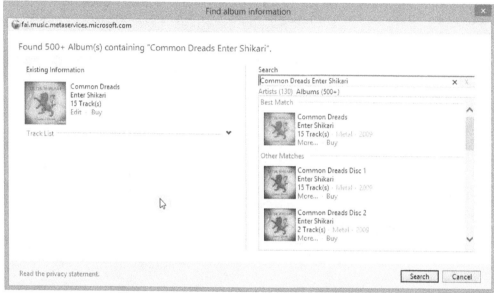

Figure 58.3 – Looking up an album online

Sometimes Windows Media Player will find the album information automatically, other times you will need to search for it yourself by entering the artist and album name into the search box. When you find a match for the album, click on it from the list and then click "Next". You will be able to confirm that the details are correct before clicking on "Finish".

The track listing will then be automatically filled out, just like in figure 58.4.

| Create playlist ▼ | Rip CD | » | | ▼ | Search | 🔍 ▼ | ⓘ |

Album	☑	#	Title	Length	Rip status
Audio CD (H:)					
Common Dreads	☑ ▸	1	Common Dreads	2:08	
Enter Shikari	☑	2	Solidarity	3:16	
Metal	☑	3	Step Up	4:40	
2009	☑	4	Juggernauts	4:44	
⭐⭐⭐☆☆	☑	5	Wall	4:29	
	☑	6	Zzzonked	3:27	
	☑	7	Havoc a	1:40	
	☑	8	No Sleep Tonight	4:16	
	☑	9	Gap in the Fence	4:07	
	☑	10	Havoc B	2:52	
	☑	11	Antwerpen	3:15	
	☑	12	The Jester	3:55	
	☑	13	Halcyon	0:42	
	☑	14	Hectic	3:17	
	☑	15	Fanfare for the Conscio...	3:45	

Figure 58.4 – Filling out track names by looking them up on the internet is much quicker than typing them yourself

We are now ready to start ripping some music. You can rip the entire CD or individual tracks, just deselect the ones you don't want. When you are ready to start ripping the disc, right click on the disc icon in the library Navigation pane (it will now be correctly named if you looked it up online) and choose "Rip CD to library".

Figure 58.5 – Starting the CD ripping process

58.3 – Copy protection options

If this is the first time you have ripped a CD, the window shown in figure 58.6 will appear.

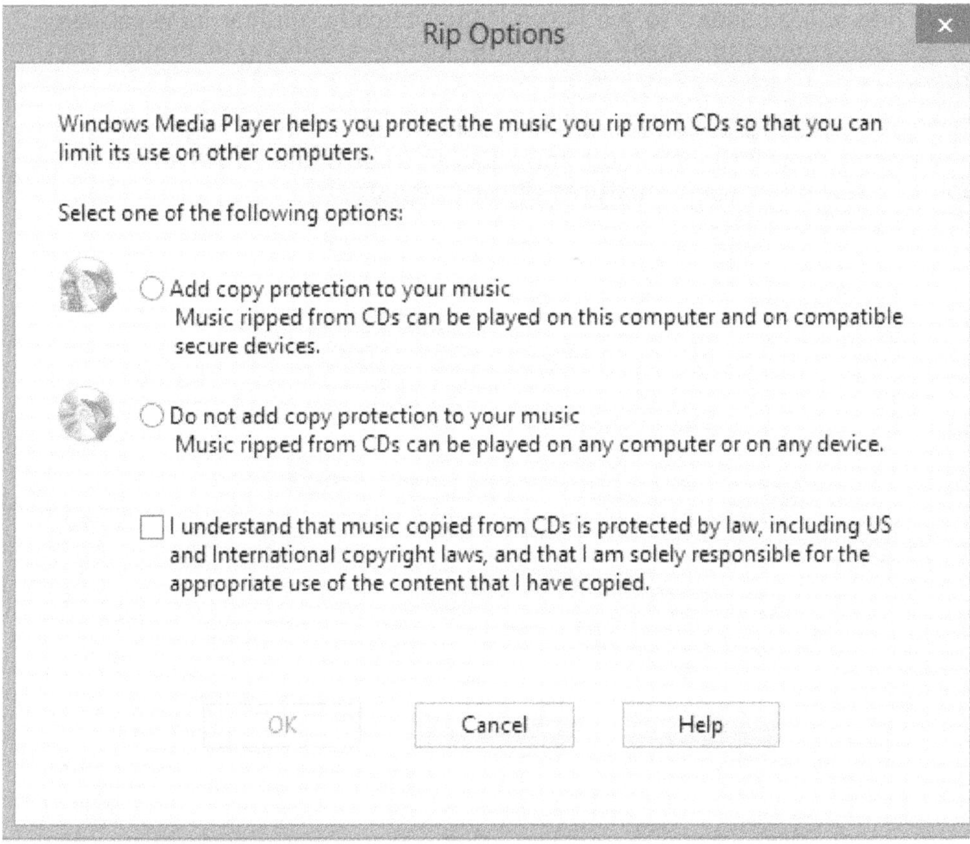

Figure 58.6 – Setting copy protection options

When ripping music from CDs, you can choose to add protection to your ripped audio files. Adding protection can help you use the media within copyright law, but it can also cause problems with some types of media players, so we recommend that you do not. You must also tick/check the box at the bottom of the window that states that you understand most music CDs are protected by copyright law. Please use the files you copy/rip from your CDs for your own personal use and do not share them with friends or on the internet.

Click on "OK" when you have selected an option and ticked/checked the box. Ripping will then begin. This window will only appear the first time you rip a CD, Media Player will remember your preferences for next time.

Media Player will then begin ripping the CD. You can continue to use the program while this takes place. When the ripping process is complete, the music files will be added to the library automatically. You can now remove the CD and enjoy your music at any time just by accessing it through the library.

That concludes this lesson on ripping audio tracks in Media Player 12. In the next lesson we will round up our introductory tour of Media Player 12 as we look at a few other useful features of the software.

Lesson 59 – Wrapping up Media Player

 In this lesson we will be going over some of the features we briefly mentioned in the other lessons, especially the media library and playlists.

59.1 – Browsing libraries

As we mentioned in lesson 57, the libraries in Windows Media Player 12 and your music library (or music folder) are linked, meaning you can browse your music collection from File Explorer or through Media Player. The media libraries also link with the appropriate tiles on the tile interface too. Browsing in Media Player can be more convenient if you want to play and browse music and video.

Just like in File Explorer, there are different views you can choose for browsing your media. If you do not like how the data is laid out in your media library, you have several options. Use the drop down box next to the search box to change views. Figure 59.1 shows where this control is.

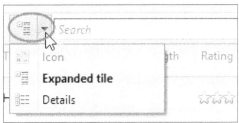

Figure 59.1 – The view options control

Depending on what type of media you are viewing, you will have several choices. Details view is useful for working with lots of tracks at once. In this view, you can set ratings by simply clicking on the stars next to the song title. Figure 59.2 shows a media library in details view.

Figure 59.2 – Media library in details view

Use the scroll control near the bottom of the window to see other columns which contain various information about your music or media files. If you don't see a scroll control here, then all the available columns are already displayed. To sort by a column, click the column once.

By right clicking on a column and choosing "Choose columns" it is possible to see a list of all the different types of information that can be displayed about the media files. Figure 59.3 shows this list.

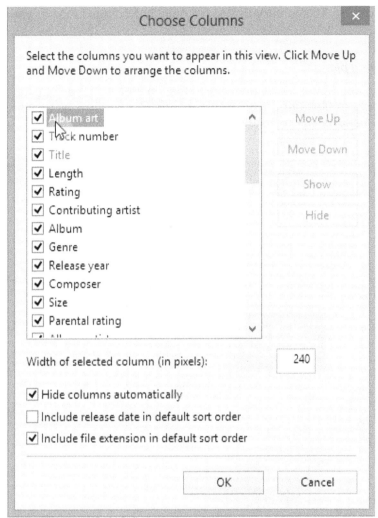

Figure 59.3 – Choosing columns to display in the media library

Of course, some categories will not be relevant to all types of media. To display a column, simply select it then click "OK", it will then appear. You can also automatically hide empty columns   by making sure the "Hide columns automatically" option is selected in this window.

You can also resize columns by dragging them, or reorder columns by dragging them to a new place. As you can see, working with Media Player is a lot like working with File Explorer. Don't forget there is also a very handy "Search" box, where you can search by artist, album, song title or any other relevant criteria. This is very useful for quickly finding things in your media library.

59.2 – Viewing pictures

We have talked about video and music files in Media Player but we did not mention picture files until now. Media Player 12 can view picture files too. Figure 59.4 shows the picture section of the media library.

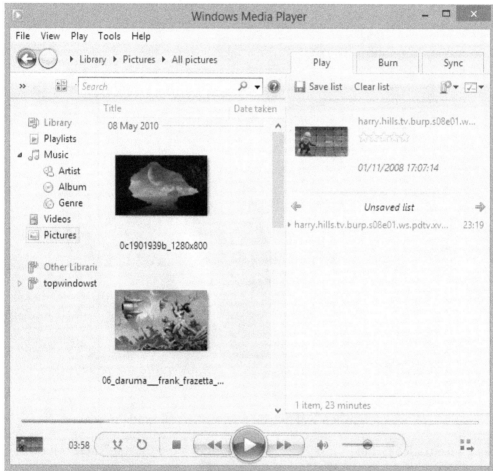

Figure 59.4 – Browsing pictures in Windows Media Player

To view pictures, just double click on them, Windows Media Player will play them as a slideshow. You can queue pictures up in a playlist just like other media, making it easy to create a custom slideshow.

59.3 – Making Windows Media Player the default player

Remember, if you work primarily with the Desktop rather than the tiles, you can make Windows Media Player the default program for opening media files. To do this, refer to lesson 19.3.

That concludes our tour of Windows Media Player 12 and this chapter. We have barely scratched the surface of the power of Windows Media Player in these lessons, do not be afraid to dive in and experiment, it is the best way to learn.

The next chapter focuses on routine PC maintenance and troubleshooting, to help keep your new PC running in tip-top condition.

Chapter 11 – Troubleshooting and Maintenance

Your PC is almost certainly the most versatile gadget you have in your home. No normal television, toaster or microwave oven could ever come close to performing as many tasks as even the most humble Windows 8 PC. This is great of course, but the downside is that PCs typically need more maintenance than regular household gadgets. Don't worry if that sounds like hard work, if you followed our advice on PC security then hopefully you won't encounter too many problems. In this chapter we will show you some simple things you can do to keep your Windows 8 machine running like new.

Lesson 60 – Uninstalling software

If you no longer use a program, it is a good idea to uninstall it. Uninstalling software frees up disk space and can free up computer resources too, if the software in question was running all the time. Sometimes it is necessary to uninstall an old program to make way for a new one. This is true in the case of most security software (i.e. firewall and antivirus packages). It is also a good idea to uninstall and reinstall a program if you are experiencing technical problems with it.

60.1 – Uninstalling tile software

To uninstall a tile based program that you downloaded from the store, simply locate the program on your Start screen and then right click on it (or select it with your finger and then swipe up from the bottom of the screen). Now, using the menu bar that appears, simply click on "Uninstall", then click "Uninstall" again to confirm. Figure 60.1 shows an example of this.

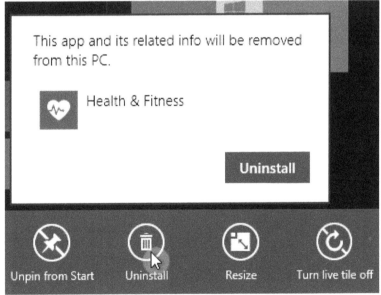

Figure 60.1 – Uninstalling a tile from the Start screen

That's all there is to uninstalling tile apps. If you want to reinstall a tile application you will need to re-download it from the store. For paid apps, as long as you use the same Microsoft account you won't need to pay for the program again. Alternatively you can simply unpin apps you don't use often and then just find them by searching.

60.2 – Uninstalling desktop software

 In this example, we are going to look at how we uninstall a typical desktop program. The actual uninstallation process will be different for every piece of software but the basic steps are usually the same.

Before you begin uninstalling any software, it is a good idea to make sure it is not running. Although a properly written uninstall script should take care of this, it never hurts to check yourself. If you do not see a window for your program, check the notification area (see lesson 30) for the programs icon. If you can see an icon, right click on it and choose "quit", "close" or "shutdown" if the option is available.

To start the uninstallation process, search for "Uninstall a program" on the Start screen and then click the icon that appears. The Control Panel will now open and show you a list of all the desktop programs installed on your PC. You may need to scroll down until you find the program you want to uninstall. Then click on it and choose "uninstall" if the option is available or "change" if it is not. Figure 60.2 shows an example of this.

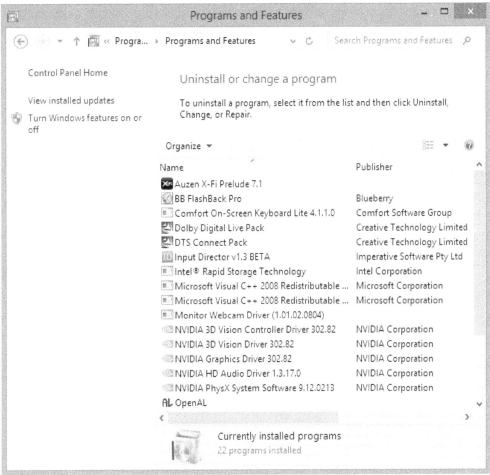

Figure 60.2 – Choosing a program to uninstall. Some software must be uninstalled by selecting "Change" while other software will have an "Uninstall" option in the same place

Once you click on "Uninstall" or "Change" the uninstallation process will begin, you should then follow the on screen prompts to remove your software. These prompts will be slightly different for every program you uninstall, but they are usually straightforward. Normally you will need to confirm that you want to remove the software when User Account Control prompts you.

Sometimes you will have to restart your PC to finish the uninstallation process. The uninstaller should offer to do this for you if it is necessary. Once your computer restarts, the uninstallation process is complete.

That concludes this short lesson on uninstalling software. In the next lesson we will take a look at how to remove temporary files and other clutter using the Disk Cleanup utility.

Lesson 61 – The Disk Cleanup utility

 In Windows 8 you can reclaim disk space and clean up temporary internet files by using the Disk Cleanup Tool. This tool was improved in Windows 7 and in Windows 8 it works in much the same way.

61.1 – Starting a disk cleanup

To start the tool, search for "cleanmgr" on the Start screen, then click on the icon that appears.

Once you click on the icon, The window shown in figure 61.1 will appear if you have more than one hard drive in your system.

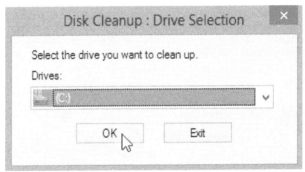

Figure 61.1 – Choosing a disk to clean up

Choose a drive to clean up by using the drop-down box control. Some computers will only have the C: drive, in which case you won't be prompted to choose a drive to clean. In this lesson we will show you how to clean the C: drive, which is usually the drive or partition that Windows is installed to. Choose the C: drive (it should be selected by default) then click "OK".

61.2 – Choosing cleaning options

The Disk Cleanup utility will then scan for temporary files. When this process is complete, the window shown in figure 61.2 will appear.

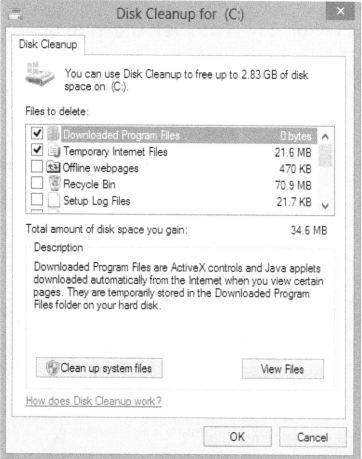

Figure 61.2 – Choosing temporary files to remove

Figure 61.2 shows the Disk Cleanup utility presenting us with a list of all the temporary files that can be deleted from the computer. If you scroll down the list and click on an item, you can see a description of the files that this cleanup option removes. In figure 61.2, the "Downloaded Program Files" option is selected, in the description we can see that this includes ActiveX and Java applets downloaded automatically. Selecting this option will not delete files you have downloaded into your downloads folder. Generally, since each option only cleans temporary files, it is safe to select them all.

For this example, we will choose every item on the list, then click on "OK". The Disk Cleanup utility will then ask us to confirm that we want to delete the files, figure 61.3 shows the window which will appear.

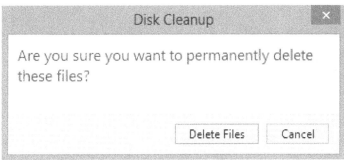

Figure 61.3 – Confirm the removal of temporary files to start the cleanup process

This is your last chance before the items are deleted. Unless there is something you really wanted to recover from the Recycle Bin or from the temporary files or error logs on your PC, it is safe to click "Delete Files". The cleanup process will then begin. When the process is complete, the utility will exit automatically. You have now cleaned the temporary files from your computer and reclaimed the disk space.

That concludes this lesson on the Disk Cleanup utility. PC maintenance really isn't as difficult as you imagined is it? In the next lesson we take a look at how we can improve system performance with the disk defragmenter tool.

Lesson 62 – Disk defragmentation

 As you go about your daily computing routine, adding files, removing files and rearranging files, the hard disk in your computer becomes more and more fragmented. File system fragmentation slows down access to files because the pieces of a file may be scattered across the disk, rather than stored together neatly. To combat this problem, the Optimize Drives tool can automatically rearrange your hard disk. The tool is easy to use and completely safe and will even run automatically. In fact, many users will not need to change the programs settings at all.

62.1 – The Optimize Drives window

To start disk defragmention manually or to change settings, open the Start screen and search for "defragment and optimize", then click on the icon to load the program. The window shown in figure 62.1 will then appear.

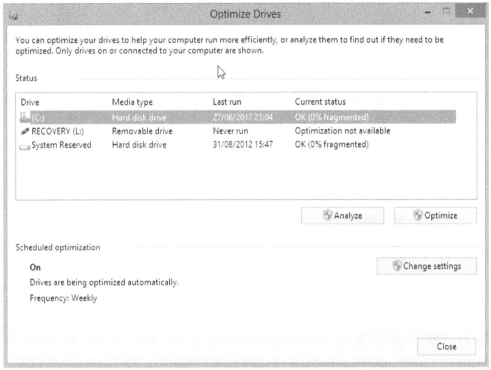

Figure 62.1 – The Optimize Drives tool

Figure 62.1 shows the main Optimize Drives tool window. From this window we can schedule regular defragmentation or manually optimize any hard disks in our computer. We will take a look at scheduled defragmentation first. Select a drive from the list in the top of the window and then click on the "Change settings" button. The window shown in figure 62.2 will then open.

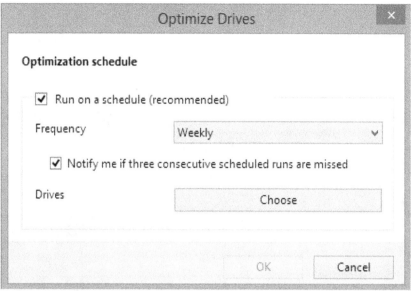

Figure 62.2 – Scheduling a defragmentation

62.2 – Setting a schedule

In this window we can choose a schedule for automatic "set it and forget it" disk optimization. When the "Run on a schedule (recommended)" option is selected, defragmentation will be automatic. By changing the "Frequency:" control, you can also choose between daily, weekly or monthly optimization. Daily is a little excessive but monthly might be suitable for a computer that isn't used frequently. Weekly will be the best option for most users.

Enabling the second tick/check box in the window will cause Windows to notify you if three consecutive scheduled runs are missed. If you have more than one hard drive or hard drive partition, click on "Choose" to choose which disks will be optimized as part of the schedule. Figure 62.3 shows the drive selection window.

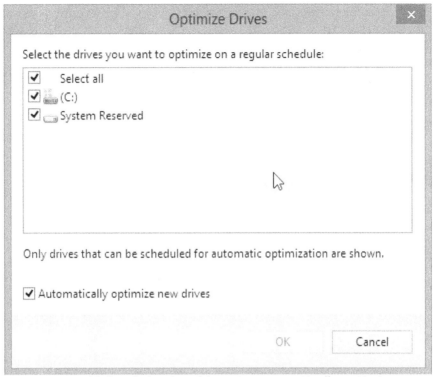

Figure 62.3 – Selecting drives to automatically optimize

In most instances you should simply select every drive available so that all your hard drives are defragmented and optimized. Click on "OK" when you are done making changes or "Cancel" if no changes were necessary. The window will then close and return you to the window shown in figure 62.2. Click on "OK" again to finish setting the optimization schedule. You will then be returned to the main Optimize Drives window as shown in figure 62.1.

62.3 – Manual defragmentation

Once you have set a schedule for disk optimization, that is really all you need to do to keep your disk defragmented and working at peak performance. If for any reason you want to do a manual disk defragment then simply choose the disk to defragment from the list near the top of the window shown in figure 62.1. Choose a disk by clicking on it and then click on the "Analyze" button.

Windows will then analyse the disk and tell you what the percentage of fragmented files is. If this value is high, you might want to go ahead and manually defragment the disk. To start a manual defragmentation, simply click on "Optimize".

Optimization will take a while, but you can use your computer for other tasks while it takes place. When the process is complete the utility will simply stop, you will not even be notified that it is done!

That is all there is to keeping your disks defragmented with the Disk Defragmenter utility.

In our next lesson, we will look at the System Restore utility. This utility can help solve serious computer problems by restoring your system settings to an earlier time.

Lesson 63 – System Restore utility

 The System Restore utility was introduced with Windows XP and has been refined in Windows Vista, Windows 7 and Windows 8. If you have a serious problem with your PC after installing a new program or piece of hardware, the System Restore utility can "roll back" to an earlier time when your PC was working correctly.

63.1 – Starting a System Restore

To start the utility, search for "recovery" on the Start screen, then click on the Recovery icon shown at the start of this lesson. The recovery section of the Control Panel will then open. Figure 63.1 shows an example of this.

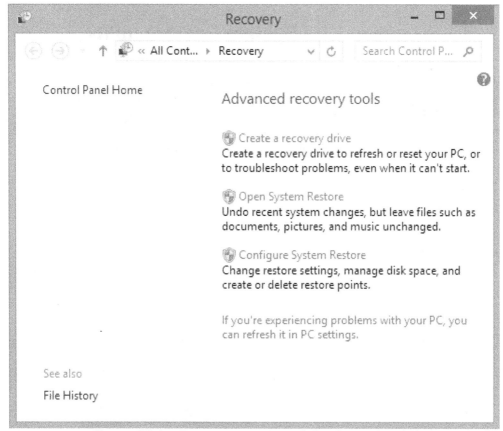

Figure 63.1 – Recovery section of the Control Panel

Click on "Open System Restore". The System Restore 'wizard' window will now open. Figure 63.2 shows this window.

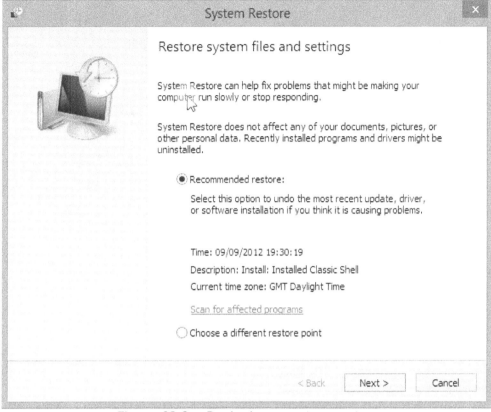

Figure 63.2 – Beginning a system restore

The System Restore tool will now guide you through the process of selecting and restoring a System Restore point. System Restore only affects system settings. Files such as pictures, videos and e-mails will not be altered. Because of this it is often more convenient to use System Restore than it is to restore from a backup when troubleshooting computer problems.

63.2 – Choosing a restore point

The System Restore utility has two options on the first window. "Recommended restore:" or "Choose a different restore point". The recommended restore option will restore from the most recent restore point. If you restore from the recommended restore point and your system still malfunctions, you can choose a different, earlier restore point. Figure 63.3 shows the window that appears if you select "Choose a different restore point".

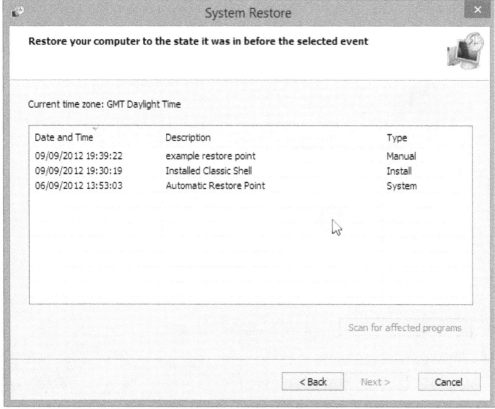

Figure 63.3 – Choosing a restore point

To choose a restore point, simply select it from the list and then click on "Next >". You can see a description of why the restore point was created, along with the date and time it was made. If you suspect that the problems you are having are down to a specific program or update you installed, you can restore to a specific restore point to test your theory.

63.3 – Restoring from a restore point

Once you choose a system restore point, you will need to confirm your selection, figure 63.4 shows the window that appears.

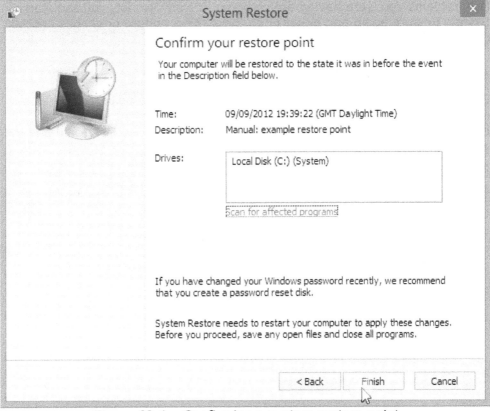

Figure 63.4 – Confirming a system restore point

This window gives us some pointers to note before we begin with the system restore process. We can "Scan for affected programs" to see if any of the programs on our computer are likely to need reinstalling after this process is completed. If you have recently changed your password, using System Restore might revert back to the old password, so make sure you can remember them both or create a password reset disk.

Since the restore process will restart your PC, you also need to close down any running programs and save your work. Click on "Finish" when you are ready to proceed.

You will receive one final warning not to interrupt the system restore process, click on "Yes" and the process will then begin. It will take several minutes to complete.

When the process is complete, the system will restart and return you to the Lock screen. You should now log back into your computer and check to see if the problems you were having are resolved. If they are not, you can start System Restore again and either undo the system restore or choose another restore point.

63.4 – Undoing a System Restore

Before the System Restore utility rolls back to a restore point, it creates a restore point containing your current configuration. That means you can easily undo a System Restore. Start the System Restore utility again and the window shown in figure 63.5 should appear.

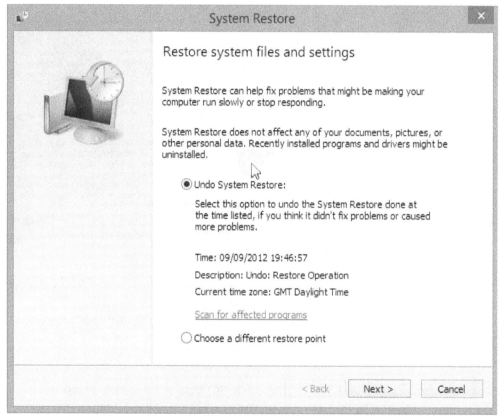

Figure 63.5 – Undoing a System Restore is easy

When you choose "Undo System Restore:" the process works in exactly the same way as when you use System Restore normally. You are in actual fact restoring from a restore point that was created before you ran System

Restore the first time!

63.5 – Creating your own system restore point

 Users can easily create their own system restore point at any time. To do this, open the Start screen and search for "create a restore point" and then click the icon that appears. The window shown in figure 63.6 will then appear.

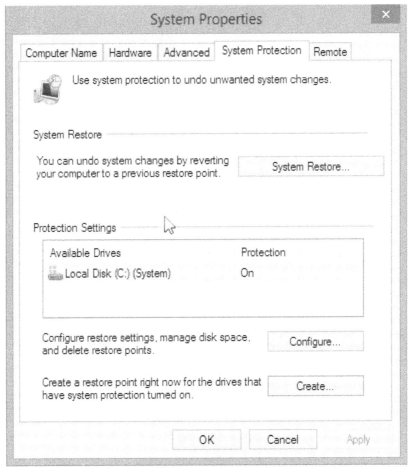

Figure 63.6 – Creating a system restore point is easy

All that you need to do to create a system restore point is choose a drive from the list in the middle of the window. Usually there is only the one drive, C:, where Windows is installed. Choose the C: drive and then click on "Create...". Windows will prompt you to name your restore point. Enter any name you like and click "Create" again. Wait a moment until Windows tells you that the restore point was created. You can now close the window and use System Restore to roll back to this point if necessary.

In the next lesson we will be taking a look at the Refresh your PC feature. This is a new maintenance tool for Windows 8 that makes repairing troublesome PCs much easier.

Lesson 64 – Refresh your PC

In this lesson we are going to look at the new "Refresh your PC" feature. This function serves two purposes. Firstly, it can be used to remove all your programs and data from your PC if, for instance, you want to sell your computer or give it away. Secondly, it can reinstall your operating system without affecting the files stored in your personal folders. This is useful if you think your operating system files have become corrupt, for instance.

To use this feature you will need to be logged in with an administrator account (you can't simply use UAC to activate this feature). To access the feature, open the Charms Bar and click on the Settings Charm. Now, click on "Change PC settings" in the bottom right of the screen. The PC settings menu will then be shown on the left of the screen. Click on the "Update & Recovery" category and then on "Recovery". You should now see the two options shown in figure 64.1, that we will be discussing in this lesson.

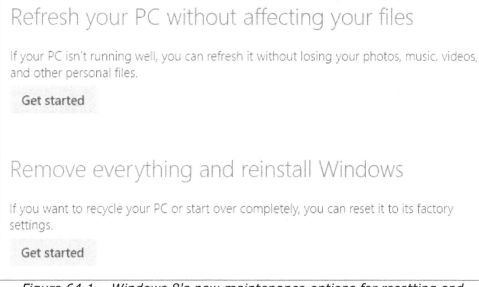

Figure 64.1 – Windows 8's new maintenance options for resetting and reinstalling your PC

In figure 64.1 we can see the two options; "Refresh your PC without affecting your files" and "Remove everything and reinstall Windows". We'll demonstrate the top option first.

64.1 – Refresh your PC

Click on the "Get started" button under Refresh your PC and the message shown in figure 64.2 will appear.

Figure 64.2 – Starting the refresh process

By using the "Refresh your PC" option you will lose any desktop programs you have installed. Many of your PC settings and customisations will also be reset to default. After the procedure is complete you can, of course, reinstall any desktop software you need. Before you resort to the Refresh feature, you should try the System Restore utility we covered in lesson 63 to undo recent changes to your PC. If you are sure you want to proceed with a Refresh, click on "Next". Windows will then notify you if it detects any programs you will need to reinstall. Click on "Next" again and you will need to wait a moment while the process starts, you may need to insert your Windows 8 installation media if prompted. When the process is ready to begin, the message shown in figure 64.3 will appear.

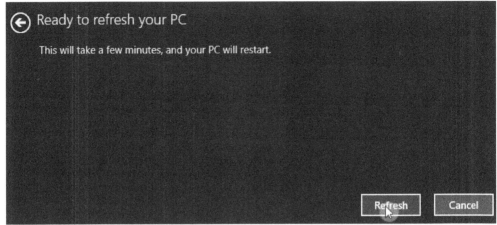

Figure 64.3 – Click on "Refresh" to begin refreshing your PC

Once you click on "Refresh", the computer will reboot. Rather than the regular Windows startup, you will see the screen shown in figure 64.4.

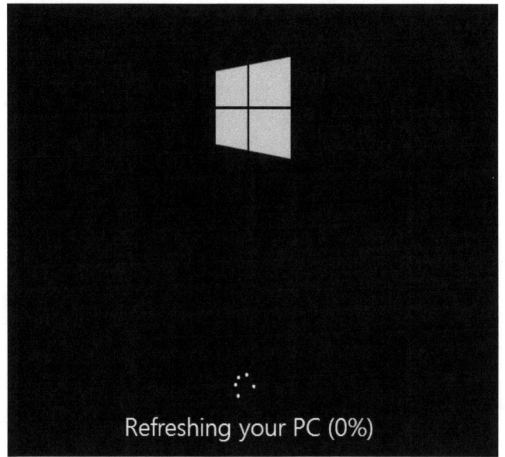

Figure 64.4 – Wait while Windows refreshes your PC

The refreshing process will take some time, when it is completed, your computer will reboot automatically. You can now log back in as normal. You will see straight away that some of your preferences have been reset and you may need to reconfigure networking settings. You should now reinstall any applications you use in desktop mode. If you go to the desktop you will find an Internet Explorer file called "Removed Apps". Double click on it to see a list of the programs that were uninstalled.

64.2 – Remove everything and reinstall Windows

The remove everything option works just like the refresh option, only it goes a step further. All of your files and folders will be removed, additional user accounts will be deleted and all software will be removed. Your PC will effectively be reset to a factory fresh state. One time you might want to use this feature is when selling or disposing of your PC. At the time of writing we were not able to confirm how thorough this process is. As we mentioned in lesson 27, it is sometimes possible (though usually difficult and time consuming) to recover deleted files on a hard drive. This means that it might be possible for an attacker to recover your deleted account settings from your Windows 8 PC after you used this feature. In practise this seems unlikely, but nevertheless something we felt we should make you aware of.

Lesson 65 – The Task Manager

Task Manager Sometimes when you work with your computer, an application will stop responding to the mouse or keyboard. When this happens, it will not be possible to close the program because the window will freeze, preventing you from doing anything with it. For (hopefully rare) situations like these, you can use the Task Manager to force the application to close. The Task Manager has been overhauled for Windows 8 and shows even more information than in previous versions of Windows.

65.1 – Starting the Task Manager

You can start the Task Manager in three ways. The first way is to open the Start screen and search for "task manager" or "taskmgr". Then, click on the icon that appears at the top, Task Manager will then open.

Ctrl   Alt   Del   If your computer is not responding normally, you may not be able to open or navigate the Start screen at all. In that case, use the following keyboard shortcut. Press and hold the Control, Alt and Delete keys together. You don't need to press them all at the same time, you can press them one after the other as long as you end up pressing all three at once.

When you press these three keys together, the screen shown in figure 65.2 will appear.

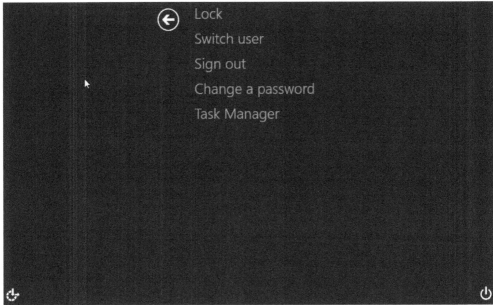

Figure 65.2 – Summon this screen by pressing the Control, Alt and Delete keys together

Choose "Task Manager" from the menu to load Task Manger.

Finally, you can also start the Task Manager by pressing and holding the Control, Shift and Escape keys together. The shift key is sometimes labelled with an up-pointing arrow on keyboards.

Figure 65.4 shows Windows 8 Task Manager open in basic view mode.

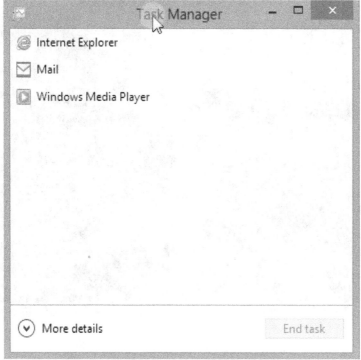

Figure 65.4 – Windows Task Manager

65.2 – Managing tasks

Task Manager shows us a list of programs that are currently running. In figure 65.4 we can see Internet Explorer and Windows Media Player, as well as the Mail tile. These programs are running and behaving normally. Occasionally a program will freeze or stop responding to mouse or keyboard input. When this happens you may need to start the Task Manager to end the program.

A program/task which has stopped responding will be marked as "Not responding". If you cannot end the program normally, select it from the list of tasks in Task Manager and then click the "End Task" button. Windows will then attempt to force the program to exit. You may see a window appear telling you that the application is not responding and that you might lose data if you proceed to force it to close. Any information you were working on in your program that was not saved will probably be lost, but if the application is no longer responding this may be the only course of action you can take.

65.3 – Processes

To access the Processes tab, firstly click on the "More details" button. This will change Task Manager into advanced mode. Now you can select the Processes tab from the top of the programs window. Figure 65.5 shows the Task Manager open on the Processes tab.

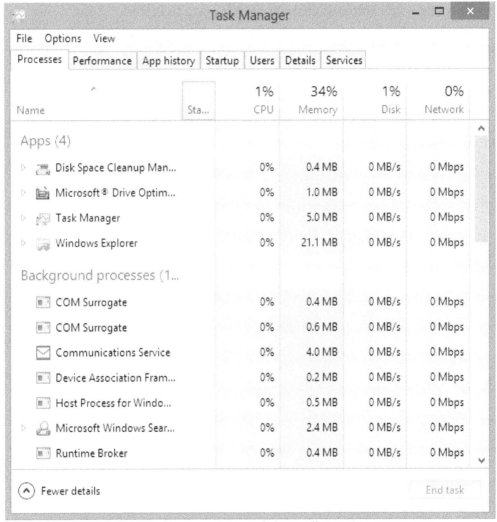

Figure 65.5 – The Processes tab lists all running processes

In this view, Task Manager gives you more details about the CPU (basically your computers brain), Memory, Disk and Network usage of all the running processes. A process might be an application, either one that is running with a window or tile or hidden in the notification area, or a subsystem or service managed by the operating system.

Just like in the basic view, you can end a process by clicking on it from the list and then choosing "End task". Be careful when ending processes, you will lose any unsaved data in the program. If you end a system process, you might make your computer unstable, forcing you to restart it.

65.4 – Other Task Manager tabs

The other tabs available in the Task Manager can occasionally be useful too, so we will take a quick tour of them now.

The Performance tab shows a graphical representation of computer resource use on your PC. Figure 65.6 shows the Task Manager open on the Performance tab.

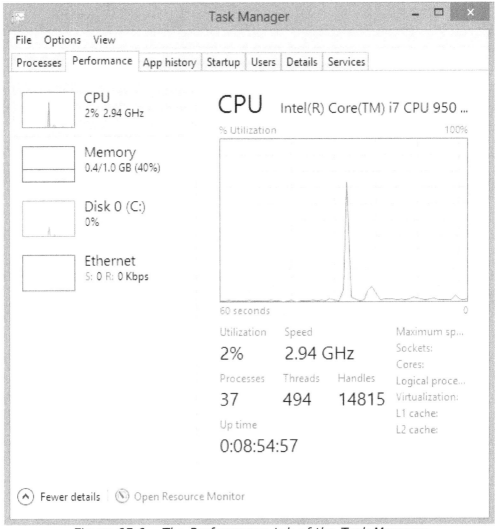

Figure 65.6 – The Performance tab of the Task Manager

You do not need to understand all the technical jargon shown in figure 65.6. The important things to note are CPU Usage and Memory. You can click on any of the small graphs on the left of the window to get a bigger view over in the right.

The CPU usage gauge is an indicator of how much computing work your PC is doing. When your computer is idle on the desktop, you should see around 0% to 3% CPU usage. If there is always some CPU activity going on pushing the meter higher, you may have some spyware or other software running in the background.

The Memory gauge is a measure of how much data the computer is working on at the moment. If this gauge is nearly full, your computer is running out of resources. Try closing some programs to free up some memory.

The Disk gauge shows how frequently your computer is writing to disk. Again, this should be low when you're not running any software.

The Ethernet gauge shows any network activity that is currently going on in the background. If you aren't running any networking or internet software, this should generally be at 0%.

New for Windows 8 is the "App history" tab. Figure 65.7 shows the Task Manager open on this tab.

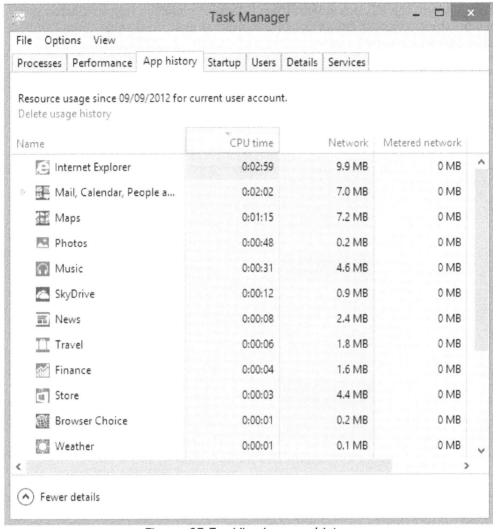

Figure 65.7 – Viewing app history

The App history tab is quite useful, as it shows CPU usage by a program over a period of time. So for instance in the Processes tab you might see spikes of CPU usage, in this tab you can see what has really been gobbling up the computing time on your PC. In figure 65.7 we can see that Internet Explorer has used the most CPU time. If you suspect a program of periodically slowing down your PC, check here to see if its CPU time count is high. Sadly, the App history tab only logs tile apps and not desktop apps.

Also new for Windows 8 is the Startup tab. Here we can see programs that start up with the PC, along with their "Startup impact". Programs listed with a high startup impact cause your PC to start slower. To disable them from starting when your PC starts, right click on them and choose "disable". If disable is greyed out for a specific program, you may need to restart Task Manager with administrator rights (run as administrator).

Next there is the Users tab. On this tab you can see which users are logged in or connected to your PC, along with a summary of how many CPU resources their programs are using. On a home PC this is usually limited to just your account.

Also new in Windows 8 is the Details tab. Figure 65.8 shows this tab open in Task Manager.

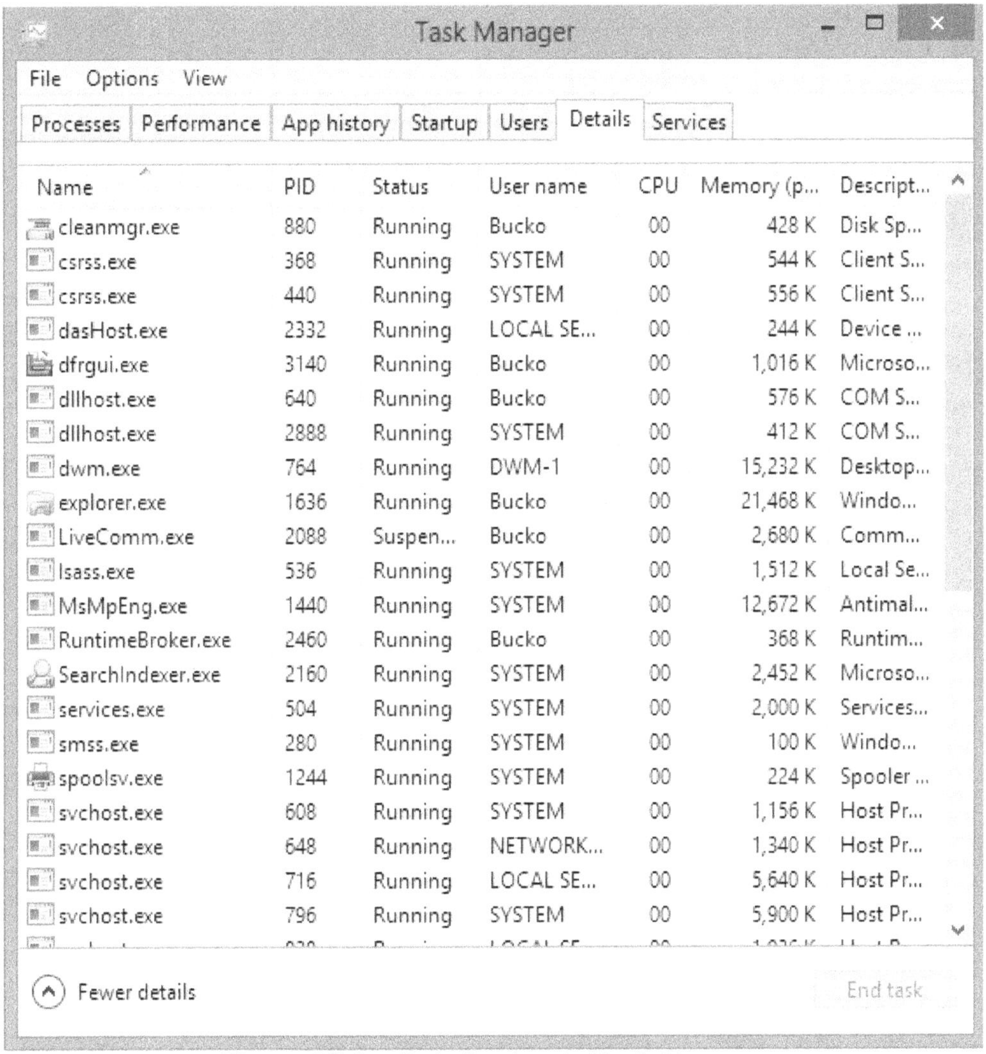
Task Manager
File Options View
Processes Performance App history Startup Users Details Services
Name PID Status User name CPU Memory (p... Descript...
cleanmgr.exe 880 Running Bucko 00 428 K Disk Sp...
csrss.exe 368 Running SYSTEM 00 544 K Client S...
csrss.exe 440 Running SYSTEM 00 556 K Client S...
dasHost.exe 2332 Running LOCAL SE... 00 244 K Device ...
dfrgui.exe 3140 Running Bucko 00 1,016 K Microso...
dllhost.exe 640 Running Bucko 00 576 K COM S...
dllhost.exe 2888 Running SYSTEM 00 412 K COM S...
dwm.exe 764 Running DWM-1 00 15,232 K Desktop...
explorer.exe 1636 Running Bucko 00 21,468 K Windo...
LiveComm.exe 2088 Suspen... Bucko 00 2,680 K Comm...
lsass.exe 536 Running SYSTEM 00 1,512 K Local Se...
MsMpEng.exe 1440 Running SYSTEM 00 12,672 K Antimal...
RuntimeBroker.exe 2460 Running Bucko 00 368 K Runtim...
SearchIndexer.exe 2160 Running SYSTEM 00 2,452 K Microso...
services.exe 504 Running SYSTEM 00 2,000 K Services...
smss.exe 280 Running SYSTEM 00 100 K Windo...
spoolsv.exe 1244 Running SYSTEM 00 224 K Spooler ...
svchost.exe 608 Running SYSTEM 00 1,156 K Host Pr...
svchost.exe 648 Running NETWORK... 00 1,340 K Host Pr...
svchost.exe 716 Running LOCAL SE... 00 5,640 K Host Pr...
svchost.exe 796 Running SYSTEM 00 5,900 K Host Pr...
Fewer details
End task

Figure 65.8 – Details view in Task Manager

This tab shows information about running processes rather like the old Task Manager did in previous versions of Windows. Again, simply click on a task and then click "End task" if you want to terminate it.

Finally, the Services tab shows which services are available on your PC. Services add extra functionality to Windows such as networking or CD recording. From this tab you can start and stop services by right clicking on them. We do not recommend doing this unless you are an advanced user and know exactly what you are doing.

65.5 – Running a program from the Task Manager

It is possible to run a program from the Task Manager. To do this, open the File menu and choose "Run new task". You will need to know where the program file is located on your computer however. In some rare instances this can be useful, if you find yourself troubleshooting a serious PC problem the Task Manager may be the only way to run a program if the Start screen wont open, for example. If you ever find the taskbar has disappeared from the desktop, you can usually restore it by starting Task Manager and opening the Run new task option and typing in "Explorer".

This is the last lesson in our PC maintenance section and it marks the end of the lessons for Windows 8! You are not finished learning about Windows 8 though, no-one ever is. Don't forget to visit Top-Windows-Tutorials.com regularly to keep up with the latest tips, techniques and tutorials for getting the most out of your Windows 8 PC.

In the last chapter we take a brief look at some popular Windows software that is compatible with Windows 8, including several desktop replacements for the tile apps that come bundled with the operating system.

Chapter 12 – And Finally...

You now know all about Windows 8, but the real purpose of an operating system is to help you run software. In this last chapter we will discuss some popular software packages that let you accomplish various computing tasks. Windows 8 comes with lots of tile software, but most users are still running PCs with keyboards and mice and desktop software works better in this instance. Remember that there are always plenty of other software recommendations on Top-Windows-Tutorials.com.

Popular Windows Software

You will always be spoilt for choice when looking for software to run on your Windows 8 machine. As the most popular operating system for home computer users, Windows has a software package to suit almost every need. In this final section, we will explore some common home computing tasks and look at some popular software packages that help you with them.

66.1 – Software recommendations

E-mail

The mail tile is nice for tablet PCs but really doesn't have the flexibility that desktop users demand. Fortunately, there are several alternatives:-

Mozilla Thunderbird (Free, see http://www.mozillamessaging.com/en-US/thunderbird/)

Reclaim your inbox with this powerful free e-mail program which includes anti-spam technologies and is extendible through plug-ins.

Microsoft Outlook (from $139.95 or $9.99 per month with a Microsoft Office suite, see http://office.microsoft.com/en-us/outlook/)

Microsoft's powerful Outlook package includes a professional e-mail package as well as a personal organiser and calendar application. It is the standard PIM (personal information manager) in many businesses.

Games

There are thousands of game titles available for Windows machines, from easy pick up and play titles to complex and in-depth simulation games.

Image and photograph editing

The Photo tile is fun for viewing your photos on a touch device, but when you want to get serious with your photographs you should check out these programs:-

Adobe Photoshop / Photoshop Elements (from $80, see http://www.adobe.com/products/photoshop/compare/)

Photoshop remains the image editing program of choice for professional photographers and artists around the world. The Elements version is an excellent choice for home photographers.

Google Picasa (free – see http://picasa.google.com/)

Enhance, catalogue and display your pictures on the desktop with this popular tool from the search engine giant Google.

Paint (bundled with Windows 8)

Windows 8 includes a basic desktop graphics utility called Paint, which can be used for simple image editing.

Paint.net (free – see http://www.getpaint.net/)

An amazing free graphics package with a feature set that rivals those found in commercially available alternatives.

Windows Live Photo Gallery (free –

see http://download.live.com/photogallery)

Another powerful tool for enhancing and cataloguing your family photos on the desktop, this time from Microsoft.

Instant messaging, video and voice chat

There are lots of great IM apps for both desktop and touch users.

Skype (tile version now bundled with Windows 8.1, desktop version is also free – see www.skype.com/)

Skype has been the market leader in internet telephony and voice over IP (VOIP) communications for several years now. What that means is, you can use your internet connection to call your friends on Skype for free. You can also use Skype to call normal telephones at rates which are often far cheaper than other services. If you have a webcam, you can also video chat with your Skype friends too!

Jitsi (free – see https://jitsi.org/)

Jitsi is the ideal video conferencing application for the privacy conscious user. Featuring strong encryption and privacy safeguards that Skype and other closed-source software cannot match.

Trillian (basic version is free – see http://www.trillian.im/)

There are several popular instant messaging services in use on the internet today. If you have friends on several services, Trillian can connect to them all through one handy interface.

Music and Multimedia

Windows Media Player and the Music tile are not the only ways your Windows 8 PC can sing and dance. There are plenty of great software packages out there that can help you discover your media in new and exciting ways.

VLC (free – see www.videolan.org/vlc/)

VLC is a popular media player with a low memory and processor overhead that is renowned for its high compatibility with a wide range of media files.

Music creation

Want to make sweet music with your PC? There are plenty of software packages that can help with that too.

Cakewalk SONAR X2 (from $99.99 – see http://www.store.cakewalk.com/)

SONAR X2 is the easiest way to turn your PC into a fully-fledged music production studio. From start to finish, SONAR will help you capture your creativity and share it with the world. With SONAR X2 you can record live instruments, vocals, or any audio source (compatible hardware permitting).

Sound Forge (from $59.95 – see http://www.sonycreativesoftware.com/soundforgesoftware)

Sound Forge Audio Studio software is the easiest way to record, edit, encode, and master audio on your PC. Includes vinyl recording and restoration to help you convert those precious old records (compatible hardware permitting).

Online safety

Children love to explore the internet, but not everything and everyone they encounter is suitable for them. Windows 8 includes a family safety module, but it needs to work in conjunction with other software to be really effective.

Optenet (From $39.95 – See http://www.optenetpc.com/)

Optenet PC is a highly effective internet filter which can filter adult and unsuitable content with minimal false positives and without making your internet run slowly.

Password Management

If you use a wide range of websites and online services then a password manager tool is essential. Most people cannot remember more than 3 or 4 unique passwords and recycling the same password over several sites is extremely bad for your online security.

KeyPass (Free, see http://keepass.info/)

If you want a free password manager but don't want to store your passwords in the cloud, look no further than the light-weight, open source password manager KeyPass.

LastPass (basic service is free, see http://lastpass.com/ and the Windows Store)

The leading password and data management service, LastPass stores your logins in a secure vault online, letting you log in securely and conveniently to websites without recycling passwords. LastPass has both a tile and desktop version meaning you can work with it seamlessly no matter how you're using your PC.

Roboform (free for up to 10 passwords, $29.95 for unlimited, see http://www.roboform.com/)

Roboform has long been one of our favourite password managers. It is preferred by many users because it offers an offline storage mode, meaning your passwords never have to be stored online. Currently however, the program runs in desktop mode only.

Social networking

The People app is one of the stand-out tiles in the Windows 8 interface and there really isn't anything on the desktop that does the same job. Nevertheless there are several programs that make social networking easier.

Tweetdeck (free – see http://www.tweetdeck.com/)

Monitor your Twitter and Facebook accounts from one handy app with Tweetdeck. Supports multiple Twitter accounts and all for free.

Yoono Desktop (free – see http://www.yoono.com/)

If you like the column layout of Tweetdeck but want a program that supports Facebook and other social networks too, try Yoono.

Web browsing

Internet Explorer is not the only way to get around the web!

Mozilla Firefox (free – see http://www.mozilla.com/firefox/)

Firefox is a popular alternative to Internet Explorer. Faster, safer, and smarter, Firefox also has a huge range of plug-ins that can be used to extend and customise the browser.

Google Chrome (free – see http://www.google.com/chrome)

Google Chrome is another very popular alternative browser. It is known for its super fast browsing speeds and simple, uncluttered interface.

Word processing and office

Microsoft Office (from $9.99 per month – see http://office.microsoft.com/)

The de-facto standard Office suite for many businesses, colleges and universities. Includes the industry standard word processor, Microsoft Word and probably the most powerful spreadsheet package in the world, Microsoft Excel.

OpenOffice.org (free – see http://www.openoffice.org/)

A fantastic Microsoft Office compatible productivity suite that is completely free! OpenOffice.org has regained the crown from plucky competitor LibreOffice by focusing on stability and speed. This book was written using OpenOffice.org Writer!

Appendix – Using Touch Gestures

At the time of writing this guide, touch PCs were something of a rarity. Because of this the lessons in this guide were written and recorded using the traditional keyboard and mouse setup. However, learning the touch equivalents shouldn't be difficult. Refer to this appendix if you are using a touch only machine or want to learn the touch equivalents for a machine with both types of controls.

Note:- Touch screens vary in capabilities, if you buy a new Windows 8 machine with a touch screen, all the gestures discussed here will work correctly. If you are upgrading an older machine, such as a Windows 7 tablet PC, then the capabilities may be more limited.

Hot corners – The hot corners are not applicable to touch. When the guide talks about using the Hot Corners, carry out the following actions instead.

Corner	Location	Touch
Start Button	Bottom Left	Swipe from the right and use the Start Charm (see lesson 3.3)
Quick Task Switcher	Top Left	Swipe from the left
Task Switcher (lesson 3.1)	Bottom left, then drag upwards	Swipe in from the left, when first app thumbnail appears, swipe back toward the left

Basic Gestures – Many of the basic gestures are the same or similar on a mouse as they are on a touch screen.

Mouse Action	Touch Equivalent
Left (or primary mouse button) click	Tap
Right click (on the tile interface, but not on a specific tile)	Swipe either from the top or the bottom of the screen
Right click (on a tile)	Use the "Swipe to select" method (see below)
Right click (on the desktop)	Press and hold with your finger
Control + Mousewheel (to zoom)	Make a pinching gesture on the screen

Many operations will work the same way with touch, for instance to drag windows, you press and hold your finger to the screen, rather than clicking and holding your mouse button. The same is true for closing tile apps (Lesson 3.4).

Swipe to select – In several of our videos you will see us selecting multiple tiles by right clicking on them. On touch hardware you can do this by flicking your finger downwards over the tile. When the tile is selected, a tick or check mark will appear over it. Be careful not to swipe your finger too far, as you will end up moving the tile instead.

Swipe from the edges – Any menu that opens from the edge of the screen can be opened on the touch screen by swiping in from that edge. The Charms Bar, for instance, always opens from the right hand side of the screen, so can be opened by swiping in from the right with your finger.

Index

32-bit..20, 22, 25, 384
    Vs. 64-bit..22
64-bit...20, 22p., 25p., 384
    And 16-bit applications...384
Action Center.......................................157, 271p., 323
Administrator accounts...
    And User Account Controls...322
    Security risk..322
Adobe Photoshop...498
ADSL...414, 416
Advertising ID...337
Alarms..371p.
    App..373
    Setting...372
Antivirus software...346, 352
    Third party...352
App Store.......................101, 105pp., 122, 145, 312, 321, 363
    Buying an app..103
    Categories..105
    Free and paid apps...102
    Rate this app..106
    Star rating..102
    Trial mode..105
    Viewing an app...103
    Write a review..106
Apps view...41p., 54pp., 165
ARM chip...**21**
Automatic updates..327, 331
Backup..
    File History..284, 290
    Image...284
    Media..285
    Methodologies..284
    Network..287p.
    Storing..289
    Strategy..284
BIOS..309
Bitlocker...21, 278
Breadcrumbs...180
Cable broadband..414
Cakewalk SONAR X2...500
Camera..372
Camera Roll..95
Cellular broadband...414
    Connecting to...415
Charms Bar...40, 46p., 50, 56p., 61p., 75, 77, 83, 99, 143, 155, 164, 310, 327, 335, 364, 366, 368, 374, 415, 417, 481, 504
Classic Shell...170p., 425

Cloud computing 146
Colour scheme..29, 406
Compatibility options..385
    Enable this program to work with OneDrive files.............388
    Reduced colour mode.......................................388
    Run in 640x480 screen resolution.............................388
    Run this program as an administrator.......................387
    Run this program in compatibility mode for....................387
    Setting...387
Compatibility troubleshooter...387
Compress drive..257
Compressed (zipped) folder..197
Computer viruses...346
    False positive..348
Contacts..
    Browsing..82
    Delete...91
    Editing..89
    Linking..90
    Pin to Start...91
    Searching...83
Context menu....167, 169, 195pp., 200, 202, 212, 223, 226, 248p., 256, 365, 385p., 388, 391, 396, 403, 425, 436, 450
    In File Explorer...195
Copy..197
Corner navigation..164
Currency converter...136
Cut..197
    On the ribbon..198
    Vs. Copy...197
Default programs...168
    Changing...168
Desktop...36, 154
    Background..157, 391pp., 404pp.
        From the internet....................................395
        On the Start screen..................................396
        Picture positioning options.........................394
        Slideshow...394
    Elements..154
    Go to when I sign in.......................................164
    Operating system..14
    Peek..159
    Shake...160
    Shortcut...166, 197
    Snap..160, 206
    Theme manager.......................................391, 404
        Automatic Colour....................................405
    Themes..404
        Downloading...407

Saving..406
Window...
    Common controls...158
    Elements..158
    Maximise..159
    Minimise..158
    Moving...159
    Resizing...159
    Restore..159
    Windows...158
Desktop PC...13, 19, 23, 163, 254
    Vs. Laptop...24
Desktop PCs..18, 24
Desktop software................21, 24, 101, 321p., 377, 380, 383, 482, 497
    Choosing..377
    Default installation directory..381
    Installing..
        Additional bundled components...382
        From optical media..379
        From the internet...380
    Uninstalling..462p.
Details pane..190p., 223, 248, 275
Devices and drives...255
Devices and Printers...409pp.
Diacritics..279
Dial up internet...415
DirectX..24, 26
Disk cleanup..465
    Options...465
Disk defragmentation...468
    Manual..471
    Scheduling..470
Dragging and dropping...202
DVD rewriter..257
E-mail...................................32p., 59, 63p., 73pp., 81, 143, 197, 312, 352, 371, 498
    Adding accounts..77
    Blind carbon copy..77
    Carbon copy...77
    Categories..74
    Forward..76
    Inbox..74
    New message...75
    Reply to..75
    Security..73
End user license agreement...380
Ethernet cable...416p.
Evernote..165, 197
Facebook...................................65, 72, 81, 83, 86, 88, 90, 92pp., 501
Family Safety..313

Fax recipient..197
File...200
    Delete...200
    Extension..242
    Lasso...211
    Move between folders...209
        On other storage devices...209
    Protected operating system...241
    Renaming...200
    Selecting multiple...211
File Explorer 18, 20, 155, 166, 168, 174pp., 181, 183, 187pp., 193, 195, 198, 206pp., 213pp., 218pp., 231pp., 242p., 254p., 281, 380, 385p., 388, 436, 439p., 444
    Address bar...178
    And homegroup...439
    And OneDrive..151
    And Recycle Bin...247
    Back/forward navigation...178
    Delete file..249
    Parent directory...178
    Ribbon..178p.
    Search tool...178, 281
    Searching..281
    See also details pane, file, folder(s)
File History..290
    Advanced settings...295
    Backup frequency..296
    Configuring..291
    Exclude folders..294
    Limitations...303
    Restore several files...301
    Restoring from...297p.
    Starting...292
File name collisions..199, 202
    Resolving manually..205
File shredding..247
Finance app...135pp.
    Watchlist...136
Firewall...340
    Software Vs. Hardware...340
    Third party...344
Floppy Disk...197, 257
Folder(s)..
    Create...194
    Customise...229
    Delete...200
    Documents..174
    Downloads...176
    Dragging...198
    Favourite...191

Icons..231
Location..228
Merging..199
Music..109
Open in new window..208, 234
Options..
    Restore Defaults...237
    View..238
Options window...233
Personal..174, 193, 255
Pictures...231
Properties...226
    General...227
Renaming..200
Reset...239
Security...227
Sharing...227
Size...227
Views...181, 238
    Content..187
    Details..182, 188
    Extra large icons...183
    List...185
    Small icons..184
    Tiles...186
    What kind of folder do you want?...230
    Working with..193
Google Chrome...501
Google mail...78
Google Mail...
    And Mail app..79
Google Picasa..498
Graphics card..22, 24
Guest networks...341
Hard drive...23, 255
    Capacity..23
    External...286p.
    Failure..283
    Internal..286
    Requirements...23
    Secondary...286p.
    Space...255
    Type..23
    Vs. RAM..22
Hardware troubleshooter..412
Hidden drives...258
Hidden files and folders..239
    Show or hide..239
Hide extensions for known file types 242

And files with similar names...244
High Definition (video)..121
Home page..421
    Change...427
Homegroups...192, 228, 434
    And media extenders...436
    Browsing..439
    Choosing file types..435
    Creating...434
    Joining...438
    Leave...436
    Password..436
    Permissions..438
    Restricting access to...436
Hot corner.......................................40, 44pp., 57, 70, 503
    Disable..164
Hotels..134
Hotmail..31, 74, 86p., 311p.
Indexing *see* Search index
Internet Explorer 11........................262p., 337, 419pp., 425, 429pp.
    Address bar..421
    Advanced settings..425
    Desktop version..419
    Download manager..428
    Favourites..423
        Add a site to..423
        Delete...425
    Main window...420
    Searching...421
    Tabs...422
        Open new...423
    Tile version...431
        Favourites..432
        Navigating..431
        Searching...431
        Tabs...433
Internet service provider..414
    Choosing..416
Jitsi...499
Jump lists..261
    Internet Explorer..262
    Windows Media Player...263
KeyPass...500
LastPass..501
Libraries...**212pp., 219, 235**
    Actual file or folder location 223
    Add a location...217
    Default save location...219
    Enable...213

In Windows 8.1...215
Manage...215
Music..215
Pictures..222
Public save location...219
Show...214
Sorting data..220
Types of locations supported..219
Vs. regular folders...214
LinkedIn..86
Links (web page)..420
Local account...
Creating...32
Lock..61
Lock screen...35p., 61, 368, 370pp., 477
Apps..371
Automatically show...371
Customisations...368
Notifications..371, 375
Picture..98, 369
Show alarms...371
Slide show..369
Mail app...62p., 73p., 76
Mail recipient...197
Maintenance window 332
Changing...333
Map network drive...259
Maps app...89, 142p.
Add a pin..143
Directions...143
Favourites...144
Map style..143
My location..143
Search..143
Memory..22p.
Requirements..23
See also RAM
Memory card reader...258
Meta data...275
Metro..20, 38
Microsoft account 25, 29, 31pp., 74, 81, 103p., 116, 146, 303, 311pp., 317, 337, 373, 462
Security risks..32
Vs. local account..31, 311
Microsoft Office...502
Modem...416
Modern applications see Tile applications
ModernMix..172p.
Mouse..

ClickLock..357
Double clicking...356
Left handed use..356
Pointer options...357
Properties window..356
Settings...355
Wheel options..359
Mozilla Firefox..501
Mozilla Thunderbird...498
Mp3..448
Multi-monitor...268
  And tiles...269
Music app..108
  Buying music..113
  Collection..108p.
  Open file..113
  Playback controls...111
  Playing music 109
  Playlists...111
  Radio...113
Music streaming..116
Navigation pane.....................175pp., 191, 213p., 235pp., 254, 439, 446, 449, 451
  Automatically expand to current folder.................................235
Netgear ReadyNAS..288
Network Locations...259
News app...122pp.
  Categories..123
  Customise...125
  News sources..124
  Search..124
  Videos..128
Notification area..155pp., 270
  Always show all icons and notifications..................................273
  Customising..271
  Hide icon and notifications...272
  Icons..271
  Network icon...271
  New Vs. old...270
  Only show notifications..272
  Show icon and notifications..272
  Volume icon..271
Notifications..
  Disable...374
  For individual applications..375
  Options...374
  Sounds...375
  System..374
Office 365..149
On the taskbar...

Tile applications..46
OneDrive..6, 146pp., 289, 303, 312
    App...**146, 149**
    Folders...147
    On the desktop...151
    Sync...148
    With File Explorer..151
OneDrive app...
    Add items..148
    Copy...150
    Cut..150
    Delete..150
    Download...150
    Make offline...150
    New folder...148
    Open with..150
    Rename..150
    Upload...148
    Viewing mode...149
OpenOffice.org...502
Operating system recovery media...285
Optenet...500
Optimize Drives..468
Outlook..31, 74, 86, 312, 498
Outlook.com..78
Paint...499
Paint.net..499
Paste...197
PC name..29
PC settings..58
    Brightness..59
    Keyboard...59
    Network...58
    Notifications..59
    Power...59
    Volume...59
People app...........................64p., 77, 81, 83p., 86p., 89pp., 143
    Options..86
    What's new..92
Photos app...................................61p., 94pp., 99, 147, 369
    Import pictures..98
    In Windows 8.1...94
    Picture browsing tools...97
    Slideshow..98
Pin...
    To Start..91, 196, 363, 365
    To taskbar...165p.
Preview pane...189p., 223
Printers...411

513

Default...411
Privacy options...335p., 338
    And desktop software...339
    General..336
    Location...337
    Webcam, Microphone and Other devices...................339
Private networks...341
Programs...
    Vs. Data..284
Quiet Hours..375
RAM..22p., 26, 384
See also Memory
Recovery media...285, 304pp., 309
Recovery partition...285, 306
Recycle Bin.........................157, 197, 200, 245pp., 425, 467
    And undelete utilities..247
    Disable..252
    Empty..247
    Files that are not sent to..249
    Folders..250
    Properties..251
    Restore all items..247
    Sending files to...248
    Window..247
Refresh your PC...481
    Removed Apps file..484
Removable drives...254p., 271
    Safely remove...271
Remove everything and reinstall Windows..................484
Ripping CDs..447
    Copy protection options...452
    Options...447
    Quality settings..448
Router..416
Satellite internet...414
Screen saver...398pp.
    3D text..399
    Configuring...399
    Downloading new...401
Search...50, 274
    Apps view...56
    Categories...51
    Everywhere...51
    Files..51
    Full-page results...53
    In File Explorer...281
    Internet...421
    Settings...51
    Web images...51

Web videos..51
Search Charm..50, 56
   In Windows 8.1...56
Search index..257, 276, 279
   Add other locations..277
   File types that are indexed...279
   Location..279
   Options...276
      Advanced..277
   Rebuild..279
Send to..196
Services...495
Settings Charm 17, 57, 61, 77, 83, 86, 99, 310, 317, 327, 335, 364, 366, 368, 374p.,
415, 417, 481
   On the Start screen..57
Share Charm..62pp., 97, 143
   Internet Explorer..63
   People app..65
   Photos app..61
Show Desktop button..157
Sina Weibo..86
Skype..375, 499
Sleep..60
SmartScreen filter..403
Social networking..65, 72p., 81, 90, 501
Solid state drive...23
   Vs. magnetic hard drive..23
Sound Forge...500
Sport app..128
   Category...129
   Favourite Sports..129p.
   Favourite Teams..130
Standard accounts..
   And User Account Controls.......................................322, 325
Standard Definition (video)..121
Standard users..
   Running as...320
   Vs. Administrators...314, 321
Start button...37, 40, 155, 162p., 171
   Right-click menu..163
Start menu.....................................14, 20, 35, 38, 41, 50, 56, 165, 169pp., 381
   Restore...169
   Vs. Start screen...38
Start screen 20, 26, 34p., 37pp., 47p., 50, 54, 57, 60, 66, 69p., 81, 91, 99, 101, 106,
122, 130, 154p., 164pp., 170, 174, 196, 254, 274pp., 281, 290, 297, 305, 310, 314,
317, 323, 329, 335, 340, 346, 360pp., 372p., 381, 385, 388, 396pp., 409, 432, 434,
438, 442, 461p., 465, 468, 473, 479, 486, 496
   Adding tiles..365
   Customise mode..361

Open...39
Personalisations..367
Pin to...365
Pin website to...432
Show administrative tools...364
Show more tiles...364
Unpin from...363
Start8..171p.
Stream (video)..
Vs. Download..121
Swipe from the edges...504
Swipe to select..504
System Image Backup..285
System Restore...303p., 473pp., 477p., 480, 482
Choosing a restore point..475
Creating a restore point...479
Undoing...478
Tablet PC...13p., 128, 265, 503
Tablet PCs..14, 21, 24, 498
Tags...274p., 281
Task Manager...486
App history...492
CPU usage...491
Details..494
Disk gauge..492
End Task...488
Ethernet gauge...492
Memory gauge..492
Performance..490
Processes...489
Services...495
Startup..493
Users..494
Task switcher...43pp., 66, 69p., 164
Alt+Tab..45
Taskbar....................155p., 158pp., 163, 165p., 174, 261pp., 273, 396, 419, 496
And Navigation properties..163, 266
And pinned apps...155
And tile applications..46
Auto-hide...266
Button..
Options...267
Buttons...266
Date and time..157
Jump lists..261
Lock/unlock..264
Moving...263p., 267
Multi-monitor options..268
Pin to..363

Preview window...156
Resizing...263p.
Toolbars..264
    Address..265
    Desktop..265
    Links...265
    New toolbar...265
    Touch Keyboard...265
This PC...176p., 180, 192, 254p., 260, 304p.
Tile applications...
    Arranging with the keyboard...70
    Closing...47pp.
    Command bar..42
    Insert...66
        From task switcher...69
        Right-click...66
        With the desktop...70
    Installing..105
    Rating..106
    Reinstall...461
    Resize control...67
    Split..70
    Title bar...49, 69
    Uninstalling...363, 461
Tiles...
    Clear personal info from...364
    Customising...361
    Groups...361
        Name..362
        Rename...362
    Live..363
    Options...363
    Photos..99
    Resize...363
    Sizes...363
    Vs. icons...39
Touch gestures...503
Travel app...132p., 135
    Best of the Web..135
    Search Hotels..135
Trillian..499
Truecrypt..278, 303
Tweetdeck..501
Twitter..65, 72, 81, 83, 86, 90, 92, 501
USB...286
USB stick drive...257
User account...
    Creating...310
    Local...

    Creating...317
    Security level...314p.
    Standard...314
    Switch...61
    See also Administrator accounts, Standard accounts, Standard users
User Account Controls...283, 320pp., 325p.
    Disable...325
    Settings..323
    See also Administrator accounts, Standard accounts
Video app...108, 117, 128
    Buying video..118
    Playback..118
Virtualization software...389
VLC...500
Volume...59, 271
Weather app..67, 70, 137pp.
    Favourites...139
    Maps...139
    Places...139
    World weather..140
WinCustomize.com..401
Windows 7........13pp., 20pp., 25, 73, 99, 153, 155p., 158pp., 162, 170, 172, 212p., 261pp., 269p., 273p., 281, 290, 323, 330, 378, 394, 402, 404, 409, 441, 443, 465, 473, 503
    Software...378
Windows 7 Superguide...2p., 16
Windows 8 backup utility..23, 284
Windows 8 Enterprise..21
Windows 8 Professional..21, 25
Windows 8 Upgrade Assistant...26
Windows 8.1...
    Upgrade...26
Windows Defender...283, 339, 346pp., 429
    Automatic scanning...351
    Detected threat...350
    Excluded files and locations...348
    Manual scan..349
    Microsoft Active Protection Service (MAPS)....................................348
    Quarantine..351
    Real time protection..347
    Starting...346
    Virus and spyware definitions...347
Windows Explorer *see* File Explorer
Windows firewall..340
    Notification settings..342
    With Advanced Security..343
Windows Live Photo Gallery..499
Windows Media Audio format..448
Windows Media Player 109, 121, 169, 219, 259, 263, 440pp., 449p., 455, 458p., 488,

499

    Columns...456
    Find album info..450
    Media library..446, 455
        Views...455
    Playback controls...445
    Playing music...443
    Playing video...444
    Running for the first time..442
    Viewing pictures...458
Windows RT...21, 24p.
    Vs. Windows 8..21, 24
Windows Store..14, 21, 24, 38, 172, 337
Windows update..327
    Advanced options..329
    Install updates automatically...331
    Manually checking for...328
    Never check for updates..332
    Recommended updates..332
    Updates for other Microsoft products....................................332
Windows Vista............................25, 155, 160, 274, 323p., 378, 473
    Software...378
Windows XP...................14, 25, 155, 254, 270, 303, 320p., 326, 378, 389, 473
    Software...378
Windows XP Tablet PC Edition...14
Wired (network)...416
Wireless (network)...416
    Connecting to...418
    Vs. Wired...416
World weather..140
XPS Document Writer..411
Yoono Desktop...501